Introductory
Transformational
Grammar
of English

Introductory Transformational Grammar of English

Mark Lester
University of Hawaii

Holt, Rinehart and Winston, Inc.
New York   Chicago   San Francisco   Atlanta
Dallas   Montreal   Toronto   London   Sydney

To my parents

Preface

This book is intended for students who have little or no background in linguistics. The book presents a great deal of information about the English language through the vehicle of transformational grammar. It has two aims in this order: (1) to give the student insight into the rules that reflect his own linguistic ability and (2) to give him some understanding of how a transformational grammar works and how it differs from other grammatical theories.

There is little in this book that is new. In fact, at a time in which transformational theory is being pulled in many directions, this book is relatively conservative. The grammar presented here attempts to convey the basic ideas of transformational grammar, ideas that would be valid in virtually any camp of transformational grammarians.

I would like to express my sincere appreciation to Professor Fred W. Householder who read an earlier version of the book, to Professor Ruth Crymes who taught much of the material in her classes, to Professor Theodore Plaister who read the manuscript, and to Naomi Hirata and Marilyn Morisato who prepared the manuscript.

M.L.

Honolulu, Hawaii
January 1971

Contents

Appendixes

Introductory Transformational Grammar of English

INTRODUCTION

An Elementary Transformational Grammar of English

The great Danish scholar of the English language Otto Jespersen wrote the following paragraph in the introductory chapter of his book *Essentials of English Grammar:*

> The chief object in teaching grammar today—especially that of a foreign language—would appear to be to give rules which must be obeyed if one wants to speak and write the language correctly—rules which as often as not seem quite arbitrary. Of greater value, however, than this *prescriptive* grammar is a purely *descriptive* grammar which, instead of serving as a guide to what should be said or written, aims at finding out what is actually said and written by the speakers of the language investigated, and thus may lead to a scientific understanding of the rules followed instinctively by speakers and writers. Such a grammar should also be *explanatory*, giving, as far as this is possible, the reasons why the usage is such and such. These reasons may, according to circumstances, be phonetic or psychological, or in some cases both combined. Not infrequently

1

the explanation will be found in an earlier stage of the same language: what in one period was a regular phenomenon may later become isolated and appear as an irregularity, an exception to what has now become the prevailing rule. Our grammar must therefore be *historical* to a certain extent. Finally, grammar may be *appreciative*, examining whether the rules obtained from the language in question are in every way clear (unambiguous, logical), expressive and easy, or whether in any one of these respects other forms or rules would have been preferable. (Jespersen, pp. 19–20)[1]

Jespersen draws a distinction between two different kinds of grammar. One kind, the prescriptive, gives a nonnative speaker a set of rules that he must follow in order to use the new language correctly. In other words, a prescriptive grammar tries to modify the learner's linguistic behavior. Jespersen obviously has considerable reservations about the value of prescriptive grammars for native speakers. Instead, he would prefer the second kind of grammar, the descriptive, which does not aim at changing behavior, but rather tries to discover what, in fact, the speaker's linguistic behavior actually is. Furthermore, a descriptive grammar may become the basis for more sophisticated investigations which will enable us to understand and explain the instinctive rules that underlie the speaker's linguistic behavior.

The need to distinguish between the two types of grammar can hardly be overemphasized. There is no need to apologize for linguistic prescriptivism as long as the basis for correction is understood by all parties concerned. In a beginning foreign language class, for instance, the views of the learner about what should or should not be said in the new language are worthless: the role of the teacher is purely prescriptive.

When dealing with native speakers of a language, the situation is naturally quite different. A child does not go to school to learn his own language in the same sense that he goes to school to learn a foreign language. He "knows" English in a way that he will never "know" any foreign language, no matter how much he is schooled in it. At this point we must distinguish sharply between two kinds of "knowing": conscious and unconscious. Most speakers, adults as well as children, do not know much about their language consciously. They do not know its history or why it works the way it does. This book is an attempt to give the reader a conscious awareness of some aspects of his own language. Unconscious knowledge is what all speakers of a language share, namely, the ability to produce, understand, and make judgments about the grammaticality and structure of sentences in their language. By the time a child comes to school he already has a vast unconscious knowledge of his language.

However, his unconscious knowledge is immature as compared to an adult

---

[1] From *Essentials of English Grammar* by Otto Jespersen, published in 1933 by George Allen & Unwin Ltd. Reproduced by permission of the publisher. [Whenever Jespersen is cited throughout this text, the reference is to *Essentials of English Grammar*.]

speaker in at least two ways. The most obvious way is vocabulary. The vocabulary of even an illiterate adult is much greater than that of a child. If we broaden the meaning of vocabulary to include the grammatical properties of the word as well as its literal denotation, the difference between the adult and the child is even greater.

A second way that an adult's unconscious knowledge is greater than the child's is in the area of what we might call role playing. Throughout the course of a day each of us shifts linguistic gears as many times as we enter into different personal and professional relationships. It is a mistake to think of the changes as being along a single axis that ranges from formal to informal. We have many different axes. We can range from shop talk to baby talk; from intimate to highly impersonal; from solemn to facetious. We talk one way to superiors, another way to subordinates; we talk one way to our children, another way to our parents; we talk one way to men, another way to women. A young child knows a few of these roles and the linguistic conventions that go with them, but his repertoire is naturally quite limited. Some of the linguistic conventions he will learn as a direct result of his schooling (for instance, the ones that pertain to some of the conventions of written English), but most he will learn as a sheer function of growing up and taking part in the various roles.

Since the publication of Jespersen's *Essentials*, the United States has seen the evolution of two new and quite different schools of language study. The first school had its roots in the 1930s, but did not gain wide recognition until after World War II. This school is commonly known as *structural* linguistics. The second new school can be dated from the publication of a monograph entitled *Syntactic Structures* by Noam Chomsky in 1957. This school is usually referred to as *transformational*. What are the main claims of these new schools, and how do they differ from each other and from what had gone before?

Both of these schools considered themselves scientific revolutions, so perhaps a good way to begin is to examine what it is that they are revolting against. The tradition that preceeded structural linguistics is called *traditional grammar*. This term means different things to different people. At its worst, it means a confused blend of prescriptive and descriptive grammars aimed at changing linguistic behavior along the most artificial lines. At its best, however, it means the work of a scholar such as Jespersen. His *Essentials of English Grammar* belongs to a long and honorable tradition, and one that is still alive. The following passage on reflexive pronouns from Jespersen's *Essentials of English Grammar* is a good example of the best kind of traditional grammar. The passage is taken from a chapter that deals with the "relations of verb to subject and object."

When the subject and object are identical, we use for the latter a so-called reflexive pronoun, formed by means of *self, e.g. I defend myself.* The pronouns are the following:

(I) myself   (we) ourselves.
(thou) thyself ⎫
(you) yourself ⎭   (you) yourselves.
(he) himself ⎫
(she) herself ⎬   (they) themselves.
(it) itself ⎭
(one) oneself (rarer one's self).

A few verbs are always used reflexively:

> She prides herself on her good looks.
> He absented himself from all committee meetings.

There is a tendency to get rid of these pronouns whenever no ambiguity is to be feared:

> I washed, dressed and shaved, and then felt infinitely better.
> He is training for the race.
> He drew back a little.
> The army retired in good order.
> The disease spread rapidly.
> You must prepare for death.

Sometimes a difference is made, or may be made, between the fuller and the shorter expression; *behave oneself* is often used of good manners and breeding, while *behave* is used for action generally: the troops behaved gallantly under fire.

> He settled himself comfortably in an easy-chair | They settled in Australia.
> No opportunity offered | He offered himself as an interpreter.

Sometimes there is an element of exertion in the reflexive use: *We kept ourselves warm by walking to and fro* is more deliberate than *we kept warm,* etc.; cf. *the soup did not keep warm* very long. *He proved himself a fine fellow* emphasizes his endeavours, while *he proved a fine fellow* merely means that people saw that he was.

It is natural that the tendency to use verbs without the reflexive pronouns is stronger in English, where these pronouns are heavy and cumbersome, than in other languages where the corresponding forms are short and light (French *se,* German *sich,* etc.).

The reflexive pronouns are also used after prepositions:

> He looked at himself in the glass.
> He lives by himself in an old cottage.

But if the preposition has a purely local meaning, the simple forms without *self* are used:

> Shut the door behind you!
> I have no change about me.
> She stood, looking straight in front of her.
> They had the whole afternoon before them. (Jespersen, pp. 111–112)

From the purely descriptive standpoint of presenting accurate information about the usage of the reflexive, this passage would be hard to improve on.

Notice that the explanations that Jespersen gives are almost always concerned with the meaning of the usage, for example, the reflexive can be deleted from the sentence when "no ambiguity is to be feared" or when the reflexive follows a preposition of "purely local meaning." Jespersen also points out that the presence or absence of a reflexive sometimes changes the meaning of the verb. For Jespersen, a descriptive grammar describes usage, and usage can be explained in terms of its effect on meaning.

THE STRUCTURAL REVOLUTION

The one book written from the viewpoint of structural linguistics that has probably had the greatest impact on the teaching of English is Charles Carpenter Fries's (pronounced *freeze*) *The Structure of English*. Let us look at the main ideas in this book in some detail in order to see how a leading structural grammarian viewed the structural revolution. The reader should bear in mind, however, that there were other structural linguists besides Fries, and that what is true for Fries may not be necessarily true for them. No field of study is perfectly monolithic.

The book begins with a distinction between prescriptive and descriptive grammars.

> The point of view in this discussion is descriptive, not normative or legislative. The reader will find here, *not* how certain teachers or textbook writers or "authorities" think native speakers of English ought to use the language, but how certain native speakers actually do use it in natural, practical conversations carrying on the various activities of a community. (Fries, p. 3)[2]

Fries bases his analysis on some fifty hours of wiretapped telephone conversations (done in the innocent days before this was illegal).

At the end of the first chapter, Fries states that the purpose of his book is to:

> challenge anew the conventional use of "meaning" as the basic tool of analysis in the area of linguistic study in which it has had its strongest hold—sentence structure and syntax. (Otto Jespersen insists, for example, "But in syntax meaning is everything." *A Modern English Grammar* (Heidelberg, 1931), IV, 291.) [Fries's footnote.] (Fries, p. 7)

In the above quote, we see one of the key ideas of structural linguistics. Linguistics cannot use meaning as a tool in the analysis of language, a position completely opposed to the basic ideas of traditional grammar. The structuralists argued that the goal of linguistic analysis is to see how meaning is

---

[2]From *The Structure of English* by Charles Carpenter Fries, copyright, 1952, by Harcourt Brace Jovanovich, Inc., and reprinted with their permission. [Whenever Fries is cited throughout this text, the reference is to *The Structure of English*.]

conveyed. Since meaning is the goal, it cannot at the same time be a means used to reach the goal, or else the discovery process is completely circular: meaning is discovered by the use of meaning. For Fries, language is a physical, observable phenomena that must be studied objectively.

The second chapter raises the question, what is a sentence? The procedure that Fries uses in this chapter is typical of the rest of the book. He first examines the possible answers that traditional grammar of the schoolroom variety provides. In this case, he cites a number of traditional definitions of the sentence (for example, "A sentence is a group of words expressing a complete thought."). He then criticizes the traditional definitions, not on the grounds that they are wrong, but on the grounds that they are inadequate definitions, that is, given just the traditional definition by itself, we could not properly sort out sentences from other groups of words that are not sentences. In short, the traditional definitions of a sentence "work" only because the user of the definitions knows how to apply them.

Fries concludes that the traditional definitions of a sentence all fail because they assume that there is some abstract, universal meaning or thought content that all sentences must share.

> The very fact, however, that the many attempts to grasp the "essence of the sentence" by this type of subtle reasoning and analysis have not given us a satisfactorily acceptable or workable set of criteria to make an acceptable definition (shown by the continual argument and dispute, and the varied attempts to form new definitions) seems to indicate that we must approach the problem from a different point of view. (Fries, p. 18)

The "different point of view" that Fries advocates is to base the definition of the sentence on its structure (its form) and not on its content (its meaning). This is the central idea from which structural linguistics gets its name: linguistic meaning can be investigated and understood only through an analysis of linguistic structures. The actual definition of a sentence that Fries proposes is quoted directly from Leonard Bloomfield's book *Language:*

> Each sentence is an independent linguistic form, not included by virtue of any grammatical construction in any larger linguistic form. (*Language,* p. 170)

This definition does not tell us how to recognize an independent linguistic form, nor does it identify the grammatical constructions that include one form in another. In order to make use of this definition of a sentence, Fries must provide some meaning-free way to define the forms and constructions that make up sentences. Fries approaches this task by the establishment of an *utterance unit.* An utterance unit is the largest possible freestanding stretch of speech. It is defined by Fries as "Any stretch of speech by one person before which there was silence on his part and after which there was also silence on his part" (p. 23). Fries then chopped up the recorded telephone conversations into sequences of utterance units, the boundaries of each unit unambiguously established by a change of speakers. Thus, by definition, an utterance unit is an independent, freestanding form not included in another form. However, as yet, it cannot be defined as a sentence, because at this point in the analysis, we have no way of knowing what is included within the utterance unit. It could be a single syllable, or a lengthy speech containing many independent sentences. Fries's next problem is to find some way to break down the utterance units into component parts. He argues that the utterance unit must contain either one sentence (defined as a freestanding form) or more than one sentence. Fries says, without much in the way of further example or justification, that it was possible through his analysis to distinguish between those utterance units that contained a single sentence and those that contained two or more sentences.

The third chapter is concerned with different kinds of sentences. Fries begins with a discussion of the two traditional ways of classifying sentence types. One type of classification distinguishes between *simple, compound,* and *complex* sentences. The other type distinguishes between *declarative, interrogative, exclamatory,* and *imperative* sentences. Fries does not object to the validity of these distinctions, but to the way that traditional grammar attempted to define them:

> Again the definitions furnish no practical help in sorting out our utterances. It is not enough to say that a sentence that "asks a question" is an "interrogative sentence," or that a sentence that "gives a command" is an "imperative sentence," or that a sentence that "makes a statement" is a "declarative sentence." No real gain derives from simply attaching technical names to the meanings "asks a question," "gives a command," "makes a statement." We are concerned with discovering just how we know that any particular sentence "asks a question," or "gives a command," or "makes a statement." In other words, how in English are these particular meanings signaled? (Fries, p. 32)

At this point, Fries turns away from any attempt to sort out sentence types on the basis of meaning. Instead, he proposes that we examine language in terms of its practical function as a means of communication. To do this, Fries turns to the discipline of psychology, and presents a model of behavior known as "stimulus-response." The classical stimulus-response model is simply

$$S \longrightarrow R$$

where S = stimulus; R = response

The stimulus-response model (often abbreviated as S-R) is a very powerful way of explaining many kinds of behavior. Fries gives the example of a cat, stimulated by the sensation of hunger, responding to the stimulus by seeking and devouring food. We could represent this in an S-R model this way:

The great advantage of the S-R model given above is its simplicity. Fries points out, however, that when dealing with human beings, the simple S-R model must be expanded to incorporate the mediation of language. A cat normally obtains food only by direct, overt physical response. Man, however, may obtain food by an indirect method—through language. Leonard Bloomfield illustrates this point by means of a parable:

> Suppose that Jack and Jill are walking down a lane. Jill is hungry. She sees an apple in a tree. She makes a noise with her larynx, tongue, and lips. Jack vaults the fence, climbs the tree, takes the apple, brings it to Jill, and places it in her hand. Jill eats the apple. (*Language*, p. 22)

The simple S-R model given above is inadequate to describe the behavior of Jack and Jill. Jill is the one stimulated by hunger, but Jack is the one who makes the overt response. Fries, following Bloomfield, proposes a more complex model to account for the effect of language on human behavior:

$$S \longrightarrow r \longrightarrow s \longrightarrow R$$

Fries illustrates the meaning of this model by means of the following diagram:

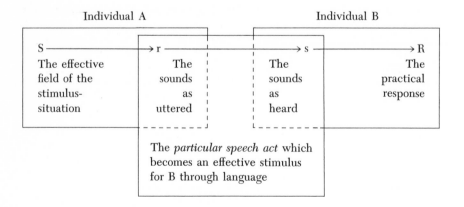

The actual speech act consists of both the *r*, the sounds uttered by individual A, and the *s*, the sounds heard by individual B. The "meaning" of any speech signal must consist, then, not only of the practical situation which stimulates the making of the particular speech sounds but also of the practical response which these particular speech sounds (through language) produce in another individual. (Fries, p. 34)

To an observer standing outside the diagram, there are three discrete events that comprise the behavior of A and B: (1) The situation that stimulates A; (2) What A says (in Fries's terminology, the *speech act*), and (3) B's action. The linguist, taking the role of the outside observer, can look at the speech act from the point of view of A (the speaker) by investigating the connection between what the speaker says and the situations that caused him to say what he did, or the linguist can look at the speech act from the point of view of B (the hearer) by investigating the connection between what B heard and the actions that B performed. In terms of Fries's diagram, the linguist can investigate speech either in terms of S (the speaker's stimulus) or in terms of R (the hearer's response).

Since World War II, both of these lines of investigation have been actively pursued. By and large, linguists have abandoned the first possibility (the correlation of the speaker's stimulus with his actual speech act) to the psychologists, because outside of highly controlled situations, it is very difficult to be certain of what the field of the speaker's stimulus actually is. Instead, the structural linguists have devoted themselves to the second alternative: the correlation of the speech sounds with the hearer's responses. Fries's belief in this line of investigation leads him to make a further assumption:

> We can proceed on the assumption that if a particular response *regularly* occurs after a speech form or a language pattern then this pattern or form "means" this response. The regularity with which the response follows the utterance of the language pattern becomes the basis for the kind of prediction of a following response that makes the functioning of language possible. (Fries, p. 36)

On the basis of this assumption, Fries can now return to his original task of categorizing the various types of single free utterances. According to the model adopted above, Fries can classify the free utterances on the basis of the type of responses they elicit: those utterances which are followed by *oral* responses are classified as questions, for example,

UTTERANCE	RESPONSE
Do you remember H____ worked in ____	Yes, yes (205)
Is Mrs. M____ there	No. Mrs. M____'s gone away on vacation (212) (Fries, p. 45)

Those utterances that are followed by *action* rather than oral responses are classified as requests, for example:

UTTERANCE	RESPONSE
Read that again will you	[Reads aloud a telegram] (239)
Just hold the phone he's on the other wire	[Waits until R____ speaks] (240) (Fries, p. 47)

Those utterances that are followed by conventional signals of attention (for example, *yes, oh, uh-huh*) are classified as statements. Fries gives an example of this type of utterance a passage in which the signals of attention are put in parenthesis:

> I wanted to tell you one more thing I've been talking with Mr. D____ in the purchasing department about our typewriter (yes) that order went in March seventh however it seems that we are about eighth on the list (I see). . . . (Fries, p. 50)

Having established a basis for classifying different types of single, free utterances, Fries next turns to the problem of analyzing the elements that make up the different types of sentences. The fourth chapter begins with a discussion of the traditional approach to sentence analysis. The passage quoted below is a clear example of the structuralists' rejection of meaning as a tool in grammatical analysis:

> In the usual approach to the grammatical analysis of sentences one must know the total meaning of the utterance before beginning any analysis. The process of analysis consists almost wholly of giving technical names to portions of this total meaning. For example, given the sentence *the man gave the boy the money,* the conventional grammatical analysis would consist in attaching the name "subject" to the word *man,* the name "predicate" to the word *gave,* the name "indirect object" to the word *boy,* the name "direct object" to the word *money,* and the name "declarative sentence" to the whole utterance. If pressed for the basis upon which these names are given to these words, one would, in accord with the traditional method, say that the word *man* is called "subject" because it "designates the person about whom an assertion is made"; that the word *gave* is called "predicate" because it is "the word that asserts something about the subject"; that the word *boy* is called "indirect object" because it "indicates the person to or for whom the action is done"; and that the word *money* is called "direct object" because it "indicates the thing that receives the action of the verb." The sentence is called a "declarative sentence" because it "makes a statement." The whole procedure begins with the total meaning of the sentence and consists solely in ascribing the technical terms "subject," "predicate," "indirect object," "direct object," and "declarative sentence" to certain parts of that meaning. "Knowing grammar" has thus meant primarily the ability to apply and react to a technical terminology consisting of approximately seventy items. It is this kind of "grammatical knowledge" that is assumed in the usual discussions of the value of "grammar" for an effective practical command of English, or for English composition, or for mastery of foreign language. It is this kind of grammatical analysis, this starting with the total meaning, *and the using of this meaning as the basis for the analysis*—an analysis that makes no advance beyond the ascribing of certain technical terms to parts of the meaning already known—it is this kind of grammatical analysis that modern linguistic science discards as belonging to a prescientific era. (Fries, pp. 54–55)

Fries begins his analysis of the sentence *the man gave the boy the money* by distinguishing between two different kinds of meaning. One kind of meaning is *lexical meaning*. The lexical meaning of *man*, for instance, is the dictionary definition of the word: it tells us what the word *man* refers to in the real world. However, what the dictionary cannot tell us is how the word *man* is used in the sentence quoted above. In the sentence *The boy gave the man the money*, the function of the word *man* is quite different from its function in the first sentence. The grammatical function of a word in a sentence is called the *structural meaning* of the word in Fries's terminology. Thus, in order to understand a sentence, we must know both what its words mean (the lexical meaning) and we must know their grammatical function within the sentence in question (the structural meaning).

Fries next addresses himself to the question of how we recognize structural meaning. He argues that structural meaning is "signalled by specific and definite devices. It is the devices that signal structural meanings which constitute the grammar of a language. *The grammar of a language consists of the devices that signal structural meanings.*" (p. 56). When the appropriate structural signals are absent from a sentence the sentence will be ambiguous because we can assign it more than one possible structural meaning. Fries illustrates this point with the sentence

Ship sails today.   (Fries, p. 62)

The sentence is ambiguous because both *ship* and *sails* could be either a noun or a verb. However, if the appropriate structural signals were present, the sentence would not be ambiguous, for example:

The ship sails today.
Ship the sails today.

In this case, *the* signals the structural meaning of *ship* and *sail* in the two sentences.

One of the deeply held tenets of structural linguistics is that the recognition of structural meaning is independent of lexical meaning. In other words, a speaker of a language does not depend on the meaning of the word in a sentence to tell him what its grammatical function is. In support of this position, Fries makes up sentences with words that have structural meaning but no lexical meaning, for example *Woggles ugged diggles* (p. 71). The fact that we know that *woggles* and *diggles* are nouns and that *ugged* is a verb means that we identify part of speech without reference to meaning.

In the fifth chapter, Fries discusses the inadequacy of the traditional definitions of parts of speech. Again, the basis of his objection to traditional definitions is not that their classification is faulty, but that their definitions are not really defining, for example:

What is a "noun," for example? The usual definition is that "a noun is the name of a person, place, or thing." But *blue* is the "name" of a color, as is *yellow* or *red*, and yet, in the expressions *a blue tie, a yellow rose, a red dress* we do not call *blue* and *yellow* and *red* "nouns." We do call *red* a noun in the sentence *this red is the shade I want. Run* is the "name" of an action, as is *jump* or *arrive. Up* is the "name" of a direction, as is *down* or *across*. In spite of the fact that these words are all "names" and thus fit the definition given for a noun they are not called nouns in such expressions as "We *ran* home," "They were looking *up* into the sky," "The acid made the fiber *red*." The definition as it stands—that "A noun is a name"—does not furnish all the criteria necessary to exclude from this group many words which our grammars in actual practice classify in other parts of speech. (Fries, p. 67)

However valid Fries's criticism of certain kinds of traditional grammars may be, it is not a valid criticism of sophisticated traditional grammarians like Jespersen. In his *Essentials of English Grammar,* Jespersen makes no attempt to define nouns, either by meaning or otherwise. He simply gives a list of typical types of nouns with the following comment: "It is practically impossible to give exact and exhaustive definitions of these [part of speech] classes; nevertheless the classification itself rarely offers occasion for doubt and will be sufficiently clear to students if a fair number of examples are given. . . ." (Jespersen, p. 66)

How does Fries go about establishing the parts of speech without reference to lexical meaning? His approach is based on the concept of *pattern-substitution*. Fries conceives the sentence to be a pattern of words in a certain grammatical arrangement. If we replace one of the words in the pattern with another word, and the grammatical pattern remains unchanged, then the two words must belong to the same grammatical class. For example, here is a set of substitutions that Fries gives:

> The *concert* was good.
> *food*
> *coffee*
> *taste*
> *container*
> *difference*
> *privacy*
> *family*
> *company* [guests]   (Fries, p. 76)

The fact that all these words are mutually substitutable means that they must belong to the same grammatical class. Fries establishes a total of four sets of substitution classes in a similar manner (these sets bear a striking resemblance to the traditional classes of nouns, verbs, adjectives and adverbs).

By the same process Fries sorts out another group of words which he calls *function words*. Function words are the converse of the four major parts of speech classes. Function words are the "little" words that are not nouns, verbs, adjectives, and adverbs. They are words like *the, and, not,* prepositions, *yes, no,* relative pronouns, and so forth. Sometimes the function word classes are called "closed" classes, as opposed to the part-of-speech classes which are called the "open" classes. For example, let us compare the "closed" class of prepositions with the "open" class of nouns. The number of prepositions is strictly limited. In a few minutes it is possible to list all currently used English prepositions. From a historical standpoint, the list is quite stable: over a period of the last hundred years, there has been practically no change at all in the list. Compare this with the list of all currently used English nouns. No one knows how many nouns there are. Even if two people had the time and patience to list all the nouns that they knew, their lists would not necessarily agree. Over a period of even several years, hundreds of new nouns come into the language and some must fall into general disuse.

There is also a great difference in the probability of occurrence of any given word from the two types of word classes. For instances, odds are good that if you write down an arbitary preposition, you will find an occurrence of it within a page or two of this book. However, if you were to arbitrarily pick a noun by putting your finger down on a page of the dictionary, the odds against your finding the same noun in a few pages are great. From the standpoint of numbers then, the function word classes consist of a small number of highly frequent words, while the part-of-speech classes consist of a large number of words, each of a relatively low average frequency of occurrence.

In the fifth and sixth chapters, Fries's point of view has been that of a linguist objectively analyzing data. As a result of that analysis he has isolated various speech classes on the basis of substitutability. These classes consist of the four part-of-speech classes of noun, verb, adjective, and adverb (though Fries gives the classes numerical labels rather than the traditional names) and a group of function word classes.

In the seventh chapter, Fries shifts his point of view:

> Now we must raise a different question. How does the user of our language recognize each of these functioning units in the stream of speech? We have insisted that unless he does recognize the differing functioning units, the separate parts of speech, he cannot respond to (or give) the necessary signals of structural meaning. This recognition, however, for the users of the language need not be in any way a conscious recognition. We mean by "recognition" here an automatic conditioned response that, in general, the naïve native speaker cannot usually analyze or describe. He must, nevertheless, respond accurately to these differing functioning units or he cannot understand the language or communicate in it. What precisely are the identifying features that operate for these practical users of the language? (Fries, pp. 110–111)

Fries's task is to identify the structural signals by which speakers actually recognize the speech class of a word. The function word classes pose no problem. Since they are small, closed classes of high frequency of occurrence they are learned as items. With the four part-of-speech classes, however, there must be some characteristics by which we can recognize the different parts of speech. It is impossible that we learn to recognize nouns the way we recognize prepositions because, as the ambiguity of *ship sails today* illustrates, one and the same word can belong to more than one part-of-speech class.

Here are structural signals by which Fries claims that speakers recognize a noun to be a noun:

a.   Contrast of form between nouns and other parts of speech. For example, noun/verb: *arrival/arrive, defense/defend;* noun/adjective: *big-ness/big, truth/true.*

b.   Compounds ending in *-one, -body, -thing, -self/selves*. For example, *someone, somebody, something, myself.*

c.   Contrast of singular versus plural forms marked by "s." For example, *boys/boy, desks/desk.*

d.   Irregular contrasts of singular and plural forms. For example, *men/man, children/child.*

e.   Possessive "s." For example, *man/man's/men/men's.*

f.   Position after determiners. For example, in the following phrase the italicized words are nouns because they follow determiners:

The *poor* and the *rich*, the very *lowest* and the very *highest* are. . . . (p. 118)

g.   Position after prepositions. For example, *at school, by telephone.*

h.   Recognition of the other parts of speech in the sentence. Fries gives as an example of this category the following newspaper headlines: (p. 119)

Bus Fares Cheap in Emergency
Bus Fares Badly in Emergency

We recognize *Fares* to be a noun in the first sentence and a verb in the second sentence because we recognize the part of speech of the word following *Fares*.

The formal characteristics of nouns that Fries gives above break down into two types: characteristics of the form of the word (groups a–e), and characteristics of position within the sentence (groups f–h). These two basic types of characteristics are also used in the characterization of the other three parts of speech.

The eighth chapter, "Structural Patterns of Sentences," distinguishes between statements, questions, and requests on the basis of different arrangements of the part-of-speech classes. To do this, Fries must introduce the notion of subject-verb agreement. If the words that are "tied" by agreement occur in the order noun-verb, then the sentence is a statement. If they occur in the order verb-noun, then the sentence is a question. Here is Fries's explanation:

(A)	(B)
1. The leader is here	1. The leaders are here
2. Is the leader here	2. Are the leaders here

As speakers of English, we respond to the first sentence of each group, *the leader is here* and *the leaders are here*, as statements of fact, not questions seeking information, nor requests for action. We respond to the second sentence in each group as questions. (Fries, p. 144)

A request is a sentence in which the verb is in the simple, uninflected form, and is not "tied" to any noun.

The ninth chapter deals with functional relationships such as subject, direct object, indirect object, object complement, appositive, and the like. Fries rejects the traditional meaning-based definition of these terms, and instead, tries to identify these relationships in terms of formal signals of structure. For example, "subject" is defined as being that noun which is "tied" by agreement with a verb. The other functional relationships are defined in terms of linguistic formulas or patterns. For example, given the pattern

determiner-noun-verb-determiner-noun

the second noun, by definition, is a direct object, for example,

The boy saw the dog.

Here is Fries's summary of the chapter:

> Our conscious experience with language has served to overstress the part that words play in the conveying of meaning. We find it difficult to believe that one could understand the meanings of all the words in a language and yet not understand a single utterance in that language. Even when the meanings that are signalled by structures are pointed out, their importance for the whole process of communication usually escapes us. That these meanings really depend upon an intricate system of formal features apart from the words as vocabulary units is not grasped easily by those who seldom try to face the facts of language objectively. (Fries, p. 201)

At the risk of dreadful oversimplification on my part, structural linguistics (as represented by Fries's *The Structure of English*) may be described as a revolutionary departure from traditional grammar in terms of what there is in language that needs to be explained. For Jespersen, explanation meant discussion of how a certain form or construction came to be used the way it is. The explanation could be semantic or purely historical. For the structural linguist, the basic question of linguistics that needed explanation was a psychological one: How does language actually work as a functional system of communication? As we have seen, this general question was narrowed to the more tractable question: How does language convey meaning? The structuralists answer to this question is, I think, fairly summed up in this quotation from Fries:

> The total linguistic meaning of any utterance consists of the lexical meanings of the separate words plus such structural meanings. No utterance is intelligible without both lexical meanings and structural meanings. How, then, are these structural meanings conveyed in English from the speaker to a hearer? Structural meanings are not just vague matters of the context, so called; they are fundamental and necessary meanings in every utterance and are signalled by specific and definite devices. It is the devices that signal structural meanings which constitute the grammar of a language. *The grammar of a language consists of the devices that signal structural meanings.* (Fries, p. 56)

For the structuralist, two basic conclusions follow from the above position:

(1) There is a one-to-one tie between structural signals and meanings which can be described adequately within the stimulus-response school of psychological behavior. The language learner comes to associate certain meanings with certain forms. As Fries puts it

> One of the earliest steps in learning to talk is this learning to use automatically the patterns of form and arrangement that constitute the devices to signal structural meaning. So thoroughly have they become unconscious habits in very early childhood that the ordinary adult speaker of English finds it extremely difficult not only to describe what he does in these matters but even to realize that there is anything there to be described. (Fries, pp. 57–58)

The role of a scientist, from the stimulus-response standpoint, is that of a detached objective observer who tries to stand outside the system he is examining. Ideally, the linguist first records a substantial body of data without prejudice as to how he thinks the language works (since each language is a unique entity that demands a unique description). He must then sift through the data and discover the linguistic forms that correlate with meaning. Any reliance on meaning to isolate the forms of the language is circular, and therefore unscientific. From this point of view, obviously Jespersen belongs to the prescientific era: Jespersen is highly subjective and relies continuously on meaning as the basis of analysis.

(2) Linguistic analysis needs to distinguish between the kind of information available to the learner and the kind of information that is not. The former will have relevance to the acquisition and use of language, while the latter will not. Historical information about the English language may be of interest to the specialist, but it is obviously irrelevant to any examination of how language conveys meaning since the typical speaker does not have historical information available to him. From this point of view, Jespersen's excursions into the history of the language are irrelevant to the central topic of how language conveys meaning.

THE TRANSFORMATIONAL REVOLUTION

For the structural grammarian, the goal of linguistics is to account for linguistic behavior. The basis of the transformational revolution is ultimately the simple observation that explanations of our linguistic behavior can not account for the extent of our linguistic knowledge. For example, Fries demonstrated the importance of structural signals by showing that if these signals were omitted from a sentence (as in newspaper headlines), the resulting sentence would be ambiguous. Chomsky points out that there are other kinds of ambiguity that have nothing to do with structural signals. A well-known example from *Syntactic Structures* is the phrase

The shooting of the hunters

This phrase can mean either (1) the hunters shot something, or (2) someone shot the hunters. Here we have one form with two different meanings. However, unlike the ambiguity of *ship sails today*, it is very difficult to see how the phrase can be made unambiguous by adding structural signals. In other words, the ambiguity of *the shooting of the hunters* is not due to a confusion as to the proper part of speech classification. There is no doubt that *shooting* is a gerund (a verb changed into a noun by the addition of *-ing*) and that *hunters* is a noun. Even knowing this, the sentence is still ambiguous.

One possible solution from a structural standpoint would be to argue that the ambiguity is due to the function word *of* in that particular pattern. In other words, when we have the sequence

gerund-of-noun

the sequence will be ambiguous in the same way that *the shooting of the hunters* is. The problem with this solution is that it does not work. Chomsky cites two phrases that appear to have exactly the same structure as *the shooting of the hunters:*

The growling of lions
The raising of flowers

Neither one of these phrases is ambiguous in the sense that *the shooting of the hunters* is. This is a fact that native speakers of English simply know. Furthermore, we know that the relation of the gerund to the noun in the two above phrases is not alike. In *the growling of lions* the relation of *lions* to *growling* is similar to the relation of *hunters* to *shooting* in the first meaning of *the shooting of the hunters,* namely, the lions growled and the hunters shot. In *the raising of flowers,* the relation of *flowers* to *raising* is similar to the relation of *hunters* to *shooting* in the second meaning of *the shooting of the hunters,* namely, someone grew flowers and someone shot the hunters.

Another frequently cited pair of sentences that illustrate the discrepancy between the information contained in the structural signals and what we actually know is the following:

John is easy to please.
John is eager to please.

In terms of sentence structure, these two sentences are identical. However, every native speaker of English knows that these two sentences are really totally different. The first sentence states that John is an easy person to please, while the second sentence states that John is eager to please us. There is nothing in the sentence structure of these two sentences that could account for the difference in the way we understand them. A possible explanation could be that the difference is in the lexical meaning of the two adjectives *easy* and *eager*. We can show that this is not the case, however, by substituting other adjectives into the same position. For example, we know that *John is difficult to please* is like *John is easy to please*, while *John is anxious to please* is like *John is eager to please*. Consequently, the difference between the two sentences is more basic than just the lexical meanings of *easy* and *eager*.

Ambiguity results when one form has two or more meanings. The opposite of ambiguity is when one meaning is embodied in two or more forms. For the sake of a term, let us call the opposite of ambiguity *paraphrase*. The classic instance of paraphrase in English is the relation between the active and passive versions of the same sentence, for example:

Active: The detective saw the accident.
Passive: The accident was seen by the detective.

In structural terms, the two sentences above are totally unrelated. The subject noun of the active sentence is *detective* while the subject noun of the passive is *accident*. The verb of the active sentence is *see* in the past tense. The verb of the passive sentence is *was* plus *see* in the past participle form. The object of the active sentence is *accident* while in the passive sentence it is *detective*. Despite these obvious differences, every speaker of English knows that in a very profound sense, these two sentences are basically the same. Furthermore, we all know that the passive is a kind of alternative version of the active, and not the other way around. Paraphrase relations are a second way in which our knowledge of the language cannot be accounted for in terms of lexical meanings of words and structural signals.

For the transformational grammarian the basic goal of linguistics is to account for what speakers know about their language. The transformational revolution is a radical shift in the kinds of questions that linguists deal with, just as the structural revolution was a radical shift away from the questions that traditional grammarians concerned themselves with. A scientific revolution is not so much a matter of changing the answers, but changing the relevant questions.

We have already seen that a native speaker of a language is aware of ambiguity and paraphrase relationships beyond what can be accounted for in terms of structural signals. What kind of knowledge does this awareness imply? For one thing, it implies that a speaker of a language, in some unconscious, intuitive way, "knows" the internal structure and the relationship of one part with another of all the sentences in his language. This knowledge does not depend on any prior exposure to each particular sentence nor does it necessarily depend on the meaningfulness or appropriateness of the sentence to some situation. Chomsky illustrates both of these points in *Syntactic Structures* with the following pair of nonsense sentences:

Colorless green ideas sleep furiously.
Furiously sleep ideas green colorless.

When Chomsky first made up these sentences, it is safe to assume that neither had ever occurred in the history of the English language. Both are unique, and both are meaningless. Yet every speaker of English knows that the first sentence, no matter how witless, is a grammatical sentence in English and that the second sentence is not. We may characterize a speaker's knowledge of his language as the ability to make judgments about sentences: he can decide whether a sentence is grammatical or not (more accurately, he can decide if two sentences are equally grammatical, equally ungrammatical, or one more grammatical than the other); he can decide whether two sentences mean the same thing or not (paraphrase); he can recognize which sentences have more than one meaning (ambiguity); he can decide if the relation of the parts to the whole in one sentence is the same as or different from the relation of the parts to the whole of another sentence. In short, the transformational grammarian is interested in linguistic knowledge.

Transformationalists disagree sharply with the theory of language acquisition that the structuralists proposed. For Fries, the child learns the language of his society by associating certain language forms with the situations that called them forth. The basic transformational objection to this theory is that the term "association" is not an explanation nor even a description of some process; it is merely a label for some unobservable process that we assume must take place. If we try to narrow the definition of "association" to some stimulus-response model so that it becomes explicit and testable, it is obviously inadequate to account for the enormous creativity of human language. Except for the passages that are directly quoted from other writers, it is a safe bet that no reader of this book can remember ever having encountered any sentence in this book before. For example the sentence

The dragon rejected the banana with a contemptuous snort and a flip of his tail.

is totally new, and yet poses no special problems of interpretation. The point is that it is perfectly normal for us to use and interpret sentences we have never encountered before. How, then, can we have any prior "association" between new sentences and the situations that call them forth?

The associationist's answer to this question is that we respond to new sentences on the basis of analogy to sentences we already know. In some sense, this is undoubtedly true, but the point is that "analogy" is no more an explanation or a description than "association" was. It is merely a label for some unobservable process that we assume must take place. Fries, to his credit, tried to make the basis of analogy precise by the concept of structural signals and sentence patterns. However, as we have seen, structural signals and sentence patterns leave a lot of our linguistic knowledge unaccounted for. How the transformationalists attempt to account for the enormous creativity of language will be discussed shortly.

The structural linguist was very concerned about discovery procedure. The structural linguist stood outside the language under examination. Fries, in investigating his own language, tried to approach it *as though it were totally foreign to him.* From his point of view, a valid scientific generalization could only come as a result of an objective examination of the relevant data. The whole point of Fries's book is to demonstrate how the structural signals of English could be discovered solely from an objective examination of a substantial block of recorded conversations, without relying on meaning.

In the transformational view, the whole question of discovery procedures is a side issue. The proof of the pudding is not in the cooking, but in the tasting. A generalization is valid just to the extent that it works. By what flash of inspiration a scientist arrives at a generalization may be a matter of great interest to the study of creativity, but it is ultimately beside the point as far as the science is concerned. The basic question we must ask of a generalization, then, is not where did it come from, but how well does it work? In other words, how valid is it? Ultimately, the structural view is that valid generalizations can be guaranteed if the proper discovery procedures are followed. The transformational view is that if the scientist is truly an objective observer of a system outside himself, and has no prior notions or prejudices about how that system works, then science is done for. Any block of data, even a very large one, has all kinds of internal structures and patterns that are purely accidental. For example, it might be the case that in a given block of language data the questions that begin with *why* all have an even number of words in them. Or it might be the case that every sentence collected on Tuesday contained at least two prepositions. It might be the case that every fifty-second sentence begins with the letter *s*. There are obviously an infinite number of possible accidental patterns that occur in any limited body of data.

We all know that these patterns are irrelevant to the way English actually works. But if we took seriously the idea of the purely objective scientist who has *no* preconceptions about what to look for in the system under analysis, we would have to admit all of these patterns as valid generalizations about the data under examination. These absurd generalizations point up the impossibility of taking at face value Fries's claim to have discovered the structural signals of English solely by an objective examination of the data. From this point of view, the structural linguists' discovery procedure has an unreal, gamelike quality. The linguist pretends that he does not know what he is looking for so that when he finds what he wants, he can claim to have found it by a rigorous, objective, scientific procedure. Fries ends up with exactly the same classifications for English that grammarians have always had. The difference is, according to Fries, that he arrived at his classifications objectively, that is, without knowing what he was looking for.

The reader should not conclude from this critical discussion that Fries's *The Structure of English* is a bad book. On the contrary, it is an outstanding piece of scholarship. It is only because scholars like Fries made the claims of structural linguistics explicit and tried to show how these claims could be met in actual practice that the discipline was able to advance.

One of the central concerns of language study has always been how language works. Each school of language study has refined and narrowed this basic question in its own way. We have already seen that the structural linguist was concerned with how language conveys meaning. The transformational linguist, on the other hand, is concerned with how we can account for linguistic knowledge, that is, the kinds of judgments that speakers make about their own language.

The transformational school has approached its question from a very special point of view—that of mathematical logic. In crude terms, the transformational linguist attempts to construct an artificial system or device that duplicates the kinds of judgments that people make. This system is what transformationalists call a grammar. A transformational grammar of English is a device that mirrors the judgments that a native speaker of English would make. In a very basic sense, a transformational grammar cannot do anything that a speaker of English cannot do. In other words, the grammar is an attempt to make explicit and conscious what the speaker of English does intuitively and unconsciously.

At this point the reader needs to bear in mind an old riddle. What has two eyes like an Indian, two arms like an Indian, two legs like an Indian, and looks exactly like an Indian, but is *not* an Indian? The answer, of course, is a picture of an Indian. A transformational grammar is a picture or model of our linguistic ability to make judgments about our language; however, it is not that ability itself; it is a device that duplicates the kind of judgments people make about their own language; it is *not* a direct statement about what goes on between people's ears. Of course, if the grammar is good, that is, if it conforms very closely to judgments we make, we would hope that the grammar would be suggestive about the mind's actual linguistic operations and provide clues to how these operations might be investigated. Considering how recent the transformational approach is, it is gratifying that such investigation has already begun to bear fruit.

Perhaps the most elementary judgment we can make about our language is to distinguish between sentences in the language and sentences that are not in the language. By *in the language* is meant *consisting only of words in that language*. This definition implies nothing about the grammaticality, truth-value, or appropriateness of the sentence. For example, *desk a of super by* is a five-word sentence in English. The fact that we also know that it is an ungrammatical sentence is not the point at question. Any speaker of English knows that the following five-word sentence is *not* a sentence in the language: *I pahn kohla wesei tui.* (In fact, it is a sentence in Ponapean, a language spoken in the Trust Territory of the Pacific.) In more specific terms, we know when a sentence is English. The device that would mirror this linguistic judgment is correspondingly elementary. Imagine a device that would take a large dictionary and then list every possible combination of all the words in the dictionary. This device would produce a listing of all possible English sentences. Any sentence that was not on the list would not be a sentence in English, although, of course, it might be a sentence in some other language.

In order to understand some of the implications of the device described above, let us pretend that there is a rare language spoken only on a remote island by a colony of deaf people. This language is exactly like all other human languages with one exception: it has only three words, *glug, aarg,* and *slish*. How many possible one-word sentences are there in this language? Obviously, three. How many possible two-word sentences are there? The first answer that might occur to you is six. The correct answer, however, is nine. To see why nine is the right answer, let us write out all the combinations. There are three combinations beginning with *glug: glug glug; glug aarg; glug slish.* There are three beginning with *aarg: aarg glug; aarg aarg; aarg slish,* and three more beginning with *slish: slish glug; slish aarg; slish slish,* for a total of nine. How many possible three-word sentences are there in this language? The answer is twenty-seven, each of the nine two-word combinations with each of the three words. In summary, we have this kind of a sequence for a language with three words: $3 : 9 : 27$. A student of mathematics would immediately recognize that the total number of sentences for each sentence length is going up by the number of the words in the language raised to the power of the number of words in the sentence. That is, the number of possible sentences one-word long is $3^1 = 3$; the number of possible two-word sentences is $3^2 = 9$; the number of possible three-word sentences is $3^3 = 27$. The number of possible sentences ten words long is 3^{10} or $3 \times 3 \times 3 \times 3 \times 3 \times 3 \times 3 \times 3 \times 3 \times 3 = 59,049$.

An important theoretical point here is that there is no such thing as the longest possible sentence even in this artificial language anymore than there is such a thing as the largest possible number. This latter claim can be proved false by taking what is claimed to be the largest possible number and adding a one to it. In the same fashion, we can prove that there is no such thing as the longest possible sentence in English (or any other natural language, even our made-up one), by adding one more word to what is claimed to be the longest possible sentence. Consequently, our imaginary language with three words contains an infinite number of possible sentences because there is no point at which we must stop making sentences longer.

Let us now apply our imaginary device to our imaginary language. Suppose we have a three-word sentence and we want to know if it is a possible sentence in the language. If the sentence in question occurs on the list of possible three-word sentences, then we know that the sentence belongs to the language. If the sentence in question does not occur on the list, then we know that the sentence does not belong to the language. Even though there is no such thing as the longest possible sentence, it is also the case that every possible actual sentence is finite in length (or else it is not a sentence): it is a three-word sentence, a ten-word sentence, a million-word sentence. Similarly, even though there is no such thing as the largest possible number, every real number is only so many digits long. Consequently, we are always assured that our device will be able to tell us if any sequence of words is a sentence in the language. All we have to do is count the number of words in the sentence under question, turn to the list of all possible sentences of that same length, and check to see if it is there.

Returning to English, let us apply the same device, using more realistic data. The *Webster's Third New International Dictionary* contains some 450,000 entries. On the basis of this dictionary, then, the number of possible one-word sentences in English is 450,000. (Remember, *sentences* here does not mean just grammatical or meaningful sentences.) The number of possible two-word sentences is $450,000 \times 450,000 = 202,500,000,000$. The number of possible three-word sentences is $450,000 \times 450,000 \times 450,000 = 91,125,000,000,000,000$. Even though the numbers have become astronomical, the same principle still holds. Our device can decide for any arbitrary string of words whether it is or is not a possible sentence in English. Obviously, in the face of numbers of such magnitude, our device is a logical abstraction rather than a practical machine.

We have seen how we can construct an elementary logical device that will duplicate the ability of humans to judge whether or not an arbitrary sentence belongs to their language. A much more interesting problem, however, is constructing a logical device that will duplicate the judgments that we make about the possible sentences of our language. The listing of all possible English sentences includes both grammatical and ungrammatical sentences. What kind of device would separate out just the grammatical ones? Let us begin by considering the magnitude of the problem. Suppose that only one sentence out of a million possible sentences is grammatical (this is an arbitrary though not totally unreasonable figure). On this basis, we would expect 91,125,000,000 grammatical three-word sentences in English. To illustrate what an enormous number this is, imagine that we could read a three-word sentence in one second. If we read continuously 24 hours a day, 365 days a year, it would take us 2,887 years to read all of them. On this same basis, it would take us 1,299,150,000 years to read all the grammatical four-word sentences. Figuring the same way, we would quickly outstrip the estimated age of the universe while still dealing with relatively short sentences.

These figures are so large that they seem unreal. Nevertheless, when we realize the possibilities of language creativity, we can understand why the transformationalists emphasize the importance of our ability to produce and understand new sentences. In short, we do not understand a sentence by searching our memory to discover what prior experience we have had with this same sentence.

In order to judge whether a given sentence is grammatical or not, we must have some very abstract capacity that does not depend on prior acquaintance with the sentence under question. The central concern for transformationalists has been to construct a logical device that would duplicate this abstract capacity. This device is a transformational grammar.

How Does a Transformational Grammar Work?

The discussion above has emphasized the infinite creativity of our language capacity. Equally impressive, however, is the speed with which children are able to acquire the language of their family. It is quite literally the case that most children are able to talk before they can tie their shoelaces. Moreover, a child acquires language without any dependence upon instruction, and largely independent of both the environment around him and of his own personality and intelligence. Barring only the very extreme cases of infant deprivation and brain damage, all children seem to acquire their language as though it were the most natural thing in the world to do.

In order to duplicate the human capacity for language in an interesting way, our logical device must be sophisticated enough to account for the infinite creativity of human language and simple enough to account for the apparent ease with which children are able to master the language of their family. As Chomsky puts it, our device must make "infinite use of finite means." The only known logical device that fits the bill is a system of recursive rules. Let us begin with a sample of what such a rule system might look like for a small piece of English.

Concrete nouns (as opposed to abstract nouns like *soul* and *idea*) may be modified by a prepositional phrase of place. One of the peculiarities of prepositional phrases of place is that they always end with a concrete noun, which, in turn, can be modified by a prepositional phrase of place, which ends in a concrete noun, and so on. For example, *the man in the store across the street by the bank under the bridge*, and so forth. After fifty or sixty prepositional phrases have been strung together, we would undoubtedly find the combination stylistically completely unacceptable. Nevertheless, there is no rule of English that puts a maximum ceiling on the number of consecutive prepositional phrases that are grammatically allowable.

Here is how a recursive rule system could duplicate our ability to make "infinite use of finite means."

Noun Phrase   ⟶   *the* Noun (Prep Phrase)
Prep Phrase   ⟶   Preposition Noun Phrase
Noun   ⟶   *bank, bridge, man, river, street, store . . .*
Preposition   ⟶   *across, by, in, near, under . . .*
              ⟶   means 'rewrite as'
                ⌢ means 'plus'
              ( ) means 'optional'
              . . . means 'the list is incomplete'

By means of a diagram called a "phrase structure tree" we can show how this rule system can generate the sequence *the man in the store across the street by the bank under the bridge.*

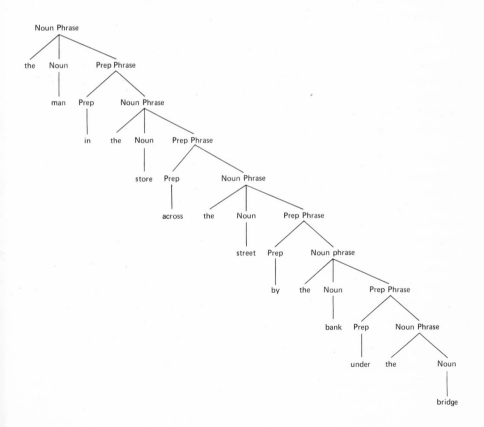

The first rule states that there is an abstract class in English called a "noun phrase," and that this noun phrase consists of two obligatory subclasses, *the* and noun, which must occur in that order, and a third optional subclass, prep phrase, which, if it occurs at all, must follow the noun.

The second rule carries on the further development of the prep phrase that made its appearance in the first rule. This rule states that the class called "prep phrase" consists of two subclasses, preposition and noun phrase, in that order. If, in the first rule, the option of including prep phrase as one of the subclasses of noun phrase is *not* exercised, then the second rule would be skipped, because in the noun phrase under development, there is no prep phrase. The last noun phrase in the sequence above, *the bridge,* is an example of noun phrase without an optional prep phrase; all the other noun phrases have a prep phrase.

The third and fourth rules rewrite the abstract classes noun and preposition as any one of the words that belong to these abstract classes. Thus, *bank, bridge,* and so on belong to the abstract class of noun; *across, by* and such belong to the abstract class of preposition. The derivation of the sequence is stopped when every abstract class has been broken down into its component subclasses and the subclasses have all been rewritten as individual words. That is, the rule system stops when there are no more abstract classes to rewrite.

A rule system is recursive when the rules loop back on themselves. In this particular case, the rule system is recursive because a noun phrase can occur as part of one of the subclasses of a noun phrase. The way the loop is broken is to rewrite a noun phrase without the prep phrase. A recursive system of this type has great generative powers. Even this miniature rule system is capable of generating an enormous number of phrases.

One of the biggest differences between a rule system approach and Fries's structural signals approach is that the rule system cannot account for its own existence. Structural linguists hoped to find a discovery procedure that would automatically reveal the significant generalizations about how a particular language works. The transformational linguist, however, simply makes up his rules as he goes along; he does not have to account for how he "discovered" his generalizations. We prefer one set of rules over another in terms of how well the rules can account for the relevant data, and in terms of the simplicity of the rules (everything else being equal, we would prefer the simpler of two sets of rules). The reader should view the rules presented here as tentative, incomplete and largely arbitrary. As our knowledge of how we acquire and use our language continues to grow, we can expect substantial modification of the rules given here.

The grammar presented here, like any recursive rule system, is based on abstract classes. In the case of a transformational grammar, the abstract classes are elements such as sentence, noun phrase, verb phrase, noun, preposition. There is no attempt made to define these abstract classes outside the rule system or to account for how we recognize them in actual practice. Ultimately, the only justification for the establishment of a particular abstract class is that rules employing this abstraction seem to work, and that the classes seem to be intuitively correct. In this respect transformational grammar and traditional grammarians such as Jespersen are in agreement. Jespersen, you recall, felt that he could give no definition by virtue of which we could identify a noun. Rather, he gave a list of nouns with the expectation that we would be able to infer the class just by seeing some sample members of it. Fries tried to give not only a description of the classes of English grammar, but also an account of how we actually recognized those classes (his definition of nouns, for instance). In this important respect, transformational grammarians and the better traditional grammarians stand at opposite poles from the structural linguists. The transformationalists argue that it is pretentious for us to advance claims about how people actually know things. Showing *what* people know and showing *how* they know it are two very different things. The transformational position is that by carefully investigating *what* people know, we may be able to start asking sensible questions about *how* they know.

Returning to the main theme of how a transformational grammar works, we can begin by saying that a transformational grammar is a recursive rule system that rewrites abstract classes as a sequence of subclasses, and that each of these subclasses is rewritten as a sequence of its subclasses until we reach the level of actual words. The starting point for the rule system is the largest abstract class, the one that includes all the others: the sentence. Again, there is no attempt to define this abstraction outside the rule system nor any attempt to account for how we recognize a sentence in actual practice.

The first rule in the grammar presented in this book is

Sentence $\longrightarrow$ Noun Phrase Auxiliary Verb Phrase.

This rule claims that all grammatical sentences in English can be traced back to a sequence of three abstract elements: a noun phrase, an auxiliary, and a verb phrase, in that order. In more traditional terms, the noun phrase functions as the subject of the sentence. The auxiliary and verb phrase together make up the complete predicate. In less formal language, then, the first rule of the grammar makes the assertion that all sentences consist of a subject and a predicate—a statement which is hardly revolutionary.

The auxiliary is the class that governs the tense of the sentence and which, if any, auxiliary and helping verbs occur before the main verb. The main verb is an abstract class that occurs as the essential part of the verb phrase. Many other abstract elements can also occur in the verb phrase, for instance, a noun phrase, which functions as the object of the main verb. As an illustration of the nature of these abstract structures, here is a sample derivation of the sentence *The detective saw the accident:*

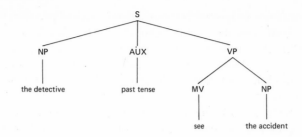

The detective is the subject noun phrase. *See* is the main verb. *The accident* is the object noun phrase. The auxiliary tells us that the main verb will be used in the past tense. The derivation does not prove that the sentence is grammatical. We knew that before we started. The rules cannot tell us anything we do not already know. They are an attempt to capture and make explicit the kinds of judgments we intuitively make about the sentences of our language. If the derivation proves anything, it proves that at least our rules are powerful enough to generate this particular given grammatical sentence.

When we began the discussion of transformational grammar, it was argued that our knowledge of English sentences could not be fully accounted by the kinds of analysis that structural linguistics offered. In particular, it was pointed out that our ability to recognize ambiguity and paraphrase seemed beyond the scope of structural linguistics. In order to deal satisfactorily with ambiguity and paraphrase we need to make a distinction between meaning and form. An ambiguous sentence is one in which there is one form but two meanings. A paraphrase relationship between two sentences is just the opposite: two different forms with but one meaning. We may represent the connection between form and meaning by the following diagram:

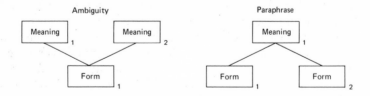

For example, the phrase *the shooting of the hunters* is ambiguous because the one form has two meanings:

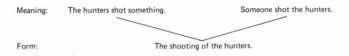

The paraphrase relation between the active and passive results from one meaning with two forms:

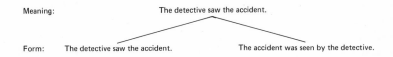

Meaning: The detective saw the accident.

Form: The detective saw the accident.   The accident was seen by the detective.

The tree diagram is a direct representation of the meaning (or equivalently, the abstract structure) of a sentence, and only indirectly and accidently a representation of its form. For example, the tree diagram of the sentence *The detective saw the accident* is nearly identical with the form of the "active" sentence, but it is quite different from the form of the "passive" version of the sentence. In this case, the active form of the sentence is closer to the abstract structure generated by the rule system than the passive form is.

In order to account for the forms of sentences, we need a second rule system to translate the abstract structures generated by the first rule system into the correct forms. This second rule system is a body of "transformational rules." The transformational rules "transform" the product of the first set of rules into the proper forms. The first set of rules are known as "phrase structure rules." The phrase structure rules generate abstract structures known as tree diagrams. The tree diagrams are a representation of the grammatical relationship between the words and abstract classes that make up the sentence, that is, the phrase structure rules account for the meaning of the sentence. The form of the sentence is accounted for by the transformational rules. In the case of the sentence represented by the tree diagram above, it has two different surface forms because we have the choice of applying or not applying the transformational rule that produces the passive. In the case of the ambiguous phrase *the shooting of the hunters*, the phrase structure rules generate two different sentences, which, because of the applications of different transformational rules, end up with exactly the same form.

In more formal terms, the tree diagram produced by the phrase structure rules represents the "deep structure" of the sentence. The transformational rules apply to the deep structure and produce as their output the "surface structure" of the sentence. In other words, the deep structure accounts for the meaning of the sentence, the surface structure accounts for the form of the sentence. The active sentence *The detective saw the accident* and the passive sentence *The accident was seen by the detective* are two different surface structures derived from the deep structure represented by the tree diagram above.

To recapitulate: ambiguity and paraphrase demonstrate that there is not a simple one-to-one connection between the meaning and the form of sentences. In transformational terms, the meaning of a sentence is accounted for by a tree diagram, which is a representation of the deep structure of the sentence. The tree diagram shows the relation of the words to each other and to the abstract classes that make up the sentence. The tree diagram is produced by the phrase structure rules. The deep structure is converted into actual form, that is, the surface structure, by the application of transformational rules. Thus the output of one set of rules serves as the input for the next set of rules. If there were no transformational rules, we could not account for the differences between form and meaning, that is, for ambiguity and paraphrase.

ORGANIZATION OF THE BOOK

A transformational grammar has two goals: (1) to generate all the sentences of a language, and (2) to provide for every sentence an analysis which conforms to our reaction to that sentence, that is, to distinguish grammatical sentences from ungrammatical ones and to analyze the internal structure of the sentences in a way that accounts for our intuitive understanding of the sentences and their relation to other sentences.

These goals are achieved (to the degree that they are achieved at all) by means of a system of rules. In order to guarantee that the system of rules will even approach the two goals, the system of rules must conform to a variety of different restraints. As there are different kinds of restraints, there are different kinds of rules conforming to those restraints. Each of the different rule types has a very definite area of the grammar as its province. Accordingly, this book is organized according to the different types of rules and their provinces. Part One deals with simple phrase structure rules; Part Two, with simple transformational rules; Part Three, with sentences combined by embedding rules; and Part Four, with sentences combined by joining rules. Since this book is not concerned with the strict mathematical formulation of the rules, let us begin with a brief overview of the province and function of the four types of rules.

Part One / Simple Phrase Structure Rules

One of the basic ideas of transformational grammar is that the sentences we normally produce and understand (what we will call surface sentences) can be derived from a number of underlying sentences of elemental simplicity. These elemental Dick-and-Jane sentences are thought to express overtly the relations that are conveyed implicitly in actually occurring surface sentences. It is further claimed that we actually understand surface sentences in terms of our intuitive grasp of the elementary sentences that make them up. The task of the simple phrase structure rule system is to generate all possible elementary sentences, and to provide each with an analysis that conforms to our intuitive feel for its meaning and structure.

Part Two / Simple Transformational Rules

Certain surface sentences seem to bear a close semantic and formal relation to other surface sentences. For example, every speaker of English knows that the sentences in the following pairs are somehow the same sentence, despite their superficial differences.

(a) John looked up the word.
John looked the word up.

(b) John gave the ball to Mary.
John gave Mary the ball.

(c) John first proposed the idea.
The idea was first proposed by John.

Furthermore, certain sentences seem to differ from other sentences in a systematic way. For instance, the following pairs of statements and questions are obviously related:

(d) John can come.
Can John come?

(e) John is here now.
Is John here now?

(f) John answered the question correctly.
Did John answer the question correctly?

In a transformational grammar, the connection between two closely related surface sentences is explained by deriving both from a single underlying elementary sentence. The difference in form between the two sentences is explained by the use of a transformational rule.

Part Three / Sentences Combined by Embedding Rules

So far we have discussed only nonrecursive rules. A recursive rule is a rule that can be applied over and over to produce longer and longer sentences. On page 25 an example was given of a recursive rule that can endlessly add prepositional phrases onto each other. Another example would be the placement of *somebody knows that* in front of any sentence to form a new sentence that we can put *somebody knows that* in front of. For example, given the sentence

Mary twisted her ankle.

we can produce a new sentence

I know that Mary twisted her ankle.

and another new sentence

He knows that I know that Mary twisted her ankle.

and another new sentence

She knows that he knows that I know that Mary twisted her ankle.

and so on.

Embedding rules combine two simple sentences to produce a more complex surface sentence by putting one sentence inside another.

Part Four / Sentences Combined by Joining Rules

Joining rules combine independent sentences to produce more complex surface sentences. The classic case of joining rules is the process of coordination. For example, the surface sentence

The doctor took an X ray, gave me a shot, and charged me $25.

comes from the coordination of three underlying elementary sentences:

The doctor took an X ray.
The doctor gave me a shot.
The doctor charged me $25.

The basic difference between joining rules and embedding rules is that the joining rules join together independent sentences at the same level without subordinating one sentence to the other. That is, the elementary sentences remain separate and equal. On the other hand, the embedding rules require a clear distinction between the "main" sentence and the embedded recursive sentence that is attached to the "main" sentence as an appendage. Furthermore, the appended underlying elementary sentence typically must undergo substantial modification before it appears on the surface, so much so that it may appear as a phrase or even a single word.

part one

SIMPLE PHRASE STRUCTURE RULES

Overview

The task of the simple phrase structure rules is to generate all possible elementary sentences. In theory, at least, the number of possible elementary sentences is finite because the number of words and the number of ways that the words can be combined (the number of sentence types or patterns) are both finite. Needless to say this finite number is quite large. In English it is convenient to say that all elementary sentences consist of three elements in a fixed order: a subject noun phrase (NP), the auxiliary (Aux), and the verb phrase (VP). We can write this statement as a phrase structure rule:

S $\longrightarrow$ NP⌢Aux⌢VP

The S means the class of all elementary sentences in the language. The arrow means 'may be rewritten as' or 'consists of the following subclasses in this order.' The ⌢ means 'joined together in this order.' Recall that one of the basic claims of transformational grammar is that all surface sentences consist of one or more elementary sentences. Thus, all surface sentences can be traced back to a series of elementary sentences, each of which consists of a subject noun phrase, an auxiliary, and a verb phrase.

THE NOUN PHRASE (CHAPTER 1)

There are several different functions that noun phrases play: subject, direct object, indirect object, object of a preposition. Chapter 1 deals with the internal structure of all noun phrases no matter what their function in the rest of the sentence is.

THE AUXILIARY (CHAPTER 2)

The auxiliary is the cover term for the present and past tense markers, and all auxiliary and helping verbs that occur before the main verb.

THE VERB PHRASE (CHAPTER 3)

The verb phrase consists of the main verb together with whatever noun phrases, adjectives, and adverbs that are necessary to make a grammatical sentence, plus the optional adverbs of time, place, manner, and so on.

The elementary sentences in all languages probably consist of these three elements (or something closely resembling them). However, the order of the elements differs from language to language. In many languages for instance the auxiliary and verb phrase come in front of the subject noun phrase. It may seen unnatural, at first glance, to put the auxiliary in front of the verb phrase, but as you will see in Chapter 2, there is considerable evidence that this is the proper order for the underlying sentences of English.

CHAPTER 1

The Noun Phrase

Overview

The noun phrase consists of three subclasses: the article, the noun, and number. In the analysis given here, there are three types of articles: the specified article, which is used when referring to a particular noun (for example, *the boy*); the unspecified article, which is used in referring to a noun whose particular identity is not known or is not important at the moment (for example, *a boy*); and the null article Ø (read "zero"). The null article is a way of describing those noun phrases that have no apparent article. For example, both noun phrases in the following sentence are said to contain the null article:

John saw Mary.

The noun and number are treated together. There is no attempt to define noun in the abstract. The discussion instead centers around the kinds of relations the noun enters into with (1) number, (2) the main verb, and (3) pronouns.

(1) All nouns must have number, but not all nouns can have both singular and plural number. In particular, a large group of nouns called *uncountable nouns* can be used in the singular only. For example, the word *dust* cannot be used in the plural:

I got some dust in my eye.
° I got some dusts in my eye.

° An asterisk indicates that the sentence is ungrammatical.

35

(2) Certain main verbs will accept only certain types of nouns as subjects. The compatability (or co-occurrence) of subject nouns and main verbs may be described in terms of a set of inherent properties (or features) that all nouns have.

(3) The chapter closes with a discussion of pronouns, with particular emphasis on the factors that govern which third person pronoun (*he, she,* or *it*) substitutes for which noun.

NP
NP $\longrightarrow$ Article $\frown$ Noun $\frown$ N*o*

$$\text{Article} \longrightarrow \left\{ \begin{array}{l} \text{specified} \\ \text{unspecified} \\ \emptyset \end{array} \right\}$$

$$\text{Specified} \longrightarrow \left\{ \begin{array}{l} \textit{the, this, that, these, those;} \text{ possessive} \\ \text{nouns and possessive pronouns} \end{array} \right\}$$

$$\text{Unspecified} \longrightarrow \left\{ \begin{array}{l} \textit{a/an, some, a few, a couple, several,} \\ \textit{much, many} \ldots \end{array} \right\}$$

$$\text{Noun} \longrightarrow \{\textit{boy, tree, idea, Mr. Brown, America} \ldots \}$$

$$\text{N}o \longrightarrow \left\{ \begin{array}{l} \text{singular} \\ \text{plural} \end{array} \right\}$$

Note: { } means 'pick only one of the enclosed elements.'

ARTICLE (ART)

In the analysis given here, the article is made up of three different and mutually exclusive subclasses: the specified article, the unspecified article and the null (or zero) article.

The Specified Article (Spec)

The specified article consists of the definite article *the*, the four demonstrative pronouns *this, that, these* and *those*, and all possessive nouns and possessive pronouns (*John's, the school's, my, our*, for example). All specified articles limit the meaning of the noun they modify to some specific or specified group. For example, when we use *the boy* or *the boys*, we make the assumption that the hearer or reader knows which particular *boy* or *boys* we are referring to, either directly, or through context. Similarly, a possessive noun or possessive pronoun specifies the noun by identifying the owner, for example, *John's car, my car.*

The demonstrative pronouns specify which of several possible referents the speaker means. *This* and *these* indicate objects relatively closer to the speaker; *that* and *those* indicate object, relatively closer to the hearer (or relatively further away from the speaker). This spacial distinction for physical objects is extended metaphorically for abstract nouns, for example, *this idea* and *that idea.*

The specification of nouns in terms of their physical location relative to the speaker and hearer is quite common throughout the languages of the world; some languages even make such specification obligatory for every concrete noun. English, of course, does not go that far, but the same distinction pops up in some verbs, for example *go* and *take* imply motion away from the speaker, while *come* and *bring* imply motion toward the speaker. Notice how odd the following sentences sound when the directions are reversed.

* Come to him.
* Go to me.
* Take it to me.
* Bring it to him.

Unspecified Articles (Unspec)

When we use a noun with an unspecified article, for example, *a boy*, we imply that it is not important that the hearer know exactly which particular boy we are referring to. The unspecified article does not necessarily mean that we could not identify which boy we had in mind; it only means that his identity is not relevant to what we want to say about him at the moment.

With the exceptions of *a/an* and *much*, the unspecified articles are used with plural nouns, for example,

many rugs
a few elephants
several houses

A/an, often called the indefinite article, is used only with singular nouns because it comes from the number *one* (as you might guess from the form *an*). *Much* is used only with a special group of nouns that can be used only in singular. This group of nouns, called uncountable or mass nouns, is discussed in the following chapter on noun features.

The Null Article (Ø)

The concept of a null article is borrowed from mathematical logic. Perhaps the best way to think of it is as a place marker. In mathematics the null is zero (0). The difference between the number *1* and the number *10* is a zero. In this case zero is a very real part of the number. It is a place marker, indicating that the number consists of two digits. In exactly the same way, the null article Ø is a place marker, indicating the position of the article within the noun phrase. Many nouns, including most proper nouns, are used with the null article, for example, *Mr. Smith, Betty, Russia, Main Street.* With other nouns, the null article often has a special meaning. Compare the italicized noun phrases in the following pairs of sentences:

> He loved *many books.*
> He loved *Ø books.*
> *Some cigarettes* are in the desk.
> *Ø cigarettes* cause cancer.
> *The candy* is delicious.
> *Ø candy* is hard on your teeth.

These nouns with null articles seem to be generalizations about the whole class of objects the nouns refer to, generalization about all books, all cigarettes, and all candy. Just to give this use of nouns a name, let us call it the "generic" use. The null article is the most common way of making a noun generic, but not the only way. For example, these two sentences both seem to be generalizing about all lions:

> Lions are the kings of beasts.
> The lion is the king of beasts.

NOUN

It is very instructive to compare how different grammars deal with the definition of a noun. Fries, you recall, attempted to give a practical definition, that is, he gave a list of formal characteristics that distinguish the class of nouns from all other parts of speech. For example, nouns can be recognized by the fact that they follow articles and by the fact that they have a contrast in form between the singular and plural (and by various other formal properties).

Now as a matter of fact, nouns are typically preceded by articles and do show a contrast of form between singular and plural. Nevertheless, the validity of the above observations tells us little about how we actually recognize nouns. Undoubtedly the presence of articles and plural endings provide important clues in the recognition of nouns, but these clues, by themselves, are not a sufficient condition for recognizing nouns. For example, in the phrase *the tall boy* we know that the *the* in front of *tall* does not make *tall* a noun. Likewise, we can only recognize the presence of a plural ending if we know the thing the ending is attached to is a noun, that is, we know that the *-s* in *books* is a plural ending only because we know *book* is a noun. By itself, the *-s* could just as well be the mark of a verb, as in the sentence

He usually books himself first class.

The problem of devising intuition-free, formal ways of recognizing the main parts of speech was taken very seriously by linguists and engineers engaged in the translation of languages by computers (machine translation). Many of the machine translation programs called for the computer to analyze the sentence into the various parts of speech. For these programs, various techniques of identifying nouns were developed. These techniques were, in effect, probabilistic guesses based on the shape of the word (for example, if the word ends in -*dom* or -*ness* it is probably a noun) and on the surrounding words (for example, if the word is between *the* and a verb, it is a noun). Some of the more sophisticated programs could identify nouns with a high degree of accuracy (but nowhere near 100 percent).

In a transformational grammar the abstract class of noun (like the other parts of speech) is undefinable except by providing an exhaustive list of all nouns in the language. The class of nouns is an abstraction which speakers of the language intuitively recognize. How speakers actually do this, that is, how their intuition works, is a psychological question of considerable difficulty. Interestingly enough, this is almost exactly the point of view that Jespersen takes in his *Essentials of English Grammar*

> In dealing with linguistic subjects it is necessary to have names for the various classes into which words fall naturally, and which are generally, but not very felicitously, called "parts of speech." It is practically impossible to give exact and exhaustive definitions of these classes; nevertheless the classification itself rarely offers occasion for doubt and will be sufficiently clear to students if a fair number of examples are given. (Jespersen, p. 66)

The task of a transformational grammar, then, is not to explain how our intuition works, but to provide a model of the language that conforms to our intuition. In a transformational grammar the abstract class of noun is generated as a subclass of the noun phrase. The abstract class noun is embodied as an actual noun by a lexical rule. A lexical rule turns to the list of nouns and picks one suitable to the noun phrase and to the sentence in which it will be used. In other words, the noun must "fit" the noun phrase and the sentence. In transformational terms, the "fit" is determined by *co-occurrence* relations. We will deal with three such co-occurrence relations: (1) the relation of the noun to number, (2) the relation of the noun to the main verb, and (3) the relation of the noun with pronouns.

The Co-occurrence of Nouns with Number

When we use a noun, we must attach number to it. In English we have two numbers: singular and plural (meaning two or more). Some languages have more than two numbers, even English used to have three numbers for the personal pronouns: singular, dual, plural (that is, three or more).

The singular ending in English is not overtly marked. In linguistic terminology, it is null (Ø). The plural marker in English takes various forms. The
most common is spelled either -s or -es, as in *day:days; picnic:picnics; box:
boxes*. Since this -s/-es ending is by far the most common ending for the plural,
it is considered to be the regular ending. English also has a number of less
common (and therefore "irregular") plural endings. Almost all of these endings
come from one of two sources: (1) borrowed foreign words that have kept
their foreign plural, for example, *one analysis–two analyses; one phenomenon–two phenomena* or (2) historical survivals of older ways of making the
plural, for example:

one foot–two feet
one tooth–two teeth
one mouse–two mice
one child–two children
one man–two men
one woman–two women
one ox–two oxen

There was a small group of nouns in Old English that made their plural without
any change in the form of the word. Some modern survivals of that group
are:

one deer–two deer
one fish–two fish
one sheep–two sheep

In Modern English the names of most fish form their plurals this way:

one tuna–two tuna
one bonito–two bonito
one perch–two perch
one angelfish–two angelfish

Oddly enough, most other marine creatures form their plurals in the regular
way:

one whale–two whales
one crab–two crabs
one eel–two eels
one shrimp–two shrimps

So far we have been talking about the singular and plural endings as though
we always had the liberty of choosing the number of the noun. Usually, of
course, we do have that liberty. However, there are some nouns that can be
used only in the singular or only in the plural. The first examples that might

occur to you are the small number of nouns that must be used in the plural: *scissors, pants, trousers, pliers, tweezers,* and so forth.

A much larger and more important group, however, are the nouns that cannot be used in the plural. The peculiarity of this group of nouns can be shown by comparing two nouns that mean nearly the same thing: *assignment* and *homework.*

> I just got a new assignment.
> ° I just got a new homework.
> Do you have many assignments?
> ° Do you have many homeworks?
> The teacher gave them one assignment for the whole month.
> ° The teacher gave them one homework for the whole month.
> The class was given two assignments.
> ° The class was given two homeworks.

Homework belongs to the group of nouns that cannot be used in the plural. A more accurate way of describing this group of nouns is to say that they cannot be counted, that is, we cannot say *one homework–two homeworks.* Since the article *a* historically means "one," we cannot say *a homework* either. There are many kinds of things that by their very nature cannot be counted: the names of gases and liquids (°*one air–*°*two airs;* °*one oxygen–*°*two oxygens;* °*one water–*°*two waters;* °*one soup–*°*two soups*), things that occur in particles (°*one dust–*°*two dusts;* °*one sand–*°*two sands*), things that occur as groups (°*one wreckage–*°*two wreckages;* °*one junk–*°*two junks*), the names of raw material (°*one zinc–*°*two zincs*), and certain kinds of abstractions (°*one fun–*°*two funs*).

Words like *homework* are often called *uncountable* or *mass* nouns. In a very real sense, these nouns do not have any number at all. However, since these nouns are used with a third-person singular form of the verb, they are usually treated as being singular. Thus, we can divide nouns into two mutually exclusive feature groups: *countable nouns/uncountable nouns.* Countable nouns occur with number, that is, they can be either singular or plural. Uncountable nouns have the form of the singular without being singular in meaning, and can never be used in the plural.

Feature systems are often graphically represented as a kind of up-side-down tree:

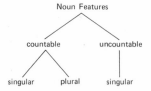

The difference between *countable* and *uncountable* is inherent within the noun, that is, some nouns are *countable* and some are *uncountable*, and you just have to know which is which. The choice between *singular* and *plural*, however, is not inherent within the *countable* noun. Each time we use a countable noun we must decide whether to make it *singular* or *plural*, depending on the situation.

The distinction between countable and uncountable nouns is valid enough, but there are two more wrinkles to be straightened out. Some nouns can be either countable or uncountable (with a change in meaning). Here are some fairly clear-cut examples with the uncountable use first:

> *Tea* is something to drink, but *a tea* is a party.
> *Youth* is the state of being young, but *a youth* is a young man.
> *Iron* is an ore, but *an iron* is for pressing clothes.
> *Lamb* is meat, but *a lamb* is a baby sheep.
> *Room* is space, but *a room* is part of a house.
> *Glass* is a material, but *a glass* is something to drink out of.

The second wrinkle is a special use of *-s* with uncountable nouns to mean something completely different from "plural." Most people would interpret the *-s* in the following words to mean not "more than one" but "different kinds of":

> A turf specialist knows a lot about *grasses*.
> The company produces dozens of *inks*.
> They export *fruits*, mostly to canneries.
> The supermarket carries *soups* I have never even heard of.

Here are some sample phrase structure trees for noun phrases:

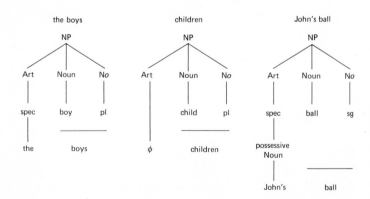

The first set of branches indicates that the class of noun phrase consists of three subclasses in a fixed order. These subclasses (Art, Noun, N*o*) are called "nodes." Each of the three nodes is broken down into its subclasses until we reach the level of actual words. The phrase structure tree is a record of which choices were made among the options allowable in the grammar. To use a fancy metaphor, the grammar is like a road map. It gives you all possible routes to all possible destinations. The phrase structure tree is the record of one particular journey. In the derivation of a particular sentence, you know both your point of origin (the abstract class "sentence") and your destination (the actual sentence that you are trying to produce).

In the example given above, we are working with a part of a sentence, but the principle is the same. We are given a sequence of words that we intuitively recognize to be an instance of an abstract class we call a "noun phrase." Our task is to show exactly how this abstract class is embodied in this particular string of words in a way that will reveal both the relations of the whole to the parts (the noun phrase to each of the words), and the relation of the parts to each other. The net result is that we have an explicit statement that (hopefully) mirrors our intuitive understanding of the words in question and gives us a way of comparing this particular string of words with other strings of words so that we can make explicit the ways in which we feel the two strings to be similar and dissimilar.

The horizontal line drawn under the Noun and No nodes indicates the operation of a set of rules that converts terminal elements into their proper form. For instance, this set of rules converts the plural node after *boy* to *-s*, but converts the pl after *child* to *-ren*. These same rules would also govern the pronunciation of the surface forms. For example, the rules would indicate that *child* when followed by a singular node is pronounced with a long *i*, but when followed by a plural node is pronounced with a short *i*. We will assume the proper operation of these rules without comment.

Exercise 1 / PHRASE STRUCTURE TREES FOR NOUN PHRASES[1]

Draw phrase structure trees for the following noun phrases:

1. Mr. Jones
2. an orange
3. these ideas
4. some sand
5. his uncle
6. glass
7. many glasses
8. the sheep (singular)
9. the sheep (plural)
10. several women

---

[1] Answers to exercises may be found at the end of each chapter.

The Co-occurrence of Nouns with Verbs

The semantic ties that bind the subject noun and the main verb together are very strong: *birds sing, fish swim, batters bat, pitchers pitch, catchers catch.* We know from our experience in the world that certain nouns "go" with certain verbs. It is possible to reflect in the grammar some of the more general semantic ties between nouns and verbs by use of features of co-occurrence. Compare the following five sentences:

The idea surprised me.
The rock fell off the table.
The celery was flourishing.
The dog sneezed.
The girl wrote out a check.

Some verbs can co-occur with any subject noun. *Surprise,* for example, can be used with all five nouns:

The idea
The rock
The celery } surprised me.
The dog
The girl

Notice, however, that when we try to use all five nouns as subjects for the second sentence, *idea* is not an acceptable subject:

° The idea
The rock
The celery } fell off the table.
The dog
The girl

With the third sentence, *idea* and *rock* are not acceptable subjects:

° The idea
° The rock
The celery } was flourishing.
The dog
The girl

With the fourth sentence, *idea, rock,* and *celery* are not acceptable:

° The idea
° The rock
° The celery } sneezed.
The dog
The girl

Finally, with the last sentence, only *girl* is an acceptable subject:

° The idea ⎫
° The rock ⎪
° The celery ⎬ wrote out a check.
° The dog ⎪
The girl ⎭

These facts suggest that as far as the co-occurrence of subject and object nouns with verbs is concerned, there is a kind of hierarchy of noun features:

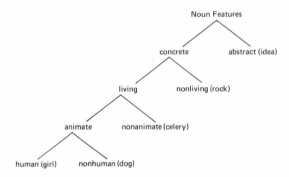

The great advantage to this type of hierarchy is that it can clearly show the similarities as well as the differences between any two nouns. For example, *girl* and *dog* differ in that *girl* is human and *dog* is nonhuman. However, they share all the other features in the hierarchy, that is, they are both animate, living, and concrete. Therefore, we can predict, that despite their differences at the lowest level of the hierarchy, *girl* and *dog* will both be acceptable subjects for a verb like *fall* (*off*), which requires only that the subject be a concrete (as opposed to abstract) noun. To take a new example, the verb *breathe* requires an animate subject, but it can co-occur with either a human or nonhuman animate noun.

What happens when a subject noun and verb do not co-occur? Is the sentence then ungrammatical? When this happens, we are aware that the sentence is not acceptable in any literal interpretation. What we usually do is make the sentence grammatical and acceptable by giving it a metaphorical interpretation. For example, we know that the following sentence is not true in any literal sense.

The idea breathed new life into them.

However, it is not ungrammatical nor meaningless. We interpret the sentence by giving the noun *idea* the property of an animate noun—we even have a special name for this: personification. This type of violation of the normal co-occurrence relations is very common, but it is only meaningful because we know what the correct co-occurrence relations are supposed to be. If we did not know the correct relations, the whole effect of deliberately violating them would be lost.

Exercise 2 / NOUN FEATURES

For the italicized nouns in the following sentences, indicate the lowest feature on the tree. The first sentence is done for you.

0. The *horse* jumped over the fence.
   Answer: nonhuman

1. The *information* was not available.
2. Several *boats* were capsized.
3. A *duck* swam across the pond.
4. I reported the *accident*.
5. The convict demanded a new *lawyer*.
6. The *cook* copied down the directions.
7. The *leaves* fell to the ground.
8. The *leaves* wilted.
9. The *computer* reported the incident.
10. The outfielder caught the *ball*.
11. The fisherman caught a *trout*.

The Co-occurrence of Nouns with Pronouns

The following chart gives the subject forms of the personal pronouns of English.

	1st person	2nd person	3rd person		
singular	I		he	she	it
		you			
plural	we		they		

The *I-you* relationship is defined automatically: *I* means the speaker, *you* means the hearer. *We* is the plural form of *I*. It does not mean that two or more people are talking in chorus. It means that the speaker is speaking not just for himself as an individual, but as the spokesman for some group of people. Similarly, *you* can mean not just a single listener, but the group that the listener represents.

One of the oddities about the English pronoun system is that the distinction between the singular and plural forms of the second person has been lost: both are *you*. Historically, there were two different second person pronouns, one for the singular and one for the plural. However, in the thirteenth century, a completely different use of the second person pronouns became established. The singular forms were used in addressing children or persons of inferior rank, while the plural forms were used as a mark of respect in talking to a superior. By the sixteenth century it was considered impolite or even insulting to address anyone with the singular forms, so these forms simply dropped out of the language and everyone used the plural on all occasions.

The third person pronouns are completely different from the first and second person pronouns, because the third person pronouns are substitutes for nouns (technically, whole noun phrases), whereas the first and second persons are not really substitutes for anything. To take an obvious example:

The boy hit *the ball.*
    he   it

as opposed to

I hit *you.*

In the third person singular there is a three-way contrast between *he/she/it*. In order to correctly use these three pronouns, we must know which nouns can be replaced by *he*, which by *she*, and which by *it*. This kind of distinction is often called "gender." Nouns that can be replaced by *he* are said to be "masculine," nouns that can be replaced by *she* are "feminine," and nouns that can be replaced by *it* are "neuter." These terms are as good as any, but they do give rise to a serious confusion when they are applied to certain European languages. In some European languages the nouns have several different sets of endings. In order to put the correct ending on the noun and on the adjective and articles that modify the noun, the speaker must know which set of endings the noun takes. Usually there is no particular pattern to which nouns go with which set of endings; consequently, a person learning the language must simply memorize the ending along with the noun. Unfortunately, these endings are also termed "genders." In some languages there are two genders (French, for example) and in other languages there are three (German, for example). Consequently, there are two completely different meanings of the term *gender:* (1) the English use, in which gender is based on the sex (or lack thereof) of the object the noun refers to, and (2) the use in certain European languages, in which gender means a particular set of endings attached to nouns and to words that modify nouns, but which have no necessary connection with the sex of the thing referred to.

In the English use of gender, an object that is not animate is automatically neuter and replaced by the pronoun *it*. Also animate nouns, if the speaker does not know (or does not care) whether the creature is a male or female, are sometimes replaced with *it* (even though mothers of small children have been known to become quite angry when asked, "What is its name?").

Many animate nouns have a built-in gender. *Waiter* is masculine, *waitress* is feminine. *John* is a boy's name, *Mary* is a girl's name. When we do not use the first name, the use of the titles *Mr., Miss,* and *Mrs.* tells the gender of the person. However, many animate nouns do not specify gender, for example *cook, teacher, student.* In a fine display of masculine superiority, the English language treats these unspecified animate nouns as masculine, that is, if we are forced to use a third person pronoun to replace a human noun when we do not know (or care about) the gender of the person referred to, we usually use *he.*

One way to envision third person pronoun substitution is in terms of a feature tree:

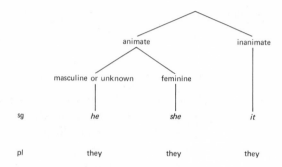

Suppose you heard this sentence out of context:

He answered it.

In this case we do not know what person the *he* is a substitution for, nor do we know what the *it* refers to—telephone, letter, question, or what. What we do know, however, is that *he* is a substitution for an animate noun and that *it* is a substitution for a nonanimate noun. We can reflect these facts in our representation of the noun phrase by using words that have no specific lexical content but which do make the distinction between animate and nonanimate. Let us agree to use the word *someone* to indicate an animate noun of unknown reference and *something* to indicate a nonanimate noun of unknown reference. We can now represent third person pronoun substitution in a phrase structure tree diagram:

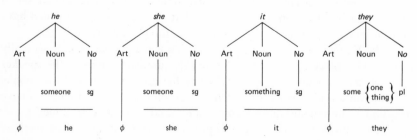

The co-occurrence features of *they* with the main verb will often dictate a choice between *someone* and *something*. For example, the subject noun phrase in the sentence

They were outraged.

obviously contains an underlying *someone*.

As with the co-occurrence restrictions between nouns and verbs, the restrictions can be violated. The most common instance of using an apparently incorrect replacement of a pronoun for a noun is the use of *she* for nouns that would normally be replaced by *it*. This is usually done as a mark of affection or familiarity. For example,

The *ship* will be recommissioned, and then *she* will be reassigned.
Our *Country*, right or wrong, but may *she* always be right!
She's a grand old *flag*, *she's* a high flying *flag*.

Another type of feature needs to be mentioned for pronouns. We have seen that the proper substitution of a third person pronoun for a noun phrase depends entirely on the intrinsic gender feature of the noun and upon the number. There is another kind of feature that is not intrinsic to the noun: case. The English pronoun system changes the form of the personal pronouns according to the function the pronoun plays within the particular sentence. For example, in the surface sentences

I saw him.
He saw me.

I and *He* are in the "subject" case, *me* and *him* are in the "object" case. Pronoun case depends on the pronoun's function in the surface structure of the sentence, not the deep structure. A clear illustration of this is in the passive transformation. When the active sentence

I saw him.

is transformed into the passive

He was seen by me.

the subject in the deep structure ends up in the object case on the surface, and the object in the deep structure ends up in the subject case. Since the determination of the case of a pronoun seems to be a feature of surface structure, all pronouns in the deep structure are in the subject case form.

We will conclude with a few general remarks about noun features. There are several different ways by which the features are determined. Some features are built-in to the noun, that is, when we pick the noun the features come along as a package deal. *Brick*, for example, is inherently common (as opposed to proper); countable (as opposed to uncountable); concrete (as opposed to abstract); and inanimate (as opposed to animate). Two other features, however, are not part of the package. We can make the word singular or plural at our pleasure, that is, number is not inherent in most countable nouns. The other feature that is not inherent in the noun is case. If we substitute a pronoun for *bricks*, the case of the pronoun (*they* or *them*) is not inherent in the word nor is it a matter of our free choice. Instead, the choice of case is entirely dictated by the grammar of the surface sentence.

Answers to Exercise 1 / NOUN PHRASES

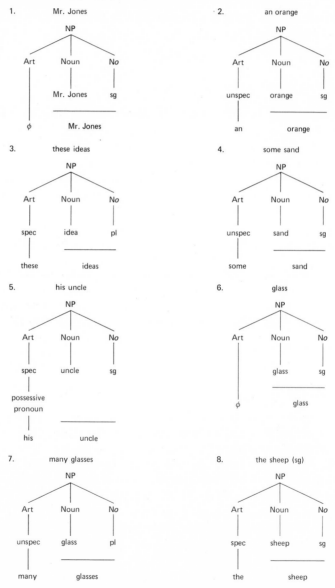

9.   the sheep (pl)

10.   several women

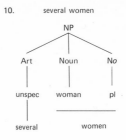

Answers to Exercise 2 / NOUN FEATURES

1. *information:* abstract
2. *boats:* nonliving
3. *duck:* nonhuman
4. *accident:* abstract
5. *lawyer:* human
6. *cook:* human
7. *leaves:* nonliving
8. *leaves:* nonanimate
9. *computer:* human

Comment: We all know that computers are not really alive. However, in this sentence, *computer* has been personified, that is, it is used with a verb that accepts only human nouns.

10. *ball:* nonliving
11. *trout:* nonhuman

Comment: The verb *catch* has two different meanings depending on the kind of object noun. With a nonliving object, *catch* means 'stop an object from falling to the earth'. With animate nouns, *catch* has a second meaning of 'trap or snare'. Actually the sentence about catching a trout is really ambiguous since a trout can be caught in the same sense that a ball is caught. This is the source for an old riddle:

Question: What is the easiest way to catch a fish?

Answer: Have someone throw one to you.

CHAPTER 2

The Auxiliary

Overview

In somewhat simplistic terms, the auxiliary is everything in the underlying sentence from the end of the subject noun phrase to the beginning of the main verb. The auxiliary is composed of tense, either present or past, as well as various kinds of "helping" verbs, which may or may not be present in any particular sentence. This grammar deals first with tense, and then with three types of "helping" verbs: modals, the perfect, and the progressive. In each case, we begin with a discussion of *form* and then move to a limited discussion of *meaning*.

TENSE

In this grammar (as in most transformational grammars), the meaning of tense is restricted to the present and past inflectional endings. Tense does *not* mean time. Every language can make the distinction between past, present, and future time, but there is no obligation for the distinction to be carried solely by the inflection of the verb. Many Asian languages have no verb inflection at all. They convey time relations by adverbs. Some European languages make subtle time distinctions in the verb inflection (Latin, for example). English and the other Germanic languages are mixed: they have a few verb inflections that partially correlate with time, but also rely on adverbs to express time relations.

In the underlying sentence, tense is generated as the leftmost element of the auxiliary. Though at first this placement seems odd, it actually captures an important generalization. The tense marker (the past or present inflectional ending) is always carried by the leftmost verb, no matter what that verb is. If there are no "helping" verbs, the tense is attached to the main verb, because that is the leftmost verb; for example, *John laughed.* However, if there are any "helping" verbs in the sentence, the main verb is no longer the leftmost verb, and consequently does not carry the tense marker. For example, if we add the modal verb *may* to the sentence above, the past tense marker will attach to *may,* not *laugh,* producing *John might laugh.*

Since the tense is generated to the left of whatever verb it will be eventually attached to, we must have some way of moving the tense marker from the left side of the verb to the right side of the verb so that it may be attached as a suffix. As you have already learned, rules that switch the order of two elements are called transformational rules. This particular transformational rule is used so often that it has a special nickname: the flip-flop rule. One of the striking things about the transformational treatment of the auxiliary is that different parts of the auxiliary seem to require the same basic flip-flop rule.

MODALS

In this grammar, the modals are nine "helping" verbs (often called modal auxiliaries) that can occur in front of the perfect: *can, may, must, shall,* and *will* in the present tense, *could, might, should,* and *would* in the past tense. One of the most difficult points about the modals is understanding what the past tense means with them. Obviously in a sentence like

It might rain tomorrow.

might is past tense in form but not past in time.

PERFECT

The perfect is the "helping" verb *have,* followed by a verb in the past participle form. It is often necessary to distinguish between the present perfect and the past perfect. When *have* is used in the present tense, it is the present perfect, when *have* is used in the past tense, it is the past perfect. For example,

Present perfect: John has eaten.
Past perfect: John had eaten.

The important thing to remember about the transformational treatment of the perfect is that the perfect really consists of two parts: the verb *have* and the past participle marker which is attached to the following verb by a flip-flop rule. In this grammar we use *-en* as the symbol for the past participle marker, even though in most cases the past participle form of the verb is the same as the simple past.

PROGRESSIVE

The progressive also consists of two parts: the "helping" verb *be* and the present participle marker *-ing*, which is attached to the following verb by a flip-flop rule. An important point that emerges from the discussion of the progressive is the distinction between "action" and "description" verbs (which is also briefly touched on in the discussion of tense). In a sentence containing an "action" verb, we may think of the subject as performing some action. In a sentence containing a "description" verb, the verb describes or defines the subject, rather than the subject doing something. Action does not necessarily mean overt, physical activity, merely that the subject does something. For example:

"Action" verb: John *slept.*
"Description" verb: John *is* sleepy.

In the first sentence, John is engaged in some action, albeit a relatively passive action in this case. In the second sentence, the verb *be* describes John's state. The distinction between "action" and "description" is not an unembodied philosophical abstraction: the two types of verbs consistently behave in overtly different ways.

AUXILIARY

Auxiliary $\longrightarrow$ Tense⌢(Modal)⌢(Perfect)⌢(Progressive)

Tense $\longrightarrow$ $\begin{Bmatrix} present \\ past \end{Bmatrix}$

Modal $\longrightarrow$ *can, may, must, shall, will*
Perfect $\longrightarrow$ *have*⌢ -EN
Progressive $\longrightarrow$ *be*⌢-ING

The second obligatory element in underlying sentences is the auxiliary. The auxiliary is made up of four components: the first obligatory, and the next three optional. The obligatory element is called "tense." Since this word means different things to different people, the sense in which it is being used here needs to be clarified. For the purposes of this grammar, tense means the present and the past inflectional ending of verbs.

Present Tense

The present tense ending takes two forms: one form is written as -s or -es. This form is used when the subject noun can be replaced by a third person singular pronoun, for example,

John sings.
He does.
Mary usually washes the dishes.

The other form of the present tense ending is null (Ø). This form of the ending is used when the subject noun is *not* the third person singular, for example,

They singØ.
I doØ.
The girls usually washØ the dishes.

Past Tense

One of the characteristics of all Germanic languages (including English) is that they have two basically different ways of making the past tense. One way, which we think of as being the "regular" way because it is the most common in Modern English, is to add on a suffix spelled -ed. for example,

We walked to school yesterday.
He colored the picture black.
They painted the house.

The other way, which we think of as being "irregular," is to mark the change from present tense to past tense by changing the vowel of the verb. For example,

come–came
dig–dug
find–found
run–ran
wring–wrung
drink–drank
see–saw
take–took

In Modern English the vowel changes look pretty chaotic. However, in Old English it is possible to see quite definite patterns in the kinds of vowel changes that took place. About the only pattern that has come into Modern English largely intact is the *ring–rang–rung, sing–sang–sung, drink–drank–drunk* pattern. This pattern can even be traced back into the prehistoric period before German, English, Latin, Greek, and Sanskrit appeared as separate languages.

There are a few groups of verbs that reflect survivals of the older patterns. One group is a hybrid: the past tense is formed with both a "regular" ending and vowel change, for example:

flee–fled
hear–heard
sell–sold
tell–told

Another group of hybrid adds -*t* instead of -*ed*. For example,

feel–felt
keep–kept
sleep–slept
think–thought

Still another group has a null (Ø) form of the past tense. For example,

I cutØ my finger yesterday.
He shedØ some light on the subject.
Jones hitØ the ball into left field.

Some more examples of this last group are

bet–bet
cost–cost
hurt–hurt
put–put
quit–quit
set–set
spread–spread

From the standpoint of the rules, it is immaterial what form the present or past tense endings actually take. Every sentence must contain tense, and tense is either present or past. For our purposes we will assume that the actual form is always correctly selected. Thus, we can indicate the tense of verbs in the following way:

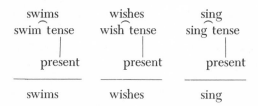

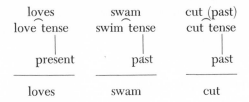

loves   swam   cut (past)

love tense   swim tense   cut tense

present   past   past

loves   swam   cut

Exercise 3 / TENSE

Draw phrase structure trees to show the derivation of the following verbs:

1. thought
2. says
3. tore
4. answers
5. did
6. whisper
7. took
8. cost (present)
9. lend
10. went

The Meaning of Present and Past Tense

We have seen how the grammar generates the present and past tense forms. Let us draw a few generalizations about the meaning of the present and past tense. At first, the meaning of present and past tense may seem obvious: present tense means 'now'; past tense means the time before 'now'. Unfortunately, this is only partially correct. The past tense usually (but not always) means past time, but the present tense has little to do with present time. For example, let us examine the meaning of the present tense in the following sentence.

Every Sunday, Red Riding Hood *takes* a basket of goodies to her grandmother.

Does the sentence mean that now, at this very minute, Red Riding Hood is on her way to her grandmother's house? Not at all. It does not tell us what Red Riding Hood is doing at this moment. It does not even tell us if today is Sunday. Even if it were Sunday and Red Riding Hood were at home in bed with a bad cold, the sentence would still be perfectly grammatical and meaningful. The present tense means that it is Red Riding Hood's normal custom to take a basket of goodies to her grandmother every Sunday. Thus, one of the most common meanings of the present tense is that the action is habitual or customary.

The meaning of habitual or repeated action is so basic to this use of the present tense that most sentences of this type are boarderline ungrammatical without an adverbial of frequency. For example, notice how stagy the following sentences sound:

John answers the phone.
The doorbell rings.
He reads a book.

If we add an adverbial of frequency, these sentences seem perfectly normal:

John *always* answers the phone.
Everytime I take a bath, the doorbell rings.
He reads a book *every chance he gets.*

Often, of course, the adverbial of frequency is not overtly expressed, but even so, it is implicit. For example, we tacitly understand the following sentence

He pays his bills on time.

as a paraphrase of

He always pays his bills on time.

So far we have discussed only "action" verbs—verbs in sentences in which the subject performs some action. The second large type of verbs in English is a group that we might call "description" verbs. This type of verb describes the subject in some way. Put another way, in a sentence with a descriptive verb, the subject does not perform any action. Perhaps the clearest case is the copula verb *be* (notice that no adverb is required):

John is very angry.

The present tense here does not imply that John is usually or normally angry; rather, it *describes* John's current condition. Here are some more examples of sentences with description verbs and no implicit adverbs of frequency:

I have a hangnail.
The book costs $3.75.
He appears to be winning.
The boat weighs nearly 400 pounds.
She looks terrible.
It seems kind of silly to me.

The reader should bear this distinction between "action" and "description" verbs in mind. There are quite consistent differences in the behavior of these two types of verbs which we will encounter throughout the grammar.

As we have seen, English (like all the other Germanic languages) has only two tenses: present and past. We have also seen that the meaning of the present tense has nothing really to do with the meaning of present time (though the past tense usually means past time). How, then, does English talk about present and future time? The answer is that English relies on several other verb constructions and on adverbs of time. Probably the most common way of talking about the present is by means of the progressive construction with a present time adverb. For example,

He is taking a shower now.

We have two common ways of talking about the future: (1) by means of the modal auxiliary *will:*

He will go to town tomorrow.

(2) by means of the progressive with a future time adverb:

He is going to go to town tomorrow.

Strictly speaking, however, the two sentences do not really mean the future, rather they mean something like, "It is his intention now to go to town tomorrow."

The Flip-Flop Rule

The auxiliary rules generate tense as the first (and only obligatory) component of the auxiliary sequence. Below are two sentences generated with the minimal development of the auxiliary, that is, with just tense:

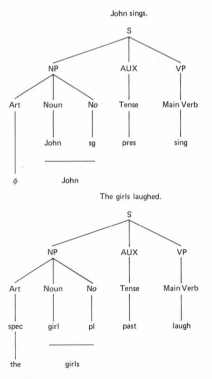

Notice that the tense is generated to the left of the main verb. In order for the pieces to come out in the right order, the tense will have to be moved to the other side of the main verb by a transformational rule. This rule, known as the "flip-flop" rule, may be formulated this way:

Tense⌢Main Verb ⟹ Main Verb⌢Tense

[*Note:* Transformational rules are written with a double-shafted arrow.]

This rule changes *John⌢Present⌢Sing* into *John⌢Sing⌢Present* and *The⌢girls⌢past⌢laugh* into *The⌢girls⌢laugh⌢past* with tense correctly attached to the verb as a suffix.

At this point the reader has every right to object. Why is tense placed on the left side of the main verb? After all, tense is a suffix, not a prefix.

Despite this obvious objection, the rule is correct the way it stands. There is a good reason why tense has to be generated in front of the main verb. You recall that tense is an obligatory element in the auxiliary, that is, every sentence must contain tense, either present or past. The other three elements in the auxiliary are optional. A sentence can have any one of the three elements, any two of them, all three of them, or none of them. Here is a sentence that has just the past tense:

John cried.

Notice what happens when we add the progressive (one of the three optional elements):

John was crying.

The main verb *cry* has now changed from the past tense form to the present participle form. The verb that is now in the past tense is the auxiliary verb *be.* Next, notice what happens when we add another optional element, the perfect:

John had been crying.

The main verb is still a present participle, but the auxiliary verb *be* has changed from the past tense to the past participle form. The perfect auxiliary verb *have* now carries the past tense ending.

Finally, adding a modal auxiliary, the remaining optional element, we get the following sentence:

John might have been crying.

This time *had* has changed back to the uninflected form *have* and the past tense ending has shifted forward to the modal auxiliary *may,* changing it to *might.*

The generalization that holds for all four sample sentences is that tense is always attached to the *first* verb. The first verb may be any one of the three optional elements, or if none of the options are picked, the main verb. As far as the rules are concerned, it does not make any difference which, if any, of the options are exercised; tense is always attached to the first verb. The function of the flip-flop rule is only to attach the tense to whatever verb follows it.

Here is a sample derivation employing the flip-flop rule:

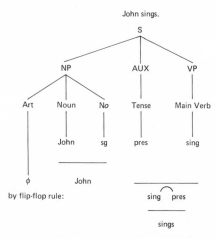

In the convention used throughout this book, the transformational rules will be listed along the left margin in the order of their application. The actual result of the application of the rule will be shown on the same line as the name of the rule. Notice that a line has been drawn over the *sing͡ pres*. This line is a way of indicating the part of the tree diagram that the transformational rule applies to. In other words, *pres͡ sing* has been transformed to *sing͡ pres* by the application of the flip-flop rule.

Exercise 4 / TENSE AND MAIN VERB

Draw phrase structure trees and show the application of the flip-flop rule for the following sentences:

1. The girl laughed.
2. The doorbells rang.
3. My shoelace broke.
4. Some children cried.
5. John lisps.

MODAL AUXILIARIES

We will deal with five modal auxiliary verbs: *can, may, must, shall,* and *will.* All of these verbs are highly irregular in form. A "regular" verb has four distinct forms, for example, *walk, walks, walked, walking.* Many "irregular" verbs have five distinct forms, for example, *sing, sings, sang, sung, singing.* The verb *be* has the greatest number of distinct forms, eight: *be, am, are, is, was, were, been, being.* The modal auxiliary verbs, however, have only a two-way contrast of form:

Verb:	can	may	must	shall	will
Present:	can	may	must	shall	will
Past:	could	might	—	should	would

Notice that there is no contrast between the third person singular and the other present forms. That is, we do not add a third person singular *-s:* °*he cans,* °*he mays,* °*he musts,* °*he shalls,* °*he wills.* Of course *can* and *will* can be used with a third person singular *-s,* but in a totally different meaning. For example,

He cans tuna.
He wills his entire estate to charity.

The past tense of four of the modals are of the hybrid type that add an ending and also change the vowel. *Must* does not have any historical past tense. If it is necessary to convert a sentence containing *must* into the past, an entirely different verb must be used as a semantic substitute. For example,

Present: John *must* go home now.
Past: John *had to* go home then.

The past tense forms of the modals have a range of meaning beyond what past tense means with other verbs. Consequently, it is possible to use modal auxiliaries that are past tense in form but not in meaning. For example,

He *could* come back tomorrow.
It *might* rain tomorrow.
I *should* feel better tomorrow.
They *would* go tomorrow if they could.

The past tense of modals is a clear illustration of the need to separate form from meaning. The phrase structure rules generate an abstract element that is necessary to account for the proper form of verbs; the name of the element has no intrinsic significance. The element means various things depending (in this particular case) on the type of verb that it is attached to. Attached to modal auxiliaries the element means one thing; attached to most main verbs, the element means something else. The name "past tense" was picked for the element because it is suggestive of the most common use.

The difference (if any) between the present tense modals *will* and *shall* has been known to cause a certain amount of anxiety among native speakers. Historically, *will* and *shall* (like many other pairs of modals) have long had partially overlapping meanings. In 1653 a grammarian by the name of John Wallis decided to do something about the wishy-washy distinction between *will* and *shall.* In his book *Grammatica Linguae Anglicanae* (*Grammar of the English Language*) he proposed that the first person use of *shall* would mean a simple, factual statement about future action, while the first person use of *will* would mean 'promising' or 'threatening' some future action. However, in the second and third persons, the two meanings would be exactly reversed: *will* would mean simple futurity; *shall* would mean promising or threatening. As far as we know, Wallis' distinction was not a very accurate reflection of the then current usage of *will* and *shall*, and certainly it is not an accurate description of present-day usage. Nevertheless, Wallis' distinction was enshrined as a rule of the language by later grammarians, and has been used to frighten children with, ever since. For most speakers of American English (including this writer), *will* and *shall* mean exactly the same thing in statements. In questions, though, they do contrast. For example, compare these two questions:

Will we dance?
Shall we dance?

The first sentence is a genuine question that asks for information. The second sentence means something like 'Let's dance'. Here are two sample derivations involving modals.

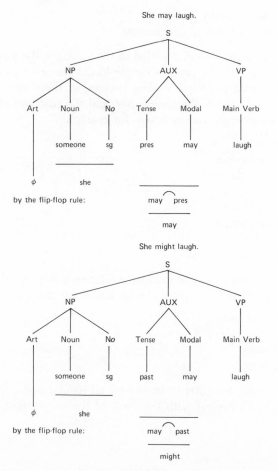

Exercise 5 / MODAL AND AUXILIARY

Draw phrase structure trees and apply the flip-flop rule for the following sentences:

1. The day will come.
2. She should resign.
3. Dogs can swim.
4. You must leave.
5. A dollar would help.

PERFECT

The *perfect* is the second optional element in the auxiliary. The perfect always consists of two pieces: the helping verb *have* plus the past participle marker, *-en*. Compare these two sentences:

I wrote a letter to my parents.
I *had* written a letter to my parents.

Notice that when the perfect is added to the auxiliary, the form of the verb after *have* changes to the past participle form. The *-en* was chosen as the symbol for the past participle ending because of those verbs that make a contrast of form between the simple past and the past participle, the most common past participle ending is *-en*, for example:

bite–bit–bitt*en*
break–broke–brok*en*
choose–chose–chos*en*
eat–ate–eat*en*
ride–rode–ridd*en*
shake–shook–shak*en*
steal–stole–stol*en*
write–wrote–writt*en*

The next most common way of marking a difference between the simple past and past participle is by a vowel change alone, for example:

begin–began–begun
drink–drank–drunk
sing–sang–sung
sink–sank–sunk

However, for many irregular verbs and for all regular verbs, the form of the past participle is identical with the form of the simple past, for example:

tell–told–told
leave–left–left
bleed–bled–bled
find–found–found
shoot–shot–shot
work–worked–worked
play–played–played
dance–danced–danced

The perfect, then, consists of *have* plus the fact that the following verb is always in the past participle form (even though most of the time the past participle form looks the same as the past). We have captured this generalization by writing the phrase structure rule for the perfect this way:

Perfect $\Longrightarrow$ have⌢-EN

Like tense, *-en* must be attached to the right-hand side of the verb that follows it. Consequently, we must invent another flip-flop rule that will put the suffix *-en* in the correct place:

-EN⌢Verb $\Longrightarrow$ Verb⌢-EN

Here are some examples of the application of this flip-flop rule:

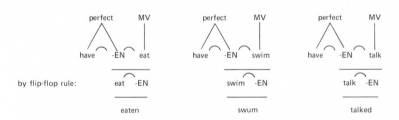

When a sentence is generated without a modal, but with the perfect, the tense will then attach to the helping verb *have*, since it is the first verb that follows the tense. When the present tense is attached to *have*, the whole construction is called the "present perfect tense"; when the past tense is attached to *have*, the construction is called the "past perfect tense." Here are three sentences with the past perfect:

He *had lived* a full life.
Mr. Smith *had chosen* to ignore the whole thing.
He *had left*.

The difference in meaning between the present and past perfect is real, but difficult to state in a few words. Often the present perfect can be paraphrased by the simple past without radically changing the meaning. For example,

> *They left.*

does not seem greatly different than the present perfect sentence,

> *They have left.*

The past perfect, however, has a much more complex time scheme. The past perfect usually describes not one period in the past, but two. Furthermore, the first period must end before or during the second. For example, the sentence

> They had left.

is understood as meaning something like

> They had already left before something happened.

Here are some more examples of the past perfect:

> The dinosaurs *had* already *died* off when the first man appeared.
> As soon as we *had finished,* we cleared off the table.
> They *had gone* to Greece when they were in college.
> He *had been* very ill that summer.

Here are some sample derivations of the perfect:

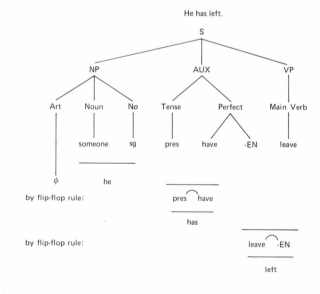

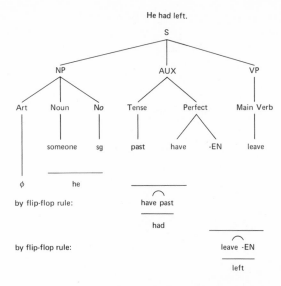

Notice that the flip-flop rules must apply twice: once to tense and once to *-en*. If *have* does not directly follow tense because of an intervening modal, tense is attached to the modal, and not to *have*. In that case, *have* is not inflected at all, that is, *have* is neither present nor past, but in the infinitive form. For example,

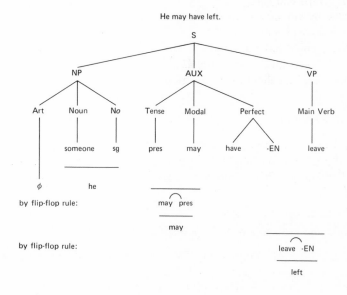

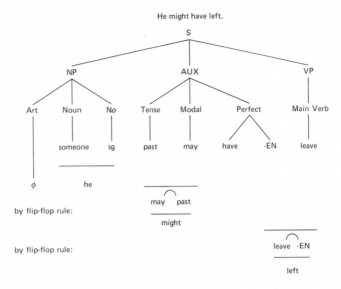

He might have left.

by flip-flop rule:

by flip-flop rule:

Exercise 6 / PERFECT

Draw phrase structure trees and apply the flip-flop rule(s) to the following sentences:

1. John has won.
2. My ships had sunk.
3. The answer may have come.
4. A cook had quit.
5. Mary could have finished.
6. Somebody must have noticed.
7. The children should have written.

PROGRESSIVE

Like the perfect, the progressive consists of two parts: the helping verb *be* and the present participle ending *-ing*, which is always attached to the verb following *be*. This attachment is governed by the third version of the flip-flop rule:

-ING⌒Verb ⟹ Verb⌒-ING

Here are some examples of the application of this rule:

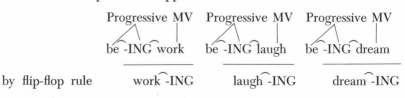

When a sentence is generated with no other optional elements in the auxiliary besides the progressive, tense is then attached to the helping verb *be*, making a contrast between the present progressive and the past progressive. For example,

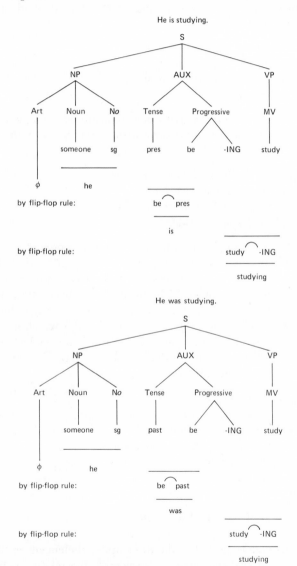

The present progressive, you recall, is commonly used to express present time, for example,

He *is* tak*ing* a shower now.

The past progressive usually indicates that at some point in the past, some action was in progress at that time, for example,

He *was* tak*ing* a shower when you called.

The present progressive can also be used with future time adverbs, but with a special meaning, for example,

I am going to the mainland tomorrow.
He is running for re-election.
John is going fishing in the morning.
We are sailing on the tide.

In these sentences, the progressive seems to mean something like "intention." We can even replace the progressive in these sentences by the verb *intend* (*to*) without radically altering the meaning:

I intend to go to the mainland tomorrow.
He intends to run for re-election.
John intends to go fishing in the morning.
We intend to sail on the tide.

In the discussion of the meaning and use of the present tense, we made a distinction between "action" verbs and "description" verbs. The "description" verbs, unlike the "action" verbs, can be used in the present tense without an implicit adverb of frequency. The distinction between these two types of verbs also carries over into the use of the progressive. Since the progressive describes action in progress, the "description" verbs, which have no action, are incompatible with the progressive. For example, if we take the same group of sentences containing "description" verbs on page 58 and make them progressive, they become ungrammatical:

° I am having a hangnail.
° The book is costing $3.75.
° He is appearing to be winning.
° The boat is weighing nearly 400 pounds.
° She is looking terrible.
° It is seeming kind of silly to me.

Final Version of the Flip-Flop Rule

The progressive is the last of the three optional elements in the auxiliary. If more than one optional element is selected, the relative position of the elements is fixed in this order: modal, perfect, progressive. Let us now generate a sentence employing all the auxiliary options:

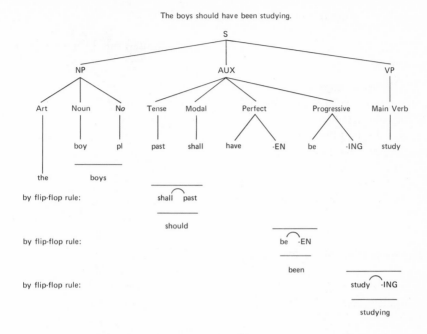

The boys should have been studying.

In order to make the operation of the flip-flop rules precise, we need to state that a flip-flop rule must apply to any ending only once. If you look at the sample derivation above, you will see that as a result of the first flip-flop, past is now to the left of *have*. We do not intend the rule to apply again to past because the result would produce the ungrammatical sequence:

° *shall had been studying*

We can simplify the expression of the flip-flop rules by combining all three rules into one. As the rules stand now, we have three separate but obviously related rules:

Tense⌢Verb ⟹ Verb⌢Tense
-EN⌢Verb ⟹ Verb⌢-EN
-ING⌢Verb ⟹ Verb⌢-ING

All three flip-flop rules attach the verb endings to the following verb. By establishing one symbol to stand for all three verb endings, we can collapse the three rules into one. The symbol used for this purpose is *Af*, which stands for *affix*. We can now write the flip-flop rule this way:

Let Af = Tense, -EN, or -ING
Af⌢Verb ⟹ Verb⌢Af

Exercise 7 / PROGRESSIVE

Draw phrase structure trees and apply the flip-flop rule to the following sentences:

1. John is singing.
2. John was singing.
3. John has been singing.
4. John had been singing.
5. John may be singing.
6. John might be singing.
7. John may have been singing.
8. John might have been singing.

Answers to Exercise 3 / TENSE

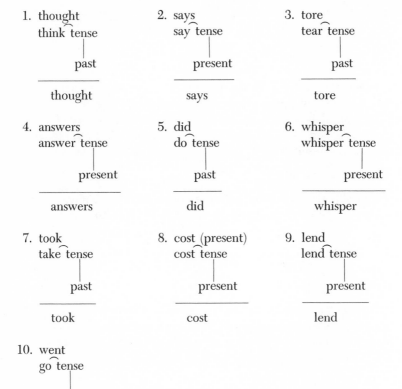

1. thought
    think ⌒ tense
            |
          past
   _____
      thought

2. says
    say ⌒ tense
            |
        present
   _____
       says

3. tore
    tear ⌒ tense
            |
          past
   _____
       tore

4. answers
    answer ⌒ tense
            |
         present
   _____
      answers

5. did
    do ⌒ tense
            |
          past
   _____
        did

6. whisper
    whisper ⌒ tense
            |
         present
   _____
      whisper

7. took
    take ⌒ tense
            |
          past
   _____
       took

8. cost (present)
    cost ⌒ tense
            |
         present
   _____
       cost

9. lend
    lend ⌒ tense
            |
         present
   _____
       lend

10. went
     go ⌒ tense
            |
          past
   _____
       went

Answers to Exercise 4 / TENSE AND MAIN VERB

1. The girl laughed.

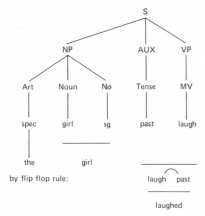

2. The doorbells rang.

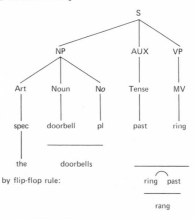

3. My shoelace broke.

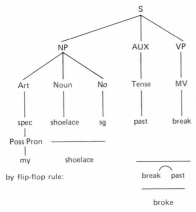

4. Some children cried.

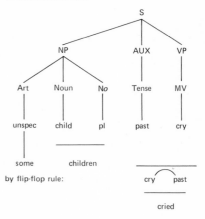

5. John lisps.

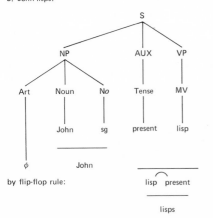

Answers to Exercise 5 / MODAL AUXILIARY

1. The day will come.

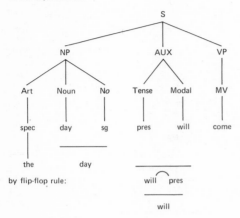

by flip-flop rule:

2. She should resign.

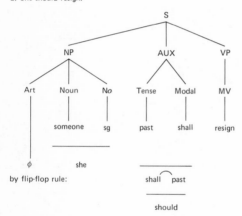

by flip-flop rule:

3. Dogs can swim.

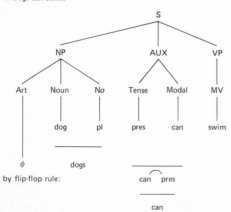

by flip-flop rule:

4. You must leave.

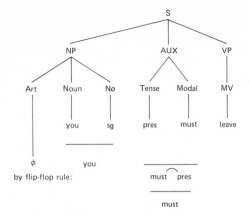

by flip-flop rule:

5. A dollar would help.

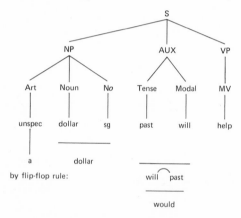

by flip-flop rule:

Answers to Exercise 6 / PERFECT

1. John has won.

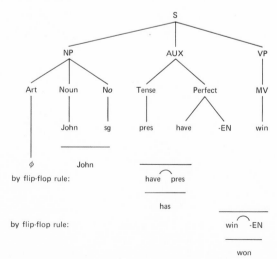

by flip-flop rule:

by flip-flop rule:

2. My ships had sunk.

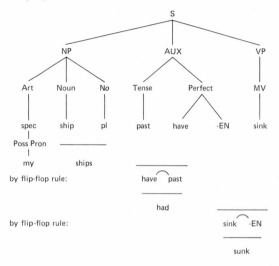

by flip-flop rule: have⌢past

                               had

by flip-flop rule: sink⌢-EN

                                              sunk

3. The answer may have come.

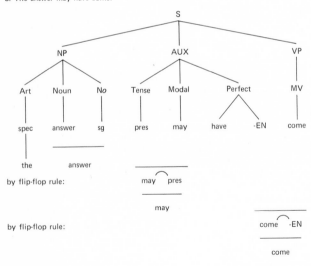

by flip-flop rule: may⌢pres

                               may

by flip-flop rule: come⌢-EN

                                             come

4. A cook had quit.

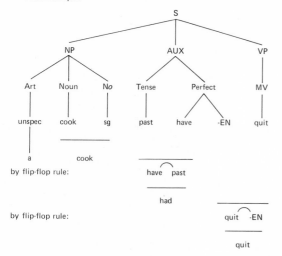

5. Mary could have finished.

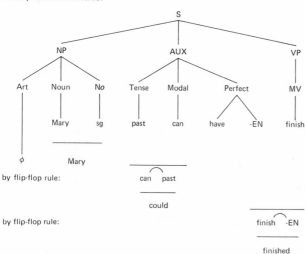

6. Somebody must have noticed.

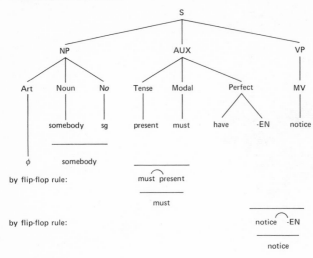

by flip-flop rule:

by flip-flop rule:

7. The children should have written.

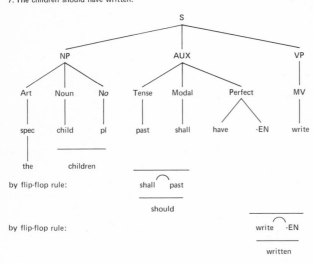

by flip-flop rule:

by flip-flop rule:

Answers to Exercise 7 / PROGRESSIVE

1. John is singing.

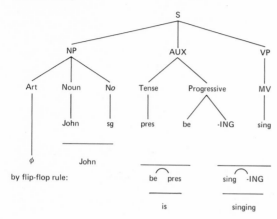

2. John was singing.

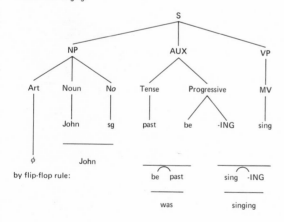

3. John has been singing.

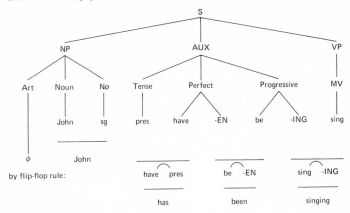

4. John had been singing.

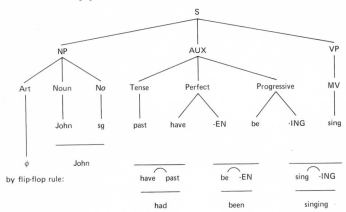

5. John may be singing.

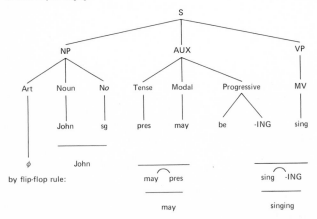

6. John might be singing.

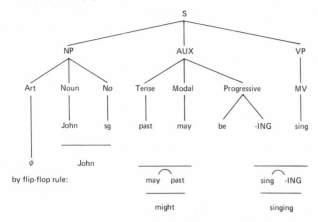

7. John may have been singing.

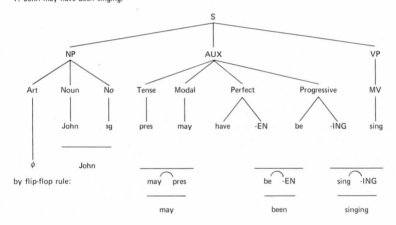

8. John might have been singing.

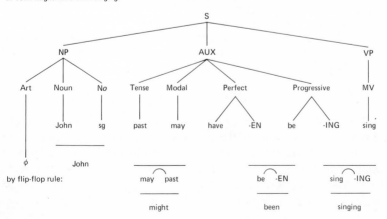

CHAPTER 3

The Verb Phrase

Overview

The verb phrase consists of three elements in this order: the main verb, the complement, and an optional element called "adverbial." The main verb and the complement are closely interrelated. The traditional terms "transitive" and "intransitive" are ways of talking about this relation. In our terminology, a transitive verb is a main verb that takes a noun phrase complement. For example, in the sentence

She sells seashells.

sells is the main verb and *seashells* is the noun phrase complement. The main verb *sell*, at least in its common usage, requires an object noun phrase. All main verbs require a subject noun phrase, but only transitive main verbs require an object noun phrase. An intransitive verb, on the other hand, does not take an object noun phrase, for example,

Jesus wept.

In this grammar, we make the generalization that all main verbs must be followed by a complement. In the case of a transitive verb, the complement is obviously a noun phrase. In the case of an intransitive verb, the complement is the null set Ø. The complement, then, is a list of the elements that main verbs take. When we select a main verb we must also select one of the elements listed under complement, even if the element we select is Ø.

The major portion of this chapter is devoted to discussions of the following nine different types of complements.

Ø
Noun Phrase
Adjective
Adverb of Place
Adverb of Motion
Noun Phrase‿Adverb of Motion
Noun Phrase‿Adjective
Noun Phrase‿Preposition‿Noun Phrase
Adjective‿Preposition‿Noun Phrase

The chapter concludes with a discussion of the way that English fuses together verbs and prepositions to form new verbs. These new units are often called "two-word verbs" (for the obvious reason that they are made up out of two words: a verb and a preposition). When a two-word verb is transitive, that is, when it takes a noun phrase complement, we must make a further distinction between separable and inseparable two-word verbs. Compare the following sentences:

John looked up the price.
John looked for the price.

In the first sentence the main verb is the two-word verb *look up;* in the second sentence it is *look for.* However, in one respect *look up* and *look for* behave quite differently. A separable two-word verb is one in which we may move the preposition to a position after the object noun phrase. For example,

John looked up the price ⟹ John looked the price up.

An inseparable two-word verb is one in which we cannot move the preposition. For example,

John looked for the price ⟹ *John looked the price for.

Thus, *look up* is a separable two-word verb, and *look for* is an inseparable two-word verb.

THE VERB PHRASE

Verb Phrase ⟶ Main Verb‿Complement‿(Adverbial)

The verb phrase in English consists of two obligatory elements and a third optional element. The first element, the main verb, is self-explanatory, at least for the moment. The second element, the complement, is not very well named. In this grammar, the term complement means anything following the main verb that is necessary to make the sentence grammatical in the intended sense. The final element, adverbial, is a loose term covering a multitude of different subclasses of adverbs. The crucial distinction between the second and third elements is that the complement is obligatory, without it the sentence is ungrammatical; while the third element, the adverbial, provides material not essential to the grammar of the sentence. The distinction between the complement and the adverbial elements is most difficult when the complement itself contains an adverb. For example,

> We put the steak *on the grill.*
> We cooked the steak *on the grill.*

In the first sentence the adverb phrase *on the grill* is a necessary part of the sentence; if it is deleted, the sentence is ungrammatical:

> ° We put the steak.

In the second sentence, *on the grill* is an optional adverbial modifier. If it is deleted from the sentence, the information that it contained is naturally lost, but the basic meaning of the sentence as well as its grammaticality are unaffected:

> We cooked the steak.

The difference between these two sentences is also shown by an optional transformational rule that deletes the noun phrase from the prepositional in the first sentence, producing

> We put the steak on.

However, if this same transformation is applied to the second sentence, the result is ungrammatical:

> ° We cooked the steak on.

Since, by definition, the grammaticality of a sentence is not affected by the presence or absence of the adverbial, it will be largely ignored from this point on.

In rough terms, the complement is simply a list of things that can occur after a main verb. For example, some main verbs can be followed by an adjective, some by a noun phrase, others by an adverb of place, and so on.

One point that needs to be clarified is what is meant by a main verb. Compare the following sentences:

> John became angry.
> John became a doctor.

From the point of view adopted in this grammar, the *become* in the first sentence is a different verb from the *become* in the second sentence. They are different because they mean different things and because they are followed by different complements. We may think of the first *become* as the one that is followed by adjectives, while the second *become* is the one that is followed by noun phrases.

There are two different types of complements: simple complements that contain no embedded sentences and complex complements that do. In this section, we will deal only with the simple complements. Complex complements will be dealt with in Part Three. Here is a list of the simple complements that we will deal with:

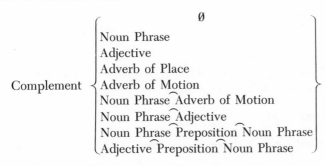

$$\text{Complement} \begin{cases} \varnothing \\ \text{Noun Phrase} \\ \text{Adjective} \\ \text{Adverb of Place} \\ \text{Adverb of Motion} \\ \text{Noun Phrase}\frown\text{Adverb of Motion} \\ \text{Noun Phrase}\frown\text{Adjective} \\ \text{Noun Phrase}\frown\text{Preposition}\frown\text{Noun Phrase} \\ \text{Adjective}\frown\text{Preposition}\frown\text{Noun Phrase} \end{cases}$$

THE Ø COMPLEMENT

The minimal complement is the null set (Ø). In traditional grammar, verbs that take a Ø complement are called "intransitive" verbs. Here are a few examples of sentences with Ø complements:

The baby slept.
She smiled.
They were working.
We laughed.

A tree diagram of the first sentence would look like this:

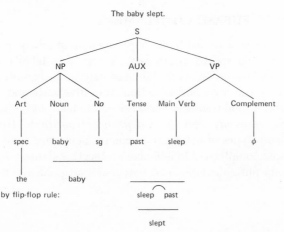

Many sentences that appear to have Ø complement may be derived from sentences with noun phrase objects. For example,

John smokes.
We won.
She sang.

might be derived from

John smokes cigarettes.
We won the game.
She sang a song.

Nevertheless, at least some verbs have a true Ø complement. Here is a famous sentence containing two clear-cut examples:

I *think*, therefore I *am*.

In this sentence, *think* means 'to have the capacity for thought' and *be*, means 'to exist'.

Exercise 8 / Ø COMPLEMENTS

Draw deep structures and apply the flip-flop rule to derive the following sentences:

1. The telephone rang.
2. Our roof leaks.
3. The baby was sleeping.
4. She will laugh.
5. I have been working.

THE NOUN PHRASE COMPLEMENT

The noun phrase is probably the most common of all complement types. It even has its own special vocabulary. A verb that takes a noun phrase complement is a "transitive" verb. We need here to distinguish between two different types of transitive verbs: "action" transitive verbs and "description" transitive verbs. Action transitive verbs are said to take *objects*, while description transitive verbs are said to take *predicate nominals*. Here are some examples of both types of noun phrase complements, first with action verbs (the noun phrase complement functioning as object), and then with description verbs (the noun phrase complement functioning as predicate nominal):

Noun phrase complements with action verbs:

The pitcher examined the ball.
The publisher reviewed the manuscript.
The lawyer sued the city.
He snapped the twig.

Noun phrase complements with description verbs:

John is a fool.
The book cost $5.95.
I weigh 175 pounds.
He has a new Mustang.

In addition to the difference in the semantic relation between the main verb and the noun phrase complement in the two types of verbs, there are several distinct formal differences as well. One difference is that we cannot easily make the "description" verb progressive. For example, let us put the example sentences above into the progressive. Notice that the sentences with "description" verbs seem ungrammatical, or at the least, very stilted.

Noun phrase complements with action verbs:

The pitcher was examining the ball.
The publisher was reviewing the manuscript.
The lawyer was suing the city.
He was snapping the twig.

Noun phrase complements with description verbs:

° John is being a fool. (Grammatical in the sense of 'pretending to act like')
° The book is costing $5.95.
° I am weighing 175 pounds.
° He is having a new Mustang.

Since the distinction between "action" and "description" is a feature of the main verb, tree diagrams for sentences containing noun phrase complements will not indicate the difference between those noun phrases that function as objects and those noun phrases that function as predicate nominals. Thus, the following tree diagram should serve for a description verb as well as for an action verb:

The pitcher grabbed the ball.

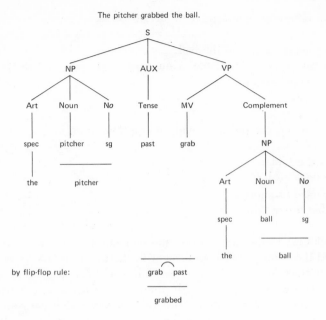

Exercise 9 / NOUN PHRASE COMPLEMENTS

Draw deep structures and apply the necessary transformational rules to produce the following sentences:

1. John broke the window.
2. I have a question.
3. The students passed the exam easily.
4. His father painted the picture.
5. Someone burned the toast.

THE ADJECTIVE COMPLEMENT

With this complement type, it is also necessary to distinguish between "action" and "description" verbs. The most common occurrence of adjective complements is after "description" verbs. These adjective complements have a special name: "predicate adjectives." Here are some sample sentences with description verbs and predicate adjectives:

Sally is silly.
It tastes great.
The soup seems watery.

However, there are also a number of highly restricted "action" verb-adjective complement pairs. Some of the pairs can be grouped into classes, though there may well be hundreds of unique "action" verb-adjective pairs. The largest single class consists of verbs like *become, continue, grow, keep, remain, stay,* and such. Examples of these are:

> He became angry.
> She grew old gracefully.
> They remained silent.
> Stay cool.

These verbs are clearly "action" verbs because they can be used in the progressive, for example,

> He was becoming angry.
> She was growing old gracefully.
> They were remaining silent.

If we add the progressive to the "description" verbs above, the resulting sentences are ungrammatical in their original meaning:

> ° Sally is being silly.
> ° It is tasting great.
> ° The soup is seeming watery.

The first sentence

> Sally is being silly.

is grammatical, but in a different sense from the original. When *be* is used as an action verb with a predicate adjective, it means something like 'acting', 'behaving', or 'pretending to be'. Some examples of the more restricted pairs of "action" verb-adjective complements are:

> The deer stood still.
> She turned red.
> His story rang true.
> The well ran dry.
> The screen went black.
> He came clean.

Here is a sample derivation of an adjective complement sentence:

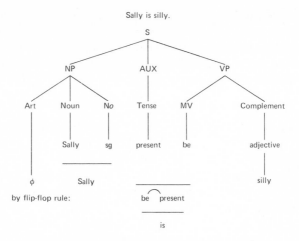

Exercise 10 / ADJECTIVE COMPLEMENTS

Draw deep structures and apply the necessary transformational rules to produce the following sentences:

1. I am happy.
2. The girl turned pale.
3. We kept quiet.
4. The man became famous.

THE ADVERB-OF-PLACE COMPLEMENT

By far the most common occurrence of the adverb-of-place complement is after the verb *be*, for example:

Your coffee is on the table.
John is at school.
The money is under the bed.

We will not draw any distinction between single-word adverbs, like *here*, and adverbial prepositional phrases, such as the ones used above. Some other verbs that take an adverb-of-place complement are *hang, lay, live, rest, shop, stand, stay*, for example:

The picture hung on the wall.
The baby lay in the crib.
The clock rested on the mantel.
I shop at Safeway.
He stood in the corner.
He stayed away.

As was mentioned before, adverbs in the complement can be confused with optional adverbs from the adverbial element. The proof that the adverbs in these sentences come from the complement is that they cannot be deleted without making the sentences ungrammatical in their original meaning. For example:

° The picture hung.
° The baby lay.
° The clock rested.
° I shop.
° He stood.
° He stayed.

Here is a sample derivation of a sentence with an adverb-of-place complement:

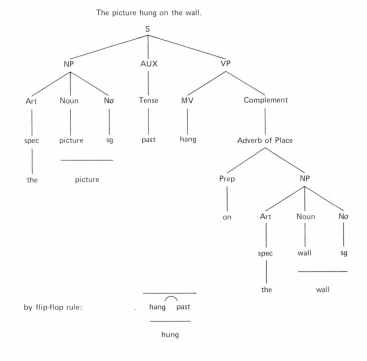

The picture hung on the wall.

Exercise 11 / ADVERBS-OF-PLACE COMPLEMENTS

Draw deep structures and apply the necessary transformational rule to produce the following sentences:

1. The dictionary is on the shelf.

2. Mr. Smith resided at 733 N. Elm Street.
3. He is here.
4. I live by the seashore.

ADVERB-OF-MOTION AND
NOUN PHRASE ADVERB-OF-MOTION COMPLEMENTS

Since these two types of complements are closely related, we will treat them together. Many features of the noun phrase adverb-of-motion complement have been commented on at the beginning of the discussion of verb phrases in reference to the sentence

We put the steak on the grill.

The prepositional phrase *on the grill* expresses motion to or from rather than just place. The distinction between adverbs of place and motion is somewhat obscured by the fact that the same question word stands for both types of adverbs:

Place: *Where* did you stay?
Motion: *Where* did you go?

The preposition *to* with adverbs of motion makes the distinction sharper, though it is not usually considered good usage. For example, most people would hesitate to write this sentence, even though it is perfectly clear:

Where did you go to?

Sometimes, however, the *to* creeps back into the sentence by sheer force of necessity. Imagine the following scene. It is a dark and stormy night. A lady is standing on a street corner trying to hail a cab. Finally one appears, and pulls up to the curb and the driver asks, "Where, lady?" In this case the speaker is forced to say "Where to." He knows where the lady is, he needs to know where she wants to go (to).

The same contrast between place and motion can be seen in the difference between *in* and *into*, and *on* and *onto*. For example:

Place: We cooked the steak on the grill.
          We cooked the steak in the oven.

Motion: We put the steak on (to) the grill.
          We put the steak in (to) the oven.

If we replace *in* and *on* in the first pair of sentences with *into* and *onto*, the result is ungrammatical:

° We cooked the steak onto the grill.
° We cooked the steak into the oven.

As was menti⬛⬛⬛⬛⬛⬛⬛⬛characteristics of the sentence

We put the steak ⬛⬛⬛

was the possibility of deletin⬛⬛⬛⬛⬛se from the adverbial prepositional phrase, producing

We put the steak on.

This deletion is not possible with adverbial prepositional phrases of place. For example:

° We cooked the steak on.
° We cooked the steak in.

Exactly the same set of relations holds between adverbial prepositional phrases of place and motion when no noun phrase follows the verb. For example, compare these two sentences:

Adverb-of-place complement: I live in that house.
Adverb-of-motion complement: I went in (to) that house.

With the adverb-of-motion complement, the noun phrase can be deleted from the adverbial prepositional phrase, but with the adverb-of-place complement, it cannot:

Place: ° I live in.   (Grammatical in the sense of 'live at the same place at which you work')

Motion: I went in.

Here are some sample sentences that have an adverb-of-motion complement.

Noun Phrase Adverb-of-Motion Complement

NP   Adv of Motion
I drove *my car* *into the garage.*

NP   Adv of Motion
The crane lifted *the cement* *up to the top floor.*

NP   Adv of Motion
The truck pushed *the car* *over to the side of the road.*

NP   Adv of Motion
The catcher threw *the ball* *back to the pitcher.*

Adverb-of-Motion Complement (without an object Noun Phrase)

Adv of Motion
The train pulled *into the station.*

Adv of Motion
Go jump *in the lake!*

Adv of Motion

She reached *into the dishwasher.*

Adv of Motion

He walked *out of the store.*

Notice that in all cases the noun phrase can be deleted from the adverbial prepositional phrase of motion:

Noun Phrase ⌒Adverb-of-Motion Complement

I drove my car into the garage ⟹ I drove my car in.

The crane lifted the cement up to the top floor ⟹

The crane lifted the cement up.

The truck pushed the car over to the side of the road ⟹

The truck pushed the car over.

The catcher threw the ball back to the pitcher ⟹

The catcher threw the ball back.

Adverb-of-Motion Complement

The train pulled into the station ⟹ The train pulled in.

Go jump in the lake ⟹ Go jump in!

She reached into the dishwasher ⟹ She reached in.

He walked out of the store ⟹ He walked out.

Here are sample derivations of the two types of complements:

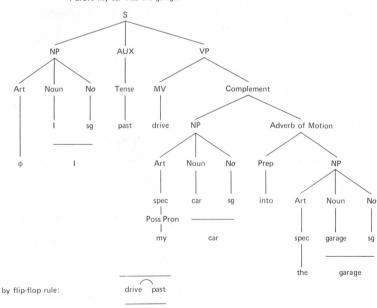

Noun Phrase ⌒Adverb of Motion Complement

I drove my car into the garage.

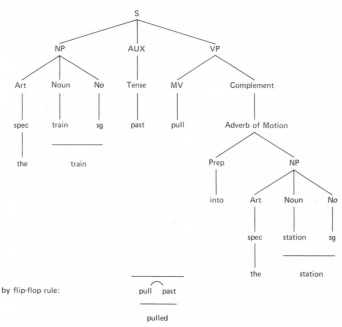

Adverb of Motion Complement

The train pulled into the station.

by flip-flop rule:

Let us call the optional transformational rule that deletes the noun phrase from the adverbial prepositional phrase of motion the "adverb-of-motion deletion rule." In addition to deleting the noun phrase, the rule also deletes the second preposition if there is more than one, so that *into* becomes *in*, *up to* becomes *up*, *out of* becomes *out*, and so forth. We may formalize this rule as follows:

$$\text{MV} \frown (\text{NP}) \frown \text{prep}_1, \frown (\text{prep}_2) \frown \text{NP} \implies \text{MV} \frown (\text{NP}) \frown \text{prep}_1$$

Applying this transformational rule to the two derivations above, we produce two new sentences (see page 96).

In these cases we have known what information was deleted from the unlerlying sentence. Suppose that we heard the sentence

John sneaked in.

without any further knowledge of the context. That is, we do not know what it was that John actually sneaked into. How would the grammar reflect this state of affairs? The grammar cannot tell you what you do not already know. In this particular case, you do not know what the exact words were in the original underlying sentence, but you do know the grammatical structure of what has been deleted, namely, a noun phrase. It has become conventional

I drove my car in.

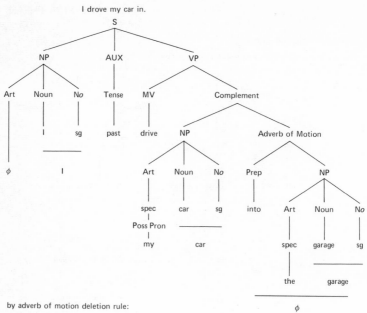

by adverb of motion deletion rule:

by flip-flop rule: drive ⌒ past

drove

The train pulled in.

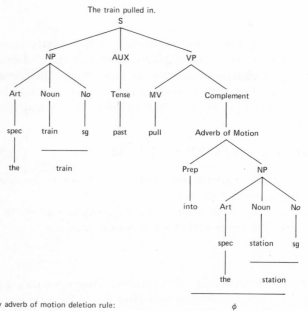

by adverb of motion deletion rule: φ

by flip-flop rule: pull ⌒ past

pulled

to represent elements of a sentence that have a grammatical structure but that do not have lexical content by the Greek letter delta Δ (which stands for dummy). The derivation of the sentence would look like this:

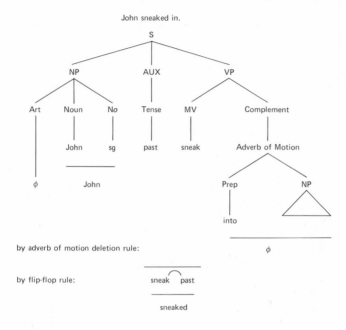

by adverb of motion deletion rule: φ

by flip-flop rule: sneak   past

                                         sneaked

Exercise 12 / ADVERB-OF-MOTION AND NP ADVERB-OF-MOTION COMPLEMENTS

Draw phrase structures and apply the necessary transformational rules to produce the following sentences:

1. The batter stepped up to the plate.
2. The train roared down the track.
3. The police forced the car over. ["to the side of the road" understood]
4. He sneaked out. ["of the theater" understood]
5. The tow-truck pulled the car out.

THE NOUN PHRASE ADJECTIVE COMPLEMENT

This complement type is highly restricted. Since the combination of verb, noun, and adjective is so idiomatic, the whole VP must be presented as a unit, for example:

carve the meat thin
eat the chicken cold

open it wide
paint it red, black, green. . . .
wash it clean
keep your powder dry

The reader should be aware that from a semantic standpoint, complements of this type are a very mixed bag. A fuller treatment would probably establish several quite distinct subtypes of complements. It might even be necessary to treat some as complex complements, that is, as complements containing independent sentences. Here is a sample derivation of a sentence with this complement type:

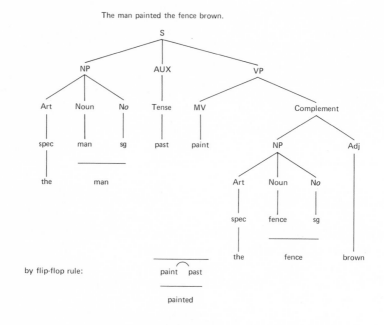

THE NOUN PHRASE PREPOSITION NOUN PHRASE COMPLEMENT

The noun phrase that occurs before the preposition is often called the "direct object" (DO), and the one that occurs after the preposition is called the "indirect object" (IO). For example, in the sentence

John gave the ball to the catcher,

the ball is the direct object noun phrase, and *the catcher* is the indirect object noun phrase. Below are some more examples of this type with the direct and indirect objects marked.

　　　　　(DO)　　　　　(IO)
I paid *the money* to *the company.*

            (DO)   (IO)
He sent *some flowers* to *her.*

               (DO)   (IO)
The boss promised *the job* to *me.*

         (DO)   (IO)
I found *a nice house* for *Gene.*

        (DO)   (IO)
He drew *a picture* for *her.*

         (DO)   (IO)
He ordered *a sandwich* for *me.*

All of the complements given above have the ability to undergo an optional transformational rule that reverses the two noun phrases and deletes the preposition. For example, we can transform

John gave the ball to the catcher.

into

John gave the catcher the ball.

Let us call this transformational rule the "object switch rule." We may formalize the rule in this manner:

     (DO)   (IO)   (IO)   (DO)
MV Noun Phrase Prep Noun Phrase $\Longrightarrow$ MV Noun Phrase Noun Phrase

Here are some more examples of the application of this rule:

        (DO)   (IO)   (IO)   (DO)
I paid *the money* to *the company* $\Longrightarrow$ I paid *the company the money.*

     (DO)   (IO)   (IO)   (DO)
He sent *some flowers* to *her* $\Longrightarrow$ He sent *her some flowers.*

          (DO)   (IO)   (IO) (DO)
The boss promised *the job* to *me* $\Longrightarrow$ The boss promised *me the job.*

       (DO)   (IO)   (IO) (DO)
I found *a nice house* for *Gene* $\Longrightarrow$ I found *Gene a nice house.*

      (DO)   (IO)   (IO) (DO)
He drew *a picture* for *her* $\Longrightarrow$ He drew *her a picture.*

        (DO)   (IO)   (IO) (DO)
He ordered *a sandwich* for *me* $\Longrightarrow$ He ordered *me a sandwich.*

About the only restriction on the use of this rule for these sentences is that the rule is usually not applied if the direct object noun phrase is a pronoun. That is, most people will prefer the untransformed version

John gave it to the catcher.

to the transformed version

John gave the catcher it.

Here are some sample derivations of sentences with NP͡ Prep͡ NP complements:

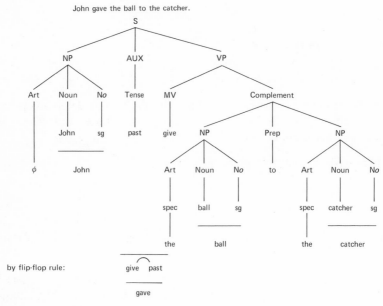

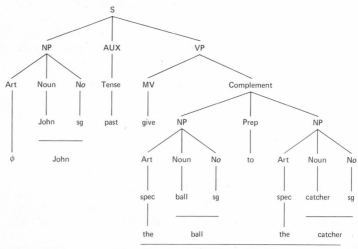

49654

Notice that the deep structures for the two sentences are identical; that is, despite their difference on the surface, the two sentences have the same underlying structure and meaning.

Here are some examples of verb phrases with NP⌢Prep⌢NP complements of a somewhat different type:

> take pity on someone
> place the troops under his command
> compensate John for his injuries
> restore the king to the throne
> provide the office with the information
> thank Mrs. Brown for her kindness
> translate the Bible into Ponapean
> play the part of a priest
> reduce the city to ashes
> leave the baby with a sitter
> fill the air with suspicion

The difference between these complements and the ones discussed above is that these NP⌢Prep⌢NP complements cannot undergo the object switch rule. For example,

> take pity on someone ⟹ ° take someone pity
> place the troops under his command ⟹ ° place his command the
> troops
> compensate John for his injuries ⟹ ° compensate his injuries John
> restore the king to the throne ⟹ ° restore the throne the king
> provide the office with the information ⟹ ° provide the information
> the office
> thank Mrs. Brown for her kindness ⟹ ° thank her kindness Mrs.
> Brown
> translate the Bible into Ponapean ⟹ ° translate Ponapean the Bible
> play the part of a priest ⟹ ° play a priest the part
> reduce the city to ashes ⟹ ° reduce ashes the city
> leave the baby with a sitter ⟹ ° leave a sitter the baby
> fill the air with suspicion ⟹ ° fill suspicion the air

It is quite common to subcategorize an underlying structure into two types in terms of the ability of the construction to undergo an optional transformation. The grammar must somehow indicate which type can "take" the transformation and which type cannot. One way of doing this is to separate the NP⌢Prep⌢NP complements into two types, say (a) and (b), and to state that by definition type (a) are those NP⌢Prep⌢NP complements that can optionally undergo the object switch rule, and type (b) are those that cannot.

A characteristic of subclass (a) is that (with rare exceptions) the preposition must be either *to* or *for*. A clear illustration of this generalization is the pair of sentences:

He took some candy to the baby.
He took some candy from the baby.

If we apply the noun phrase switch rule to both sentences, the result is grammatical only for the first sentence:

He took some candy to the baby $\Longrightarrow$ He took the baby some candy.
He took some candy from the baby $\Longrightarrow$ ° He took the baby some candy.

Put another way, we know the transformed sentence

He took the baby some candy.

can only mean to the baby and not from the baby.

Exercise 13 / NP͡ PREP͡ NP COMPLEMENTS

1. Indicate whether the following verb phrases contain a type (a) or a type (b) complement [type (a) can undergo the object switch rule, type (b) cannot]:

   a. ask John for his help
   b. take John for a fool
   c. write a letter to Santa Claus
   d. report the accident to the police
   e. steal candy from a baby
   f. mail the report to the commission
   g. sell a new car to the customer
   h. sell John on the idea
   i. draw a picture of her
   j. receive a message from the clerk
   k. play a song for her
   l. sweep the dirt under the rug
   m. take John for a ride
   n. do anything for money

2. Draw the phrase structure and apply the necessary transformational rules to produce the following sentences:

   a. The boys repeated their story to the judge.
   b. We built the children a tree house.
   c. I sold John on the idea.
   d. The boss promised me a job.
   e. He ordered me a sandwich.

THE ADJECTIVE PREPOSITION NOUN PHRASE COMPLEMENT

The complement is used with the verb *be*. Here are some sample sentences containing this complement:

John is *honest about his shortcomings.*
He is *afraid of the dark.*
I am *happy about my grade.*
It is *sensitive to heat.*
We are *uneasy about the situation.*
She is *fearful of the outcome.*
The message was very *frank about the possibilities.*
I am *conscious of the difficulty of the task.*
He is very *angry about it.*

Notice that all the adjectives are descriptive of a mental state. If other types of adjectives are used in this complement type, the result is ungrammatical, for example:

° I am slender about it.

Here is a sample derivation of this complement:

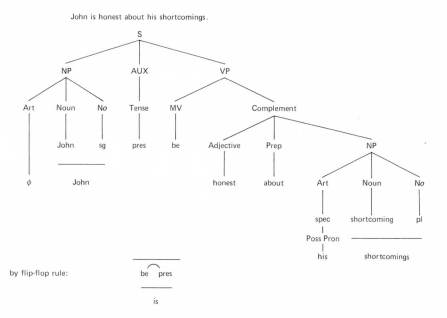

WAYS OF MAKING NEW VERBS

Every language has a continual need to make up new verbs. One of the most common ways of making up new verbs in the Indo-European languages has been to fuse together a verb stem and preposition to make a new verb. In Latin, the preposition was attached to the beginning of the verb. Here are some examples of verbs made this way that have come into English:

compel Lat *com* 'with, together' + *pellō* 'drive, force'
comprehend Lat *com* 'with, together' + *prehendō* 'grasp' (*pre* is also itself
  a preposition)
devour Lat *de* 'down, from' + *vorō* 'swallow'
detain Lat *de* 'down, from' + *teneō* 'hold'
exceed Lat *ex* 'out' + *cedō* 'Go away, withdraw'

Many English verbs are made with prepositions prefixed in the Latin manner, for example:

bypass	overestimate
downplay	overlook
forget	understand
forgive	upset
offset	withdraw
outlast	withstand
overcome	

However, most English preposition-verb combinations are made with the preposition used as a suffix rather than a prefix. This deviation from the Latin model has turned the English way of suffixing prepositions into something of a second-class citizen (and in its own native land, too), even though the English way is as ancient as the Latin. On the other hand, much of the stigma of the verb + preposition combination is due to the very fact that these forms are new, that is, they appear first as slang or part of a specialized technical jargon. If the combination withstands the passage of time, it becomes an unobjectionable part of the English vocabulary.

New Intransitive Verbs

Here are some examples of new intransitive verbs (verbs with a Ø complement) made by adding a preposition to the verb stem:

I *give up.*
The fire *went out.*
The battery has *run down.*
The firecrackers *went off.*
His promotion finally *came through.*
The ship *came about.*
We finally *gave in.*
Christmas will soon *come around.*
something will *turn up.*
The batter *struck out.*
She *passed out.*
Stop in sometime.

Even the verb *be* can be used as an intransitive verb if it has a suffixed preposition:

The batter *is up.*
The batter *is out.*
The game *is over.*

Here is a sample derivation of a sentence with an intransitive verb + preposition construction

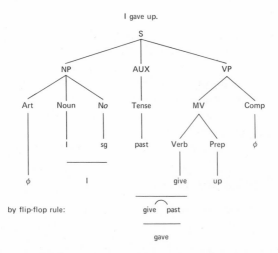

New Transitive Verbs

Compare these two sentences:

John looked up the word.
John looked up the wall.

In the first sentence the verb *look* enters into a construction with the preposition *up* to produce a new verb which means something like 'check on, as in a dictionary or reference work'. The most likely interpretation of the second sentence is that the verb *look* is followed by an adverbial prepositional phrase of place. Thus, the relationship between the main verb and the following preposition is quite different in the two sentences despite their apparent surface similarity. The difference between the two sentences is also shown in their pronunciation. In the first sentence the preposition bears a relatively heavy degree of stress, even louder than the verb that proceeds it while in the second sentence the preposition is said with minimal stress. Here are some more examples of new transitive verbs with their meanings:

She *called up* her parents.	call up = 'telephone'
I *took back* the broken pump.	take back = 'return'
He *brought up* his own name.	bring up = 'mention'
The ship *shot down* the attacking planes.	shoot down = 'destroy an aircraft by gunfire'
The army *took over* the country.	take over = 'assume control of'
The boxer *knocked out* his opponent.	knock out = 'render unconscious by a blow'
She *brushed off* her old hat.	brush off = 'dust'
He *made up* the whole story.	make up = 'fabricate'
The company *turned down* his offer.	turn down = 'reject'

The combination of a verb and a preposition to make a new transitive verb is so common that these verb constructions have a special name: "two-word verbs." One of the pecularities of all the Germanic languages is that many (but not all) two-word verbs can undergo an optional transformational rule that separates the preposition from its verb and moves it after the object noun phrase. These two-word verbs are called "separable" because the preposition can be separated from the verb. We may represent this transformational rule, which we will call the "separable preposition switch rule," in the following manner:

$$\text{MV} \frown \text{Prep} \frown \text{NP} \implies \text{MV} \frown \text{NP} \frown \text{Prep}$$

All of the new transitive verbs given above are of the "separable" type. Applying the separable preposition switch rule to these sentences we get:

John *looked up* the word $\implies$ John *looked* the word *up*.
She *called up* her parents $\implies$ She *called* her parents *up*.

I *took back* the broken pump $\Longrightarrow$ I *took* the broken pump *back*.
He *brought up* his own name $\Longrightarrow$ He *brought* his own name *up*.
The ship *shot down* the attacking planes $\Longrightarrow$ The ship *shot* the attacking
planes *down*.
The army *took over* the country $\Longrightarrow$ The army *took* the country *over*.
The boxer *knocked out* his opponent $\Longrightarrow$ The boxer *knocked* his oppo-
nent *out*.
She *brushed off* her old hat $\Longrightarrow$ She *brushed* her old hat *off*.
He *made up* the whole story $\Longrightarrow$ He *made* the whole story *up*.
The company *turned down* his offer $\Longrightarrow$ The company *turned* his offer
down.

For those verbs that permit the separable preposition switch rule, the application of the rule is optional in all cases but one. If the object noun phrase is a pronoun, the rule becomes obligatory:

° She called up them.

must be transformed to

She called them up.

If the object noun phrase is not a pronoun, the application of the rule is optional; that is, we can have either

She called up her family.

or

She called her family up.

The two-word verbs that *cannot* undergo the optional transformational rule are called "inseparable two-word verbs" because the preposition cannot be separated from the verb. The following sentences contain inseparable two-word verbs. When we attempt to apply the separable preposition switch rule, we get ungrammatical results.

We *depended on* him $\Longrightarrow$ ° We *depended* him *on*.
The hunters *shot at* the deer $\Longrightarrow$ ° The hunters *shot* the deer *at*.
I *checked into* the story $\Longrightarrow$ °I *checked* the story *into*.
I have never *heard of* him $\Longrightarrow$ °I have never *heard* him *of*.
John *got over* his cold $\Longrightarrow$ ° John *got* his cold *over*.
We *learned about* Turing machines $\Longrightarrow$ ° We *learned* Turing machines
about.
I *ran across* an odd fact $\Longrightarrow$ °I *ran* an odd fact *across*.
She will *stand by* him $\Longrightarrow$ ° She will *stand* him *by*.
I will *look after* him $\Longrightarrow$ °I will *look* him *after*.

The subclassification of transitive verb + preposition units into separable and inseparable two-word verbs is essentially the same kind of subclassification that we made of NP͡ Prep͡ NP complements into type (a) and type (b). That is, a construction generated by the phrase structure must be classified into two different types according to the ability of the construction to undergo an optional transformational rule. As with type (a) and type (b) NP͡ Prep͡ NP complements, the user of the language must simply know whether a given transitive two-word verb is separable or inseparable in order to use it correctly.

If a verb can be joined with a preposition in order to make a new verb, there is nothing to prohibit this new verb from joining with another preposition to make a second new verb. Although this is an unlikely sounding series of events, it is actually fairly common with two-word verbs. Here are some examples of new transitive verbs made by joining a second preposition to the two-word verb:

We *ran out of* milk.
The boy *talked back to* his teacher.
He *tried out for* the team.
He *put up with* a lot of nonsense.
Watch out for the car!
He *brushed up on* his French.
They *found out about* it.
She *dropped out of* school.

Here are some sample derivations of transitive verbs made from verb + preposition combinations:

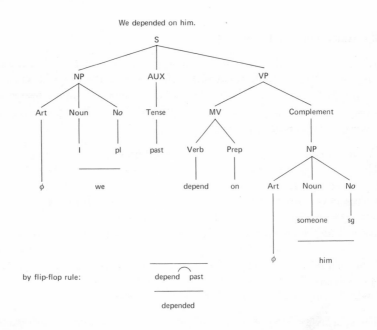

She called her family up.

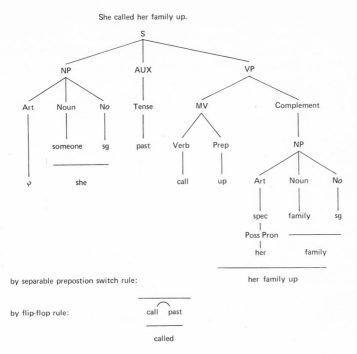

by separable prepostion switch rule:

by flip-flop rule:

called

He tried out for the team.

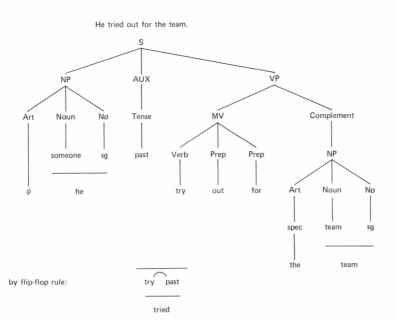

by flip-flop rule:

tried

Exercise 14 / VERB + PREPOSITION COMBINATIONS

Draw phrase structures and apply the necessary transformational rules to produce the following sentences:

1. Your time is up.
2. The general looked the situation over.
3. I forgot about it.
4. I took it down.
5. He found out about it.

Answers to Exercise 8 / Ø COMPLEMENTS

1. The telephone rang.

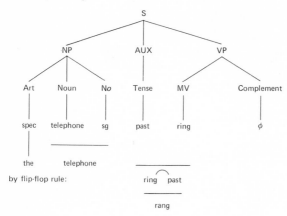

2. Our roof leaks.

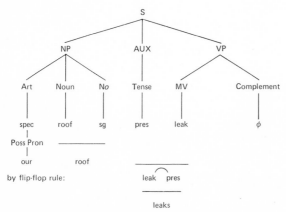

3. The baby was sleeping.

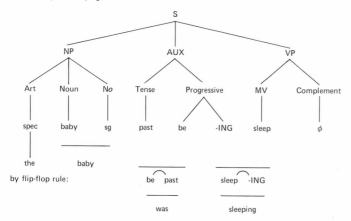

4. She will laugh.

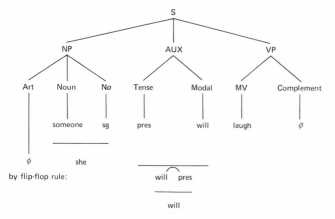

5. I have been working.

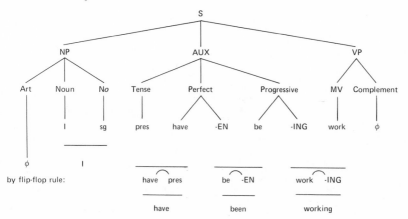

Answers to Exercise 9 / NOUN PHRASE COMPLEMENTS

1. John broke the window.

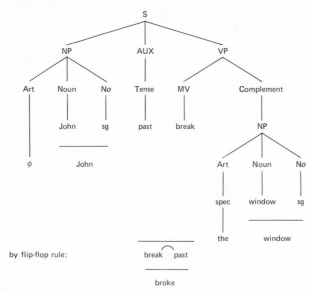

2. I have a question.

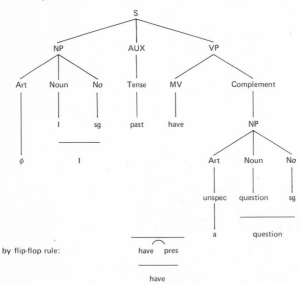

3. The students passed the exam easily.

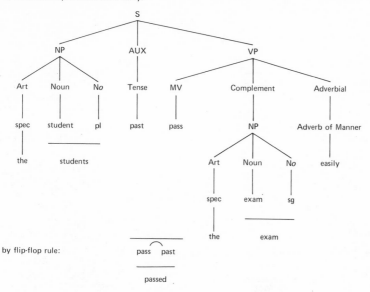

by flip-flop rule:

4. His father painted the picture.

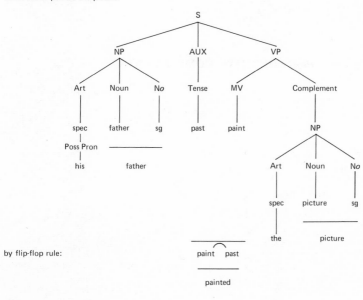

by flip-flop rule:

5. Someone burned the toast.

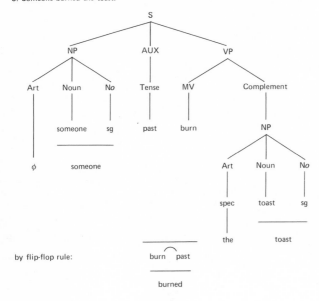

by flip-flop rule:

Answers to Exercise 10 / ADJECTIVE COMPLEMENTS

1. I am happy.

2. The girl turned pale.

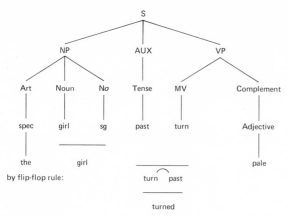

3. We kept quiet.

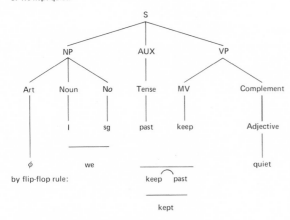

4. The man became famous.

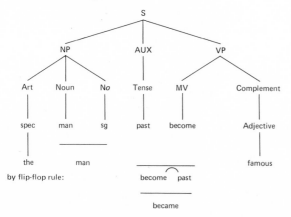

Answers to Exercise 11 / ADVERBS-OF-PLACE COMPLEMENTS

1. The dictionary is on the shelf.

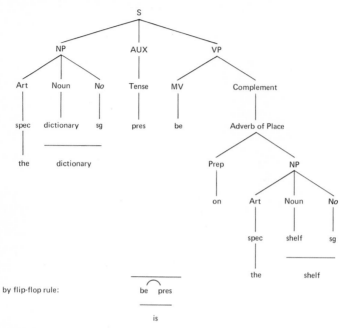

by flip-flop rule:

2. Mr. Smith resided at 733 N. Elm Street.

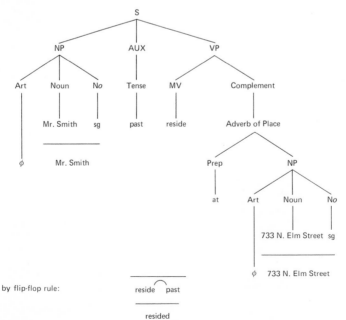

by flip-flop rule:

3. He is here.

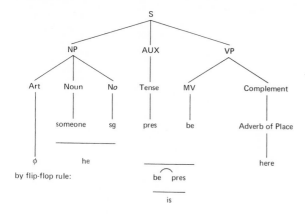

by flip-flop rule:

4. I live by the seashore.

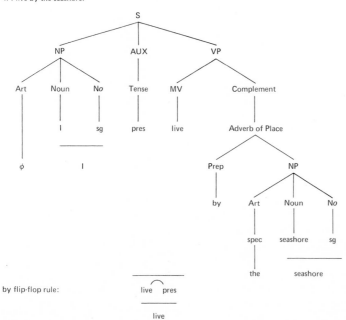

by flip-flop rule:

Answers to Exercise 12 / ADVERB-OF-MOTION AND NP͡ ADVERB-OF-MOTION COMPLEMENTS

1. The batter stepped up to the plate.

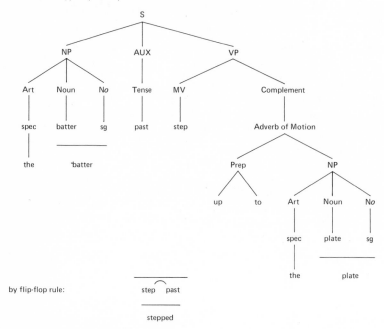

by flip-flop rule:

step͡ past

stepped

2. The train roared down the track.

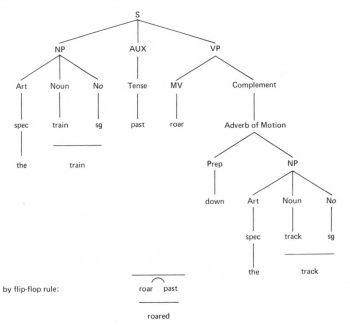

by flip-flop rule:

roar͡ past

roared

3. The police forced the car over [to the side of the road].

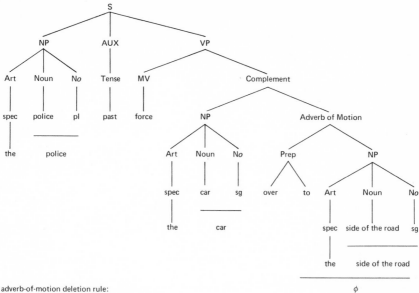

by adverb-of-motion deletion rule:

by flip-flop rule: force ͡ past

forced

4. He sneaked out [of the theater].

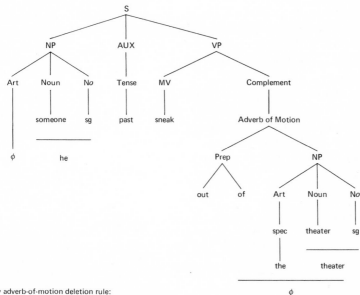

by adverb-of-motion deletion rule:

by flip-flop rule: sneak ͡ past

sneaked

5. The tow truck pulled the car out.

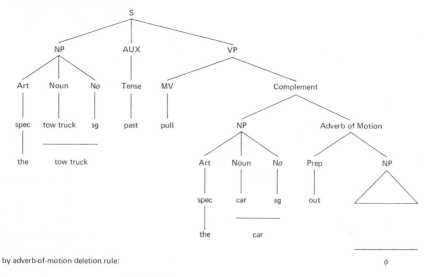

by adverb-of-motion deletion rule: ϕ

by flip-flop rule: pull͡ past

                                      ─────────
                                        pulled

Answers to Exercise 13 / NP͡ PREP͡ NP COMPLEMENTS

1. a. ask John for his help *Type (b)*
   b. take John for a fool *Type (b)*
   c. write a letter to Santa Claus *Type (a)*
   d. report the accident to the police *Type (b)*
   e. steal candy from a baby *Type (b)*
   f. mail the report to the commission *Type (a)*
   g. sell a new car to the customer *Type (a)*
   h. sell John on the idea *Type (b)*
   i. draw a picture of her *Type (b)*
      COMMENT: *draw her a picture* would mean *draw a picture for her,* not *of her.*
   j. receive a message from the clerk *Type (b)*
   k. play a song for her *Type (a)*
   l. sweep the dirt under the rug *Type (b)*
   m. take John for a ride *Type (b)*
   n. do anything for money *Type (b)*

2.a The boys repeated their story to the judge.

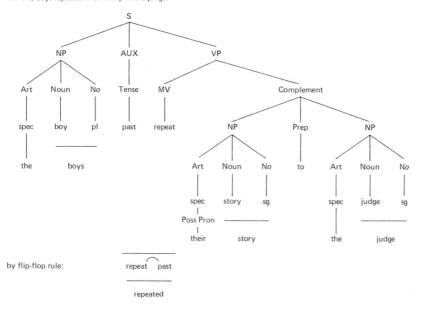

by flip-flop rule:

repeat ⌒ past

repeated

2.b. We built the children a tree house.

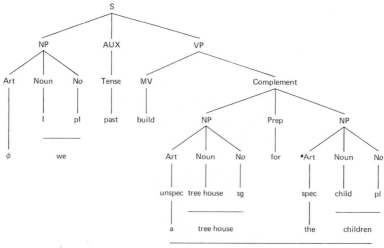

by object switch rule: the children a tree house

by flip-flop rule: build ⌒ past

built

2.c. I sold John on the idea.

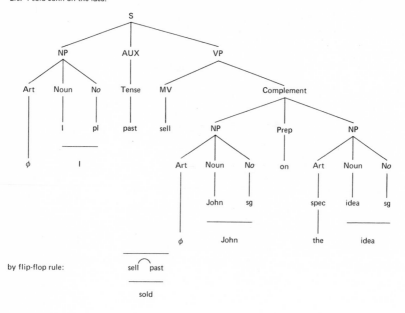

by flip-flop rule: sell ⌒ past
                        ─────────
                          sold

2.d. The boss promised me a job.

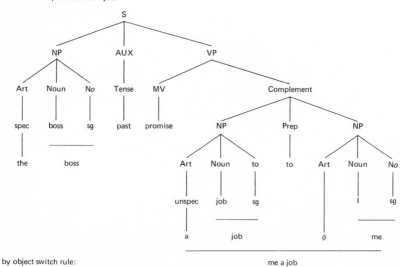

2.e. He ordered me a sandwich.

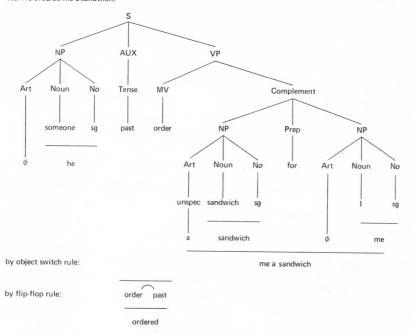

by object switch rule: me a sandwich

by flip-flop rule: order   past

                            ordered

Answers to Exercise 14 / VERB + PREPOSITION COMBINATIONS

1. Your time is up.

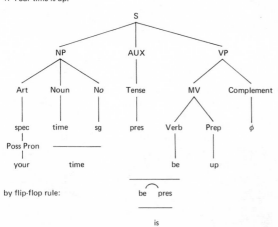

by flip-flop rule: be   pres

                    is

2. The general looked the situation over.

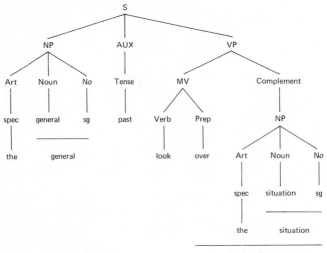

by separable preposition switch rule: the situation over

by flip-flop rule: look⌢past

                                  looked

3. I forgot about it.

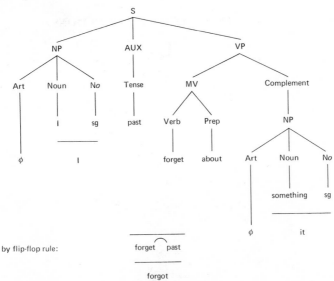

by flip-flop rule: forget⌢past

                          forgot

4. I took it down.

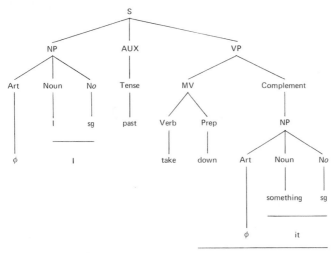

by separable prepostion switch rule: it down

by flip-flop rule: take⌢past

         took

5. He found out about it.

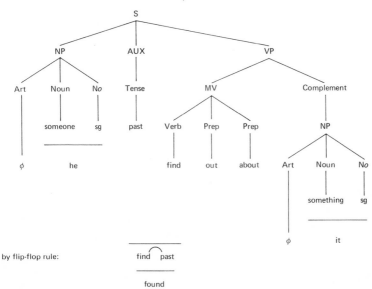

by flip-flop rule: find⌢past

        found

part
two

SIMPLE
TRANSFORMATIONAL
RULES

Overview

The grammar presented up to now produces the basic sentences that underlie the more complex sentences that we actually use in speaking and writing. All of the basic sentences generated by the grammar of Part One are active (rather than passive), statements (rather than questions), affirmative (rather than negative), and neutral (rather than containing commands or any special emphasis). Obviously passives, questions, negative statements, and emphatic sentences play a large role in actual language use. How then are these sentences generated by the grammar?

One theoretically possible way to produce these four different sentence types would be to have a separate set of basic rules for each. The grammar would then consist of at least five parts: the rules that generate active, affirmative, neutral statements; the rules that generate passive sentences; the rules that generate questions; the rules that generate negative statements; and the rules that generate commands and emphatic sentences. It is conceivable that some languages work that way. However, no one has ever found one that does, and it seems pretty unlikely that anyone ever will. Such enormous reduplication seems to go against the grain of human languages. All known languages use a quite different principle: they have just basic set of rules that generate active, affirmative, neutral statements. These sentences can then be turned into passives, questions, negative statements, or commands by making some variation in the form of the underlying statement. This variation may be achieved by adding or deleting a word or phrase, or by rearranging some of the words in the basic sentence, or even by changing the way the sentence is pronounced. In transformational terms, passives, questions, negative statements, commands, and emphatic statements are produced by applying certain transformational operations to the basic underlying sentence. In this section, we will examine some of these transformations.

CHAPTER 4

The Passive

Overview

The phrase structure rules produce "active" sentences. "Passive" sentences are created from certain types of active sentences by an optional transformational rule. This rule reverses the subject and object noun phrases, inserts a *by* in front of the original subject noun phrase which now follows the main verb, and adds *be͡* -EN to the auxiliary. For example, the passive version of

John saw the accident.

is

The accident was seen by John.

An important restriction on the formation of passive sentences is that only those sentences containing "action" transitive verbs can be transformed into the passive.

A rule closely associated with the passive is the "agent deletion rule." This rule deletes the original subject noun phrase (and the *by* that precedes it). Applied to the passive sentence above, this rule would convert

The accident was seen by John.

to

The accident was seen.

The passive rule is formalized here as a sequence of three elementary (and unordered) rules: the noun phrase switch rule that reverses the subject and object noun phrases, the *by*-insertion rule, and the be͡ -EN insertion rule.

THE PASSIVE

The passive is an optional transformational operation that converts underlying active sentences into the passive. Here are some corresponding active and passive sentences:

Active: John hit the ball.
Passive: The ball was hit by John.
Active: The explosion injured several bystanders.
Passive: Several bystanders were injured by the explosion.

Active: An inexperienced reporter wrote the story.
Passive: The story was written by an inexperienced reporter.

The function of the passive is to shift the focus of attention away from the subject noun phrase and onto the object noun phrase. Sometimes the passive is employed because the subject noun phrase is unknown and irrelevant, and sometimes because the subject noun phrase is so obvious that it seems redundant to mention it. For example, compare the active and passive versions of these two sentences:

Someone made my camera in Japan.
My camera was made in Japan.
My mother bore me in Chicago.
I was born in Chicago.

There is one important restriction on the application of the passive transformational rule: the noun phrase in the complement must function as an object, not as a predicate nominal. You recall in the discussion of noun phrase complements in Chapter 3 that we drew a distinction between "action" transitive verbs and "description" transitive verbs. "Action" transitive verbs take object noun phrase complements while "description" transitive verbs take predicate nominal noun phrase complements. Put another way, the passive transformation can only apply to sentences containing "action" verbs. As illustration of this point, listed below are the four examples of "description" transitive verbs that were given in Chapter 3.

John is a fool.
The book cost $5.95.
I weigh 175 pounds.
He has a new Mustang.

If we try to apply the passive to these sentences, the results are ungrammatical:

John is a fool $\Longrightarrow$ °A fool is been by John.
The book cost $5.95 $\Longrightarrow$ °$5.95 was cost by the book.
I weigh 175 pounds $\Longrightarrow$ °175 pounds was weighed by me.
He has a new Mustang $\Longrightarrow$ °A new Mustang was had by him.

From a semantic standpoint, the fact that transitive "description" verbs do not undergo the passive transformation is not surprising. In sentences with transitive "action" verbs, the passive focuses attention on the thing acted upon, rather than on the actor. Since the actor/acted-upon relation does not exist in sentences containing a "description" verb, the passive does not exist either.

Another difference between "action" and "description" verbs (but not necessarily limited just to transitive verbs) follows from what has been said. Adverbs of manner indicate the manner or way in which the action of the sentence was performed. As you might guess, adverbs of manner cannot be used in sentences containing "description" verbs because "description" verbs have no action. For example, if we add adverbs of manner to the "description" sentences above, the results are ungrammatical or at best, very stilted:

°John is *accidentally* a fool.
°The book *sadly* cost $5.95.
°I weigh 175 pounds *solidly*.
°He has *badly* a new Mustang.

Thus, only those sentences with transitive verbs that can readily accept adverbs of manner can undergo the passive.

Before we try to formalize the passive, let us examine some corresponding active and passive sentences:

Active	*Passive*
John broke the glass	$\Longrightarrow$ The glass was broken by John.
John may break the glass	$\Longrightarrow$ The glass may be broken by John.
John is breaking the glass	$\Longrightarrow$ The glass is being broken by John.
John has broken the glass	$\Longrightarrow$ The glass has been broken by John.
John may have broken the glass	$\Longrightarrow$ The glass may have been broken by John.
John has been breaking the glass	$\Longrightarrow$ The glass has been being broken by John. (?)
John may be breaking the glass	$\Longrightarrow$ The glass may be being broken by John. (?)
John may have been breaking the glass	$\Longrightarrow$ The glass may have been being broken by John. (?)

The last three passives may not be fully grammatical for all people. Many people avoid using the passive when the auxiliary contains the progressive plus another optional element.

The passive transformation can be broken down into a group of elementary transformational operations. The order in which these are presented is solely a matter of convenience, since there is no compelling evidence that indicates that the operations are relatively ordered. They are:

(1) NP switch rule: the subject NP and object NP change places.
(2) *by* insertion rule: *by* is inserted between the main verb and the following NP (which was the original subject).
(3) *be -EN* insertion rule: *be -EN* is inserted between the last element of the auxiliary and the main verb.

Let us go through the generation of several passives in slow motion:

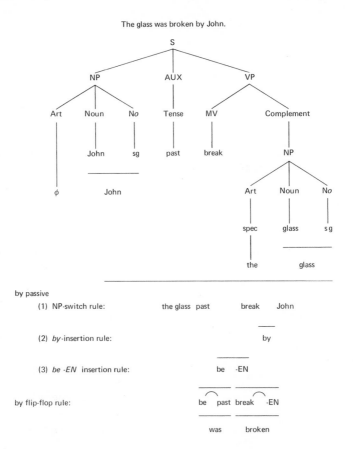

The glass was broken by John.

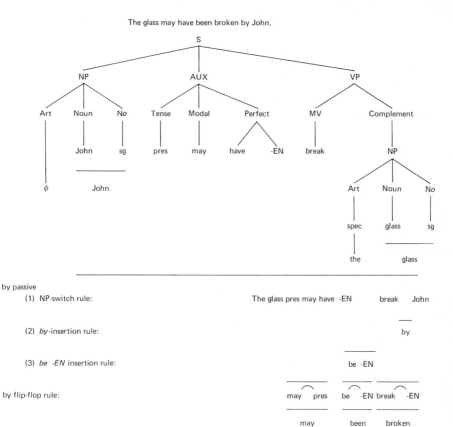

The glass may have been broken by John.

by passive

(1) NP-switch rule:

(2) *by*-insertion rule:

(3) *be -EN* insertion rule:

by flip-flop rule:

A rule that is closely associated with the passive is the "agent deletion rule." This rule deletes the original subject and the *by* in front of it converting

The glass was broken by John.

into

The glass was broken.

This rule may be applied to any passive sentence. We may formalize the agent deletion rule in the following way:

be⌢-EN⌢MV⌢by⌢NP ⟹ be⌢-EN⌢MV

It would be simpler to write the rule this way:

by NP ⟹ Ø

but this would have the effect of deleting any prepositional phrase that began with *by*, for example,

The ashtray was by John ⟹ ° The ashtray was.

Since the only source of *be -EN* is the passive transformation, the first form of the agent deletion rule guarantees that the rule will delete only the right type of prepositional phrase.

Often, when we are presented with a passive sentence with the agent deleted we do not know what the exact subject was in the underlying active sentence, as, for example, in the passive sentence

My camera was stolen.

The grammar can only reflect what we actually know, namely that the underlying subject noun phrase has the feature of an animate noun. Here is a derivation for the sentence is question:

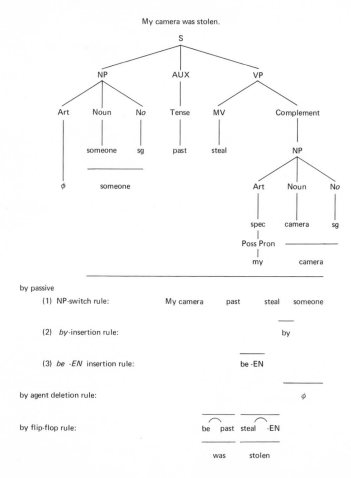

Exercise 15 / PASSIVE AND AGENT DELETION

Draw phrase structure trees and apply the necessary transformational rules to generate the following sentences:

1. He is respected by everybody.
2. The school was being evaluated by the board.
3. My day was ruined.
4. Jones must have been hit by the pitch.
5. The accident was reported.

Answers to Exercise 15 / PASSIVE AND AGENT DELETION

1. He is respected by everybody.

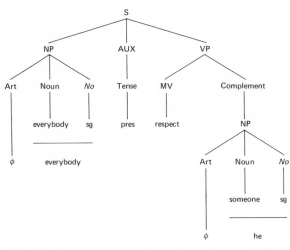

by passive

    (1) NP-switch rule: he pres   respect   everybody

    (2) *by*-insertion rule: by

    (3) *be -EN* insertion rule: be -EN

by flip-flop rule: be   pres respect -EN

                             is   respected

2. The school was being evaluated by the board.

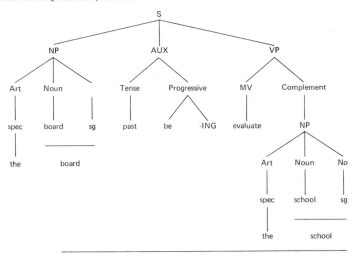

by passive
   (1) NP-switch rule: The school   past be-ING   evaluate   the board

   (2) *by*-insertion rule: by

   (3) *be -EN* insertion rule: be -EN

by flip-flop rule: be past be -ING   evaluate -EN

                             was   being   evaluated

3. My day was ruined.

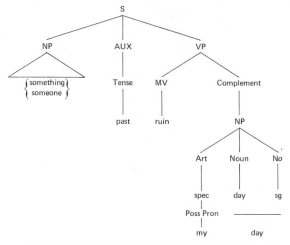

by passive
(1) NP-switch rule: my day past   ruin   { someone / something }

(2) *by*-insertion rule: by

(3) *be -EN* insertion rule: be   -EN

by agent deletion rule: φ

by flip-flop rule: be past   ruin -EN

                                 was   ruined

4. Jones must have been hit by the pitch.

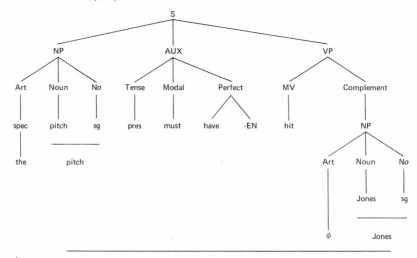

by passive

(1) NP-switch rule: Jones   pres   must   have -EN   hit the pitch

(2) *by*-insertion rule: by

(3) *be -EN* insertion rule: be -EN

by flip-flop rule: must⌒pres   be⌒-EN hit⌒-EN

                                      must   been   hit

5. The accident was reported.

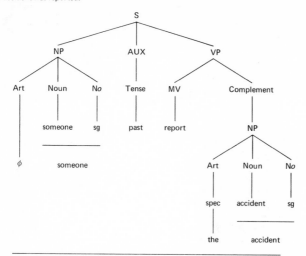

by passive

    (1) NP-switch rule: the accident past   report   someone

    (2) *by*-insertion rule: by

    (3) *be -EN* insertion rule: be -EN

by agent deletion rule: φ

by flip-flop rule: be   past report -EN

                       was   reported

CHAPTER 5

Questions

Overview

This chapter deals with two types of questions: (1) *yes-no* questions that expect a "yes" or "no" answer, for example, *Is it dinner time yet?* and (2) question-word questions that begin with a question word (*who, what, why,* and so on) and which ask for specific information, for example, *What is for dinner?*

The basic assumption of this chapter is that both types of questions are derived from underlying statements by transformational rules. It turns out that the rules which are necessary to convert underlying statements into questions are also quite closely connected with the rules that make underlying statements negative (Chapter 6) and give them special emphasis (Chapter 7).

There are two transformational rules necessary to convert underlying statements into *yes-no* questions. The first rule is called the "yes-no question switch rule." A switch rule changes the relative position of two or more elements in the underlying statement. This particular switch rule reverses the order of the subject noun phrase and some parts of the auxiliary. If the auxiliary contains any optional helping verb (recall that tense, the leftmost constituent of auxiliary, is obligatory), the tense plus the first helping verb move in front of the subject noun phrase. Thus we have the following statement-question pairs formed by the operation of the *yes-no* question switch rule:

Statement: John may come. (Modal)
Question: May John come?

Statement: John has gone.   (Perfect)
Question: Has John gone?
Statement: John is going.   (Progressive)
Question: Is John going?

This version of the *yes-no* question switch rule is also used in one other situation: when the main verb is *be:*

Statement: John is crazy.   (Main Verb *be*)
Question: Is John crazy?

However, when no optional element has been picked from the auxiliary, and the main verb is not *be*, we must use a slightly different version of the *yes-no* question switch rule. In this version, the only thing that is moved to the first position in the sentence is the tense, for example:

Statement: John stubbed his toe.
Question: *Past* John stub his toe?

We now need to invoke the second transformational rule: the "*do*-insertion rule." This is a very general rule that applies any time that the tense (either past or present) has been separated from a verb. *Do* is a verb substitute that unconnected tenses are attached to, but that has no particular meaning of its own. For this reason it is often called a "dummy" verb. Applying the *do*-insertion rule to the question above we produce a much more normal looking sentence:

Did John stub his toe?

As was mentioned above, these rules are necessary for other parts of the grammar as well. For instance, in the production of question-word questions we need only add one more rule to the two discussed above: the "question-word switch rule." A question-word question is derived from an underlying statement that has something missing. More accurately, it has an element with grammatical function but no lexical content. For instance, the question

Where is my toothbrush?

is presumed to be derived from an underlying statement

My toothbrush is SOMEWHERE.

The *SOMEWHERE* indicates that the statement contains an adverb of place as the complement. It also indicates that we cannot embody this particular adverb of place with words, because we do not know what the words are. In short, if we knew where the toothbrush was, we would not have to ask. The first step in the question-word switch rule is to replace the element that has grammatical function but no lexical content with the appropriate question word (*where* in the case of adverbs of place). The question-word switch rule then moves the question word to the first position in the sentence (after the prior operation of the *yes-no* question switch rule). For example, we would first apply the *yes-no* question switch rule to the underlying statement

My toothbrush is SOMEWHERE

producing

Is my toothbrush SOMEWHERE?

By the question-word switch rule the *SOMEWHERE* would be replaced by that appropriate question word and then moved to the first position in the sentence, producing

Where is my toothbrush?

QUESTIONS

The various ways that English changes a statement into a question by changing only the intonation will not be discussed here. Rather, we will concern ourselves with questions that are formed by some change in the grammar of the underlying sentence. The basic type of question in English is the *yes-no* question. As you might guess, a *yes-no* question is a question that anticipates "yes" or "no" as the answer, for example:

Is your name John?
Will he be able to go?
Have they been here before?
Is he living there now?
Can you come?

These *yes-no* questions are formed from the underlying statement by moving the first verb to the front position in the sentence. (In more technical language, it is moved in front of the subject noun phrase):

NP		NP
Your name is John	$\Longrightarrow$	*Is your name* John?
NP		NP
He will be able to go	$\Longrightarrow$	*Will he* be able to go?
NP		NP
They have been here before	$\Longrightarrow$	*Have they* been here before?
NP		NP
He is living there now	$\Longrightarrow$	*Is he* living there now?
NP		NP
You can come	$\Longrightarrow$	*Can you* come?

For earlier stages of the language this generalization would have been very powerful indeed. For example, here are some *yes-no* questions from Shakespeare's play *As You Like It:*

> Know you where you are?
> Called your worship?
> Looks he as freshly as he did?
> Change you color?
> Speak you so gently?
> Begin you to grow upon me?

In Modern English, these *yes-no* questions would be said this way:

> Do you know where you are?
> Did your worship call?
> Does he look as fresh as he did?
> Do you change color?
> Do you speak so gently?
> Do you begin to grow upon me?

For Shakespeare, the first verb in any sentence could be moved to the first position in order to transform the underlying statement into a *yes-no* question. Obviously, as the examples above show, the case is a little more complicated in Modern English.

To understand the Modern English way of transforming the underlying statement into a *yes-no* question, we must first look at the verb *following* tense (assuming that the flip-flop rule has *not* yet been applied). In gross terms, tense can be followed by one of two types of verbs: (1) a modal or helping verb from one of the optional elements in the auxiliary, or (2) if no verb from the auxiliary is used, the main verb. As our first approximation of the *yes-no* question rule, we may make this generalization: if the tense is followed by a verb generated from any of the optional elements of the auxiliary, *both the tense and the auxiliary verb move to the front part of the sentence as a unit.* For example, these underlying statements are transformed by the *yes-no* rule into questions (with the subsequent application of the flip-flop rule assumed):

> With modals
> John *past can* come $\implies$ *past can* John come?
>   could
> He *pres will* be ready soon $\implies$ *pres will* he be ready soon?
>   will
> I *past may* be surprised $\implies$ *past may* I be surprised?
>   might
> We *pres may* go $\implies$ *pres may* we go?
>   may

With the perfect

John *past⌢have* -EN come ⟹ *past⌢have* John *-EN⌢come?*
                                               <u>had</u>   <u>come</u>

He *pres⌢have* -EN be ready ⟹ *pres⌢have* he *-EN⌢be* ready?
                                         <u>has</u>   <u>been</u>

I *pres⌢have* -EN be surprised ⟹ *pres⌢have* I *-EN⌢be* surprised?
                                         <u>have</u>   <u>been</u>

We *pres⌢have* -EN go ⟹ *pres⌢have* we *-EN⌢go?*
                                  <u>have</u>   <u>gone</u>

With the progressive

John *past⌢be* -ING come ⟹ *past⌢be* John *-ING⌢come?*
                                  <u>was</u>   <u>coming</u>

He *pres⌢be* -ING be good about it ⟹ *pres⌢be* he *-ING⌢be* good about
it?   <u>is</u>   <u>being</u>

We *pres⌢be* -ING go ⟹ *pres⌢be* we *-ING⌢go?*
                              <u>are</u>   <u>going</u>

When the tense is followed by the main verb directly, the *yes-no* rule takes this form: *move just the tense by itself to the first position in the sentence.* The following sentences do not contain any optional verbs from the auxiliary, and consequently, the tense is next to the main verb in the underlying sentence:

John *past* come ⟹ *past* John come?
The phone *past* ring ⟹ *past* the phone ring?
The fish *pres* seem to be biting ⟹ *pres* the fish seem to be biting?
He *pres* have a headache ⟹ *pres* he have a headache?

As the sentences now stand, they are not only ungrammatical but unpronounceable. We now need to invoke a very powerful transformational rule: whenever tense (either present or past) is *not* followed immediately by a verb *for whatever reason,* put in a *do* directly after the tense. As you will see later on, this rule, which we will call the "*do*-insertion rule," is not confined just to the production of *yes-no* questions, but is used in many areas of the grammar. Applying the *do*-insertion rule (and then the flip-flop rule) to the above sentences, we produce the following grammatical (and pronounceable) questions:

    past John come? ⟹ *past⌢do* John come?
                               do⌢past
                                <u>did</u>

    past the phone ring? ⟹ *past⌢do* the phone ring?
                                        do⌢past
                                        <u>did</u>

pres the fish seem to be biting? $\Longrightarrow$ $\overset{\frown}{pres\ do}$ the fish seem to be biting?

$$\frac{\overset{\frown}{do\ pres}}{do}$$

pres he have a headache? $\Longrightarrow$ $\overset{\frown}{pres\ do}$ he have a headache?

$$\frac{\overset{\frown}{do\ pres}}{does}$$

If we were to apply the *yes-no* rule as it stands to sentences in which the main verb is *be,* the results would be ungrammatical, for example:

° Do you be hungry?
° Does John be a policeman?
° Do we be near a drugstore?
° Did he be angry?

In order to prevent this ungrammatical application of the *yes-no* rule, the *yes-no* rule needs to be modified to permit *be* to be moved with tense to the first position of the sentence no matter what *be's* grammatical function is. With this modification, the *yes-no* rule would apply this way to the example sentences above:

You *pres* be hungry $\Longrightarrow$ $\overset{\frown}{pres\ be}$ you hungry?

$$\underset{are}{}$$

John *pres* be a policeman $\Longrightarrow$ $\overset{\frown}{pres\ be}$ John a policeman?

$$\underset{is}{}$$

We *pres* be near a drugstore $\Longrightarrow$ $\overset{\frown}{pres\ be}$ we near a drugstore?

$$\underset{are}{}$$

He *past* be angry $\Longrightarrow$ $\overset{\frown}{past\ be}$ he angry?

$$\underset{was}{}$$

Let us attempt now to formalize the transformational rules that we have invoked for dealing with *yes-no* questions. These rules can be made very compact by requiring that the rules be applied in a definite relative order. The first rule we discussed converts the statement

Your name is John.

into the *yes-no* question

Is your name John?

This rule applies when the tense in the underlying statement is followed by any one of the following: a modal auxiliary, the helping verb *have,* the helping verb *be,* or if none of these optional elements have been selected, the main verb *be.* Let us call this rule the "*yes-no* question switch rule 1." We may write the rule this way:

Let V_{aux} = the first optional element in the auxiliary *or*, if no optional element has been selected, the main verb *be*

Yes-no question switch rule 1: $NP \frown Tense \frown V_{aux} \Longrightarrow Tense \frown V_{aux} \frown NP$

Here are some examples of this rule:

John *past* may come $\Longrightarrow$ *past* may John come?
           might

John *pres* have -EN go $\Longrightarrow$ *pres* have John -*EN* go?
         has   gone

John *pres* be -ING go $\Longrightarrow$ *pres* be John -*ING* go?
        is   going

John *pres* be crazy $\Longrightarrow$ *pres* be John crazy?
       is

What happens when rule 1 cannot apply? In other words, what happens when it is the case that no optional element has been selected from the auxiliary and the main verb is not *be*? In that case, the tense moves to the first position by itself. Let us call this rule the "*yes-no* question switch rule 2." We may write the rule this way:

Yes-no question switch rule 2: $NP \frown Tense \Longrightarrow Tense \frown NP$

Notice that if a sentence undergoes rule 1, the resulting transformed sentence cannot also undergo rule 2 because rule 1 has already moved the tense in front of the noun phrase. For the same reasons, if a sentence undergoes rule 2, it could not then undergo rule 1. These two rules are said to be "disjunctive." Disjunctive rules are rules that are mutually exclusive as far as their application to any one sentence is concerned. That is, we may apply either one or the other but not both. Furthermore, these rules are relatively ordered. That is, it makes a difference which order we apply them in. For example, if we applied rule 2 to this underlying statement

John *pres* be sick.

we would produce this ungrammatical *yes-no* question (assuming further the application of the *do*-insertion rule):

° Does John be sick?

Put another way, rule 2 is the general rule for making *yes-no* questions in English. Rule 1 deals with an important class of exceptions to rule 2. Rule 2 only becomes a valid generalization for all sentences if we first apply rule 1 to eliminate all the exceptions. This same pattern for rules is found throughout transformational grammars: first deal with the exceptions, then make the general rule.

Stated now in technical language, the *yes-no* question switch transformation is a pair of ordered disjunctive rules. In order to generate a *yes-no* question, we first see if we can apply rule 1 to the underlying statement. If we can, we must then skip rule 2 altogether. If we cannot apply rule 1, then we must apply rule 2. All *yes-no* questions, then, result from the application of either rule 1 or rule 2 (but never from the application of both).

The *do*-insertion rule is applied after the operation of the *yes-no* question switch rule and before the flip-flop rule. The *do*-insertion rule must be applied whenever the tense has been separated from a following verb. This separation may be brought about by a transformational rule which moves tense away from the verb (as the *yes-no* question switch rule 2 does), or by the placement of some element between the tense and its verb. The *do* is inserted into the sentence to "carry" the tense marker. Since it has no meaning of its own, *do* is sometimes called a "dummy" verb. Another way of looking at this rule is to consider that the flip-flop rule is obligatory for each occurrence of tense. In those cases where the flip-flop rule cannot apply because tense is not followed by a verb, then we must supply a *do* to make the flip-flop rule work. We may formalize the operation of the *do*-insertion rule this way:

Let X = any element *except* a verb

do-insertion rule: Tense $\frown$ X $\Longrightarrow$ Tense $\frown$ *do* $\frown$ X

We can now restate the *yes-no* rule in its final version for American English: If tense is followed by a modal, the helping verb *have*, or the verb *be* (either as a helping verb or as a main verb), tense and the following verb move *as a unit* to the first position in the sentence. On the other hand if the tense is followed by a main verb (except *be*), tense moves *by itself* to the first position in the sentence, and the *do* insertion rule must be applied.

For British English, the story is a little different. Compare the following sentences:

British: Have you been sick?
American: Have you been sick?
British: Have you the time?
American: Do you have the time?

British and American English treat the helping verb *have* the same way: it is moved to the first position of the question along with tense by the *yes-no* rule. However, British and American English differ in their treatment of *have* as a main verb. In American English *have* is just like any other main verb; when the *yes-no* rule is applied to sentences containing *have* as a main verb, tense is moved by itself to the first position in the sentence and then the *do*-insertion rule must be applied. In British English, *have* is like *be*: it moves to the first position with tense whether it is a helping verb or a main verb. Thus, in American English, in order to correctly use the *yes-no* rule, we must sharply distinguish between *have* used as a main verb and *have* used as a helping verb. This is a clear illustration of the importance of the underlying structure of a sentence in the proper application of the transformational rules. Here are some sample derivations of *yes-no* questions.

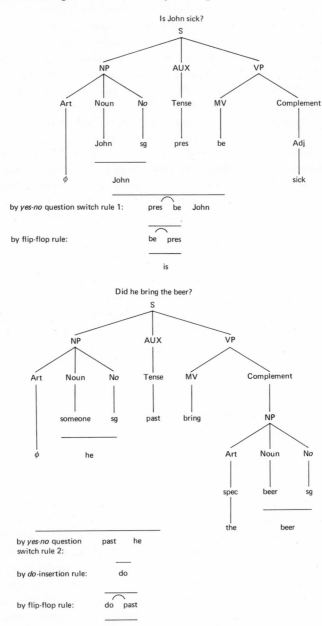

Exercise 16 / YES-NO QUESTIONS

Draw the phrase structure and apply the necessary transformational rules to produce the following sentences:

1. Can John come?
2. Do you know Mr. Smith?
3. Has something hurt him?
4. Does he have the answer?
5. Did John call you up?

QUESTION-WORD QUESTIONS

The second major type of question is called a "question-word question" because the question begins with a question word, for example: *who, whom, which, what, where, when, why, how often, how much, how many*. Question-word questions ask for specific pieces of information, not just agreement or disagreement. For example compare the following questions and answers:

Q. *What* is your major?   A. My major is *French.*
Q. *Who* are you?   A. I am *Mr. Phelps.*
Q. *Where* have you been?   A. I have been *out.*
Q. *When* can you come?   A. I can come *anytime you like.*
Q. *How much* money is missing?   A. *$50* is missing.
Q. *How often* will he call?   A. He will call *about once a day.*

The italicized word or phrase in the answer is the piece of information that the question was eliciting. It is perfectly grammatical to delete from the answer everything except the desired information, for example:

Q. *What* is your major?   A. *French.*
Q. *Who* are you?   A. *Mr. Phelps.*
Q. *Where* have you been?   A. *Out.*
Q. *When* can you come?   A. *Anytime you like.*
Q. *How much* money is missing?   A. *$50.*
Q. *How often* will he call?   A. *About once a day.*

How do we know that the appropriate answer to the first question is *French*, and not *Mr. Phelps* or *out?* Obviously the question words call forth certain kinds of answers. *What* has a co-occurrence relationship with nonanimate noun phrases, *who* with animate or human noun phrases, *where* with adverbs of place, *when* with adverbs of time, *why* with adverbs of reason, and so on.

Our basic assumption is that all questions are derived from corresponding underlying statements. What kind of statements underlie question-word questions? Let us take, for example, the question *Where have you been?* The minimal assumption about the underlying statement is that *you* is the subject noun phrase, *pres have -EN* is the auxiliary, and *be adverb of place* is the verb phrase.

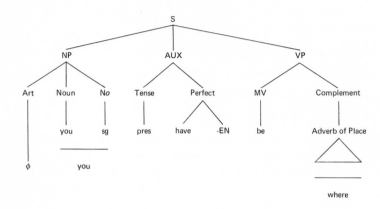

The underlying statement must contain one element that has grammatical function but no lexical content. Recall that the Greek letter delta Δ is used for this purpose. In the sentence above, this element is the complement. When this element is replaced by the appropriate question word (*where* in this case), the hearer or reader knows that the question is asking him to supply one specific piece of information: an adverb of place. In order for a question-word question to exist, it must contain one grammatical element that can be replaced by a question word. The first step in the generation of the surface form of the question, then, is to replace that element with the appropriate question word.

It would appear that the next step in the process of transforming the underlying statement into a question would be to move the question word to the first position in the sentence, that is, changing the underlying

you pres have -EN be *where*

into

where you pres have -EN be.

This solution creates a new problem since the *yes-no* rule would then move tense and the following helping verb to the first position in the sentence, producing

° *pres* have where you -*EN* be.
   have   been

We could correct the operation of the *yes-no* rule by setting up a condition; for example, that the tense goes to the first position in the sentence except when the first element in the underlying sentence is a question word. With a little tinkering, the *yes-no* rule could be made to produce the proper results.

However, if we reorder the two transformations so that the *yes-no* switch rule comes first, and then we move the question word to the first position, we can always get the proper results without having to complicate the *yes-no* rule with special conditions. For example, by the *yes-no* rule, the underlying statement

you *pres* have -EN where

is transformed into

pres have you -EN be where.

Next, by the rule that switches the question word to the first position in the sentence (let us call this the "question-word switch rule") the final form of the question is achieved:

pres have you -EN be where ⟹ where *pres* have you -E͡N be?
⎽⎽⎽⎽⎽⎽⎽⎽⎽⎽⎽⎽   ⎽⎽⎽⎽⎽⎽⎽⎽
have   been

The *yes-no* rule and the question-word switch rule show how the relative ordering of transformational rules can simplify the description of the generation of the surface form.

The interdependence of the *yes-no* and question-word switch rules is shown very clearly in the generation of these two questions *Who(m) did Bill see* and *Who saw Bill.*

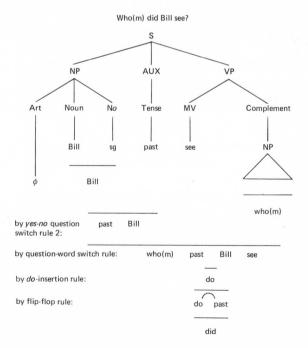

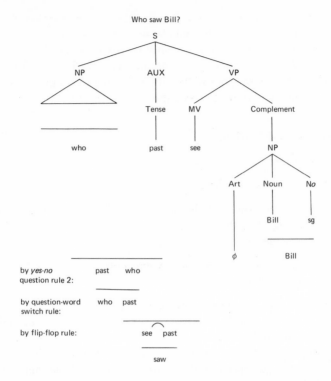

The question word in the first sentence comes from the underlying object while in the second sentence, it comes from the underlying subject. In the generation of the first question, *yes-no* question switch rule 2 separates the tense from the following main verb, so the *do*-insertion rule is required. However, in the generation of the second sentence, the question-word switch reverses the operation of question switch rule 2 and leaves tense right back where it started from, next to the main verb. Thus the *do*-insertion rule cannot be employed.

We have already seen that in earlier stages of the language, *yes-no* questions were made by moving the tense to the first position of the sentence along with whatever verb followed, even a main verb, so that the *do*-insertion rule was not necessary, for example:

Know you where you are?
Called your worship?

The same general pattern holds true for the formation of question-word questions. Here are some question-word questions from *As You Like It:*

How looked he?
What said he?

How like you this?
Where dwell you?
Where learned you that oath?

In Modern English, we would have to use *do:*

How did he look?
What did he say?
How do you like this?
Where do you dwell?
Where did you learn that oath?

As an exercise, the reader might work out the rules that govern the generation of question-word questions for Shakespeare.

Exercise 17 / QUESTION-WORD QUESTIONS

Draw the phrase structure and apply the necessary transformational rules to produce the following sentences:

1. Who knows the answers?
2. Where is a telephone?
3. What did you see?
4. When does the program start?
5. Who(m) did you want?
6. Why did he call you up?

Answers to Exercise 16 / YES-NO QUESTIONS

1. Can John come?

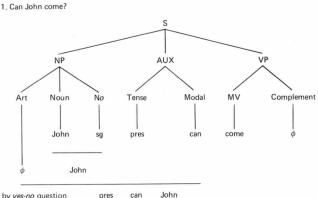

2. Do you know Mr. Smith?

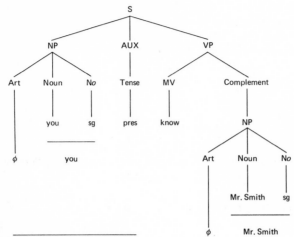

by *yes-no* question   pres   you
switch rule 2:
                          ——
by *do*-insertion rule: do

by flip-flop rule: do   pres

                               do

3. Has something hurt him?

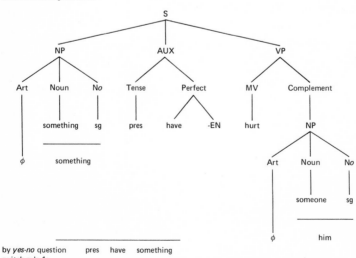

by *yes-no* question   pres   have   something
switch rule 1:

by flip-flop rule: have   pres   hurt   -EN

                              has   hurt

4. Does he have the answer?

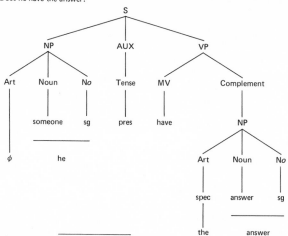

by *yes-no* question   pres   he
switch rule 2:

by *do*-insertion rule: do

by flip-flop rule: do   pres

                   does

5. Did John call you up?

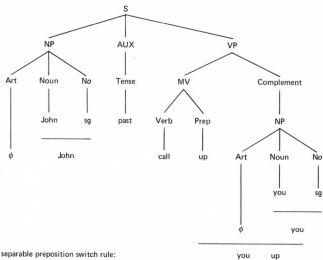

by separable preposition switch rule: you   up

by *yes-no* question   past   John
switch rule 2:

by *do*-insertion rule: do

by flip-flop rule: do   past

                 did

Answers to Exercise 17 / QUESTION-WORD QUESTIONS

1. Who knows the answers?

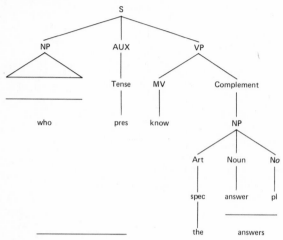

by *yes-no* question switch rule 2:		pres	who
by question-word switch rule:		who	pres
by flip-flop rule:		know ⌢ pres
			knows

2. Where is a telephone?

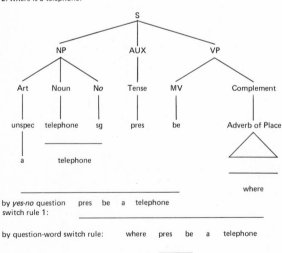

by *yes-no* question switch rule 1:   pres   be   a   telephone

by question-word switch rule: where   pres   be   a   telephone

by flip-flop rule: be ⌢ pres

is

3. What did you see?

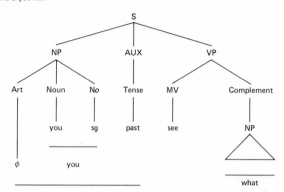

by *yes-no* question   past   you
switch rule 2:

by question-word   what   past   you   see
switch rule:

by *do*-insertion rule: do

by flip-flop rule: do   past

                                did

4. When does the program start?

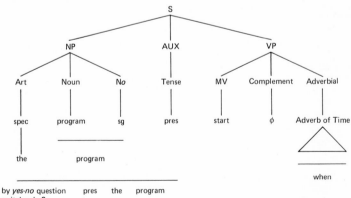

by *yes-no* question   pres   the   program
switch rule 2:

by question-word switch rule: when   pres   the   program   start

by *do*-insertion rule: do

by flip-flop rule: do   pres

                                does

5. Who(m) did you want?

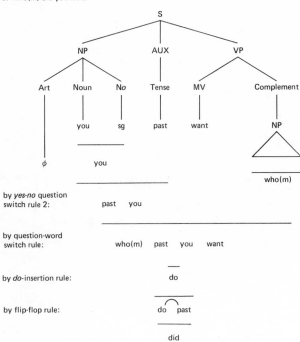

by *yes-no* question
switch rule 2:   past   you

by question-word
switch rule: who(m)   past   you   want

by *do*-insertion rule: do

by flip-flop rule: do   past

                                         did

6. Why did he call you up?

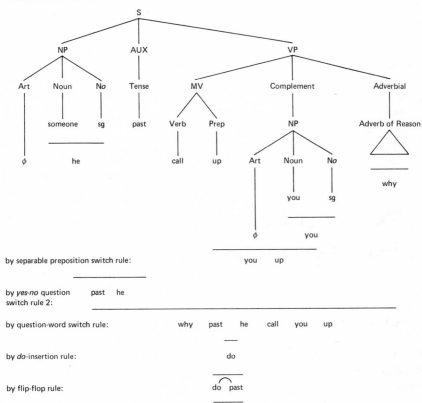

by separable preposition switch rule: you up

by *yes-no* question   past   he
switch rule 2:

by question-word switch rule: why   past   he   call   you   up

by *do*-insertion rule: do

by flip-flop rule: do past

                        did

CHAPTER 6

Negative Statements

Overview

This chapter deals with two separate but closely related areas of grammar: (1) sentences made negative by the use of *not*, and (2) the derivation of question tags. Question tags are tacked on to the end of statements in order to get a confirming response from the hearer. For example, the *isn't it* in the sentence *It is hot, isn't it?* is a question tag.

The placement of *not* is governed by the "*not*-insertion rule." When the underlying statement contains a helping verb or the main verb *be*, *not* is inserted directly after the first verb. For example:

I will *not* be able to come. (Modal)
He has *not* been feeling well. (Perfect)
John is *not* going. (Progressive)
He is *not* ready yet. (Main Verb *be*)

However, when there are no helping verbs and the main verb is not *be*, the *not* is inserted between tense and the main verb; tense is thus separated from a following verb, and the *do*-insertion rule must be used. For example, the negative of

He saw the steamroller.

is

He did not see the steamroller.

Notice that the placement of *not* is governed by the same conditions that govern the way in which questions are formed.

One of the most striking things about question tags is the negative-positive reversal. That is, if the main sentence is affirmative, the tag is negative; if the main sentence is negative, the tag is affirmative. For example,

Main Sentence	Tag
It is hot,	isn't it?
It isn't hot,	is it?
It rained,	didn't it?
It didn't rain	did it?

The form of the question tag is completely determined by the form of the main sentence. In other words, the tag consists of elements that are either copied from the main sentence (the tense and the subject noun phrase) or are determined by the nature of the main sentence (the positive-negative reversal). The last part of this chapter is devoted to a formalization of the *question tag rule*. The question tag rule operates under much the same conditions as the rules governing the production of questions and negative statements. In particular, if the tense in the main sentence is followed by a helping verb or *be* used as a main verb, both the tense and the verb following tense are copied in the question tag. However, if tense is followed directly by a main verb other than *be*, the tense alone is copied in the tag, thus requiring the use of the *do*-insertion rule (as in *It rained, didn't it?*).

NEGATIVE STATEMENTS

There are many ways of negating a statement. We will confine our attention to the use of *not*. It would seem a simple matter to insert *not* after the verb, for example:

I will *not* be able to come.
He has *not* been feeling well.
John is *not* going.
He is *not* ready yet.

As you can see, *not* is placed after the first helping verb or the main verb *be*. What happens, however, when there is no optional element from the auxiliary, that is, when tense is next to the main verb (other than *be*)? Here are some examples of sentences of this sort:

° You *pres* not know what I mean.
° He *past* not see the steamroller.

The sentences come out like an Indian talking in a grade-B movie. Obviously, in order to be grammatical these sentences must use the *do*-insertion rule:

You do not know what I mean.
He did not see the steamroller.

Notice that the conditions governing the placement of the *not* are identical to the conditions for the operation of the *yes-no* question switch rule: the auxiliary verbs and the main verb *be* work one way, and all main verbs (except *be*) work the other way. We can even use the same cover symbol V_{aux} to describe the first condition. If tense is followed by V_{aux}, then the *not* is placed directly after the V_{aux}; if tense is followed by a main verb other than *be*, the *not* is placed after tense and in front of the main verb. We may write this rule, which we will call the "*not*-insertion rule," in the following manner:

not-insertion rule:

(Let V_{aux} be defined as in the *yes-no* question switch rule)
1: Tense $\widehat{\ }$ V_{aux} $\Longrightarrow$ Tense $\widehat{\ }$ V_{aux} $\widehat{\ }$ *not*
2: Tense $\widehat{\ }$ Main Verb $\Longrightarrow$ Tense $\widehat{\ }$ *not* $\widehat{\ }$ Main Verb

1 and 2 are disjunctive and ordered. That is, we first try to apply 1. If the conditions for its application are met, we apply the rule and skip 2. If the conditions for its application are not met, then we must skip 1, apply 2.

As an automatic consequence of the application of *not*-insertion rule 2, the *do*-insertion rule must also be applied, since tense is not followed by a verb. Here are some sample derivations of sentences with *not* in them (the rule that contracts *not* to *n't* would be given in the phonological component, the set of rules that govern the pronunciation of the surface structure):

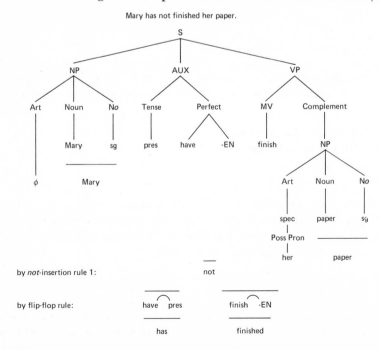

Mary has not finished her paper.

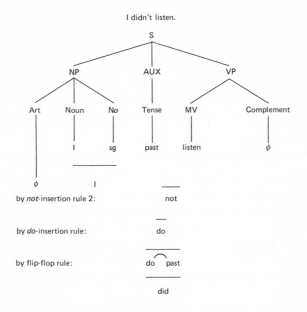

I didn't listen.

Exercise 18 / NEGATIVE SENTENCES

Draw the phrase structure and apply the necessary transformational rules to generate the following sentences:

1. We cannot win.
2. The class did not meet.
3. The plumbers are not coming.
4. The clock does not work.
5. I do not get it.

QUESTION TAGS

Question tags do not really turn statements into questions. Rather, they request the hearer to react to or confirm the speaker's statement. The italicized portions in the following sentences are question tags:

It is hot, *isn't it?*
It isn't hot, *is it?*
It rained, *didn't it?*
It didn't rain, *did it?*

Perhaps the most striking peculiarity of the question tag is the nega-tive-positive reversal between the tag and the main sentence: if the main sentence contains *not,* then the tag is affirmative; if the main sentence is affirmative, then the tag must contain *not.* The tag must also contain a verb in the same tense as the main sentence, and a noun phrase that is identical with the subject noun phrase of the main sentence. In short, given the main sentence we can always predict exactly what the tag will be.

The rules governing the question tag must copy parts of the main sentence onto the tag—clearly this is the case with the tense and the subject noun phrase. The copying of the verb that is connected to tense in the main sentence is more complicated. In the four question-tag sentences cited above, three of the four copy the verb along with the tense. Only the third sentence

It rained last night, didn't it?

does not copy the verb. Obviously in this case the tense is copied by itself, and consequently the tag must employ the *do*-insertion rule to carry the tense. We can account for the data with this generalization: if tense in the main sentence is followed by V_{aux} or *do* (from the operation of the *do*-insertion rule), then the V_{aux} and *do* are copied onto the tag along with tense. If the tense in the main sentence is followed by a main verb other than *be* (remember the *do* from the *do*-insertion rule is not a main verb), then the tense is copied by itself.

One of the interesting consequences of this generalization is that it must assume that the *do*-insertion rule has already applied to the main sentence before any of the rules for making the question tag are applied. That is, for the question tag to come out right, we must assume a fixed relative order of application of the different rules involved: first we apply all of the rules for the main sentence except the flip-flop rule, then we apply rules for copying the question tag. There are many similar instances of a relative ordering of independent transformational rules.

We may formalize the question tag rule in the following way:

(a) The main sentence contains *not:* (the square brackets [ ] mean the rule holds for either *do* or V_{aux})

$$\text{NP}^\frown \text{Tense}^\frown \begin{bmatrix} do \\ V_{aux} \end{bmatrix}^\frown not^\frown \text{X} \implies \text{NP}^\frown \text{Tense}^\frown \begin{bmatrix} do \\ V_{aux} \end{bmatrix}^\frown not^\frown \text{X} \underbrace{\text{Tense}^\frown \begin{bmatrix} do \\ V_{aux} \end{bmatrix}^\frown \text{NP}}_{\text{tag}}$$

(See Examples (a)$_1$ and (a)$_2$ below)

(b) The main sentence does not contain *not:*

1: $\text{NP}^\frown \text{Tense}^\frown V_{aux}^\frown \text{X} \implies \text{NP}^\frown \text{Tense}^\frown V_{aux}^\frown \text{X} \underbrace{\text{Tense}^\frown V_{aux}^\frown not^\frown \text{NP}}_{\text{tag}}$

(See Example (b)$_1$ below)

2: $\text{NP}^\frown \text{Tense}^\frown \text{X} \implies \text{NP}^\frown \text{Tense}^\frown \text{X} \underbrace{\text{Tense}^\frown not^\frown \text{NP}}_{\text{tag}}$

(See Example (b)$_2$ below)

The two rules in (b) are ordered and disjunctive. Here are some sample derivations employing these rules:

Example (a)₁:

It isn't hot, is it?

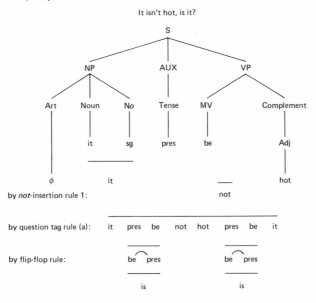

by *not*-insertion rule 1:

by question tag rule (a):

by flip-flop rule:

Example (a)₂:

It didn't rain, did it?

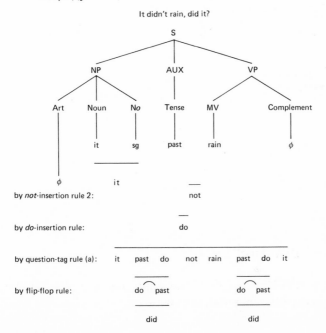

by *not*-insertion rule 2:

by *do*-insertion rule:

by question-tag rule (a):

by flip-flop rule:

Example (b)₁:

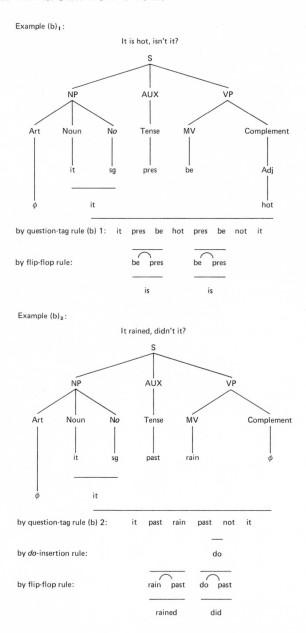

by question-tag rule (b) 1:   it   pres   be   hot   pres   be   not   it

by flip-flop rule: be pres   be pres

                                                  is   is

Example (b)₂:

It rained, didn't it?

by question-tag rule (b) 2:   it   past   rain   past   not   it

by do-insertion rule: do

by flip-flop rule: rain past   do past

                                              rained   did

Exercise 19 / QUESTION TAGS

Draw phrase structure trees and apply the necessary transformational rules to produce the following sentences:

1. John has answered the letter, hasn't he?
2. He won't fail, will he?
3. The ships didn't sink, did they?
4. I finished the story, didn't I?
5. The shower doesn't leak, does it?

Answers to Exercise 18 / NEGATIVE SENTENCES

1. We cannot win.

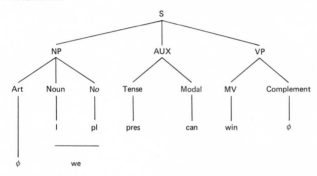

·by *not*-insertion rule 1:   not

by flip-flop rule: can   pres

                                                         can

2. The class did not meet.

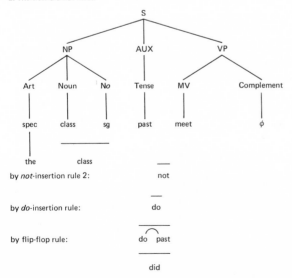

by *not*-insertion rule 2:   not

by *do*-insertion rule: do

by flip-flop rule: do   past

                                                   did

3. The plumbers are not coming.

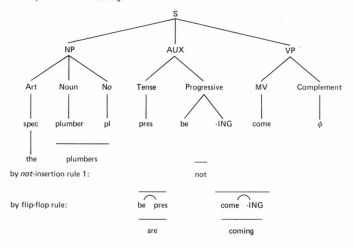

by *not*-insertion rule 1:

by flip-flop rule:

4. The clock does not work.

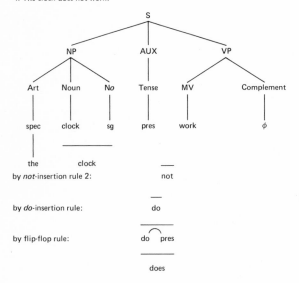

by *not*-insertion rule 2:

by *do*-insertion rule:

by flip-flop rule:

5. I do not get it.

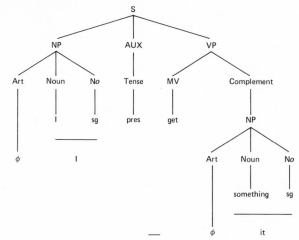

by *not*-insertion rule 2: not

by *do*-insertion rule: do

by flip-flop rule: do pres

do

Answers to Exercise 19 / QUESTION TAGS

1. John has answered the letter, hasn't he?

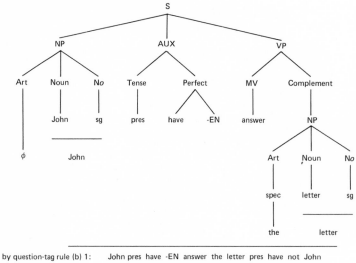

by question-tag rule (b) 1: John pres have -EN answer the letter pres have not John

he

by flip-flop rule: have pres answer -EN have pres

has answered has

[*Note* that the pronoun replacing *John* in the tag is in the subject form even though it is in an apparent object position in the surface sentence. Why?]

2. He won't fail, will he?

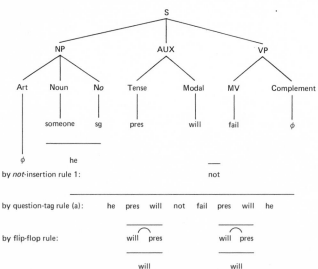

by *not*-insertion rule 1: not

by question-tag rule (a): he pres will not fail pres will he

by flip-flop rule: will pres will pres

will will

3. The ships didn't sink, did they?

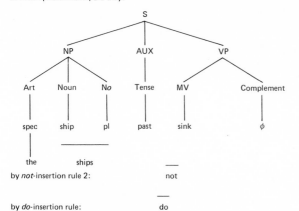

4. I finished the story, didn't I?

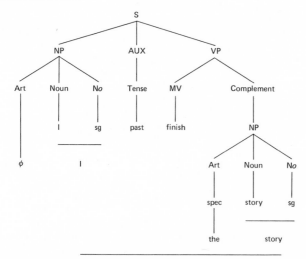

5. The shower doesn't leak, does it?

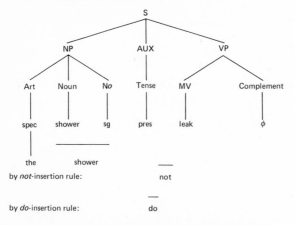

by *not*-insertion rule: not

by *do*-insertion rule: do

by question-   the shower pres do not leak pres do the shower
tag rule (a):   _____

                                                                                            it

by flip-flop rule: do pres   do pres

                            does   does

CHAPTER 7

Emphasis and Commands

Overview

In this chapter we deal with two different kinds of emphases: (1) whole sentence emphasis, in which the truth value of the whole sentence is asserted, and (2) element emphasis, in which a word or grammatical element is singled out for special attention. The chapter closes with a brief discussion of sentences that give commands.

The rules governing whole sentence emphasis are closely related to the rules governing questions and negative statements. When the underlying statement contains a helping verb or the main verb *be*, whole sentence emphasis is marked by extra heavy stress on the first verb following tense, for example:

He *coúld* win, after all! (Modal)
I *háve* seen a lawyer! (Perfect)
She *ís* telling the truth! (Progressive)
John *wás* sick after all! (Main Verb *be*)

However, when tense is followed directly by a main verb other than *be*, we must apply the *do*-insertion rule. For example, the emphatic version of

I saw a lawyer.

is

I *díd* see a lawyer!

We can account for this use of *do* by imagining that there is an abstract element called "EMP" (for emphasis) that represents the presence of extra heavy stress. EMP is inserted into the sentence by a rule exactly parallel to the *not*-insertion rule. If tense is followed by a helping verb or by the main verb *be*, EMP is inserted after the verb following tense; however, if tense is followed directly by a main verb other than *be*, EMP is inserted between tense and the main verb, thus requiring the use of the *do*-insertion rule.

There is a second kind of emphasis that stresses individual words or grammatical elements. Individual word emphasis is achieved by placing extra heavy stress on the word or element we wish to emphasize. This is called "contrastive stress" because it contrasts two words of the same type. For example, if we place contrastive stress on the word *small*, we are placing special emphasis on the contrast of *small* versus *big*, as, for example, in the following sentence:

John saw a *small* dog.

The contrastive stress singles out the dog's size as being of special importance.

In addition to giving special emphasis to individual words by means of contrastive stress, English also can place special emphasis on entire grammatical elements (which may consist of one or more words). In this chapter we deal informally with two families of transformational rules that do this: (1) the "cleft" family, and (2) the "predicate" family. Taking the sentence

The plane circled the field.

as our starting point, here are some of the ways that we can place special emphasis on certain grammatical elements by means of the two families of rules:

Cleft:
    Subject Noun Phrase: What circled the field was *the plane.*
    Object Noun Phrase: What the plane circled was *the field.*
    Verb Phrase: What the plane did was to *circle the field.*
Predicate:
    Subject Noun Phrase: It was *the plane* that circled the field.
    Object Noun Phrase: It was *the field* that the plane circled.

The final part of the chapter deals with commands. The unequivocal form of command in English is the imperative sentence, a sentence with no overt subject noun phrase, for example,

Go away.
Stop that.
Bring me the file on Smith.

Traditional grammar assumed that there was an "understood" *you* subject in imperative sentences. The chapter concludes with a discussion of this claim and produces evidence from the form of tag questions to support the traditional analysis.

THE EMPHATIC SENTENCE

We will include under this heading both sentences that have some special emphasis and sentences that have been transformed from statements into commands. In English, there seem to be two basically different kinds of emphasis. One kind of emphasis asserts the truth value of the whole sentence, while a second kind of emphasis singles out one particular element within the sentence for special emphasis. For the sake of convenience, let us call the first type of emphasis "whole sentence emphasis," and the second type "element emphasis."

Whole Sentence Emphasis

Whole sentence emphasis is achieved by placing extra heavy stress on the pronunciation on the first optional element from the auxiliary that follows tense, or on the main verb *be*, for example:

With a modal auxiliary:
He *coúld* win, after all!
You *múst* be quiet!

With the perfect:
So he *hád* been lying!
I *háve* seen a lawyer!

With the progressive:
She *ís* telling the truth!
They *wére* hiding there!

With *be* used as a main verb:
But he *ís* a Korean!
John *wás* sick after all!

However, as you might guess, when tense is followed directly by a main verb other than *be*, the *do*-insertion rule is applied, for example:

He *díd* win, after all!
I *díd* see a lawyer!
She *dóes* know the answer!
We *dó* have a new telephone!

If we imagine the presence of emphatic stress as being indicated in the grammar as an element, say, by the symbol EMP, we can then account for the placement of the stress and the use of the *do*-insertion rule in exactly the same way as we did with *not*. If tense is followed by a helping verb or *be* as a main verb, *EMP* is placed *after* the first helping verb or *be*, for example:

He *past* can EMP win, after all.
      could

I *pres* have EMP *-EN* see a lawyer.
   have   seen

She *pres* be EMP *-ING* tell the truth.
    is   telling

John *past* be EMP sick after all.
      was

If tense is directly followed by a main verb other than *be*, EMP is placed directly after tense (and before the main verb), for example:

He *past* EMP win, after all.
I *past* EMP see a lawyer.
She *pres* EMP know the answer.
We *pres* EMP have a new telephone.

Since tense is not now followed directly by a verb, the *do*-insertion rule automatically applies:

He *past do* EMP win, after all.
     did

I *past do* EMP see a lawyer.
  did

She *pres do* EMP know the answer.
    does

We *pres do* EMP have a new telephone.
    do

In the phonological part of the grammar, EMP will be realized as extra heavy stress on the preceding verb.

    We may formalize the "EMP insertion rule" as follows: (let V_{aux} be defined as in the *yes-no* question switch rule)

   1. Tense $\frown$ V_{aux} $\Longrightarrow$ Tense $\frown$ V_{aux} $\frown$ EMP
   2. Tense $\frown$ Main Verb $\Longrightarrow$ Tense $\frown$ EMP $\frown$ Main Verb

Rules 1 and 2 are disjunctive and ordered. If the conditions for rule 1 are not met, then rule 2 will automatically apply. Since 2 separates tense from a following verb by inserting EMP, the *do*-insertion rule must also be applied. Here are several derivations of emphatic sentences:

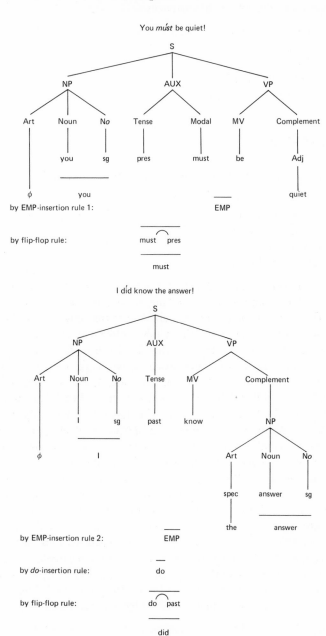

Exercise 20 / SENTENCE EMPHASIS

Draw the phrase structure trees and apply the necessary transformational rules to generate the following sentences:

1. She *míght* be telling the truth!
2. I *ám* coming!
3. He *díd* have a car!
4. He *hád* stolen a car!
5. The package *díd* turn up!

Element Emphasis

Any word in a sentence can be given contrastive stress, for example:

Jóhn saw a small dog.
John *sáw* a small dog.
John saw *á* small dog.
John saw a *smáll* dog.
John saw a small *dóg*.

This kind of element emphasis is called "contrastive stress" because it contrasts two words of the same type. By giving contrastive stress to *John* we are asserting that it was *John* and not somebody else that saw a small dog. When we stress *saw*, we are not giving the whole sentence an emphasis (or else we would use *do*), but we are stressing that John did in fact *see*, not *hear* or *imagine*, the dog. By stressing the article *a*, we emphasize that it was just one dog, not several, and that the dog was not otherwise specified (or else we would have used *the*). Likewise, *small* is contrasted with *big* and *dog* with *cat* or whatever else John could conceivably have seen. From the standpoint of grammar, contrastive stress would be indicated by placing the extra heavy stress marker EMP after the word to be given contrastive stress. The phonological rules would govern its actual realization into sound.

English, like most other languages, has ways of giving special emphasis, not just to single words but to entire grammatical units. This emphasis is accomplished by a diverse group of transformational rules that invert the normal sentence order to give prominence to certain elements.

There are at least two different families of transformations that invert the underlying sentence in order to give emphasis to a particular grammatical element. One of these families of transformations is called the "cleft." For example, let us take this underlying sentence: *The plane circled the field.* The cleft transformation that emphasizes the subject noun phrase is

What circled the field was *the plane.*

The cleft that emphasizes the object noun phrase is

What the plane circled was *the field*.

The cleft that emphasizes the entire verb phrase is

What the plane did was (*to*) *circle the field*.

Here is another underlying sentence: *John saw Mary at the park yesterday*. The cleft that emphasizes the subject noun phrase is

Who saw Mary at the park yesterday was *John*.

The cleft that emphasizes the object noun phrase is

Whom John saw at the park yesterday was *Mary*.

The cleft that emphasizes the adverb of place is

Where John saw Mary yesterday was *at the park*.

The cleft that emphasizes the adverb of time is

When John saw Mary at the park was *yesterday*.

The cleft can also emphasize predicate adjectives, for example from the underlying sentence *John is hungry* we can generate the cleft.

What John is is *hungry*.

The mechanism of the cleft transformation is quite complex. The grammatical element being emphasized is moved to the end of the sentence, the verb *be* is then put between the end of the original sentence and the element being emphasized. A relative pronoun appropriate to the element being emphasized is placed at the beginning of the sentence. If the element being emphasized is the verb phrase, then *do* must be inserted after the original subject noun phrase.

The second family of inversion transformations is less complex to describe because it employs a version of the question-word switch. For the sake of a label, we will call it the "predicate" family of transformational rules. Let us take as a sample underlying sentence *John saw Mary at the park yesterday*. If we choose to emphasize the subject noun phrase we get

It was *John* who saw Mary at the park yesterday.

If we emphasize the object noun phrase we get

It was *Mary* whom John saw at the park yesterday.

If we emphasize the adverb of place we get

It was *at the park* that John saw Mary yesterday.

If we emphasize the adverb of time we get

It was *yesterday* when John saw Mary at the park.

This type of inversion transformation moves the element being emphasized to the first position of the sentence, follows that element by the appropriate relative pronoun, and then places *It tense be* in front of the emphasized element, with the tense taken from the tense of the underlying sentence.

Commands

There are many ways of telling people to do things. For example, commands are often presented as questions:

Will you close the door?
Do you mind stopping that?

If the context is clear enough, even a statement can serve as a command. For instance if a person in a room looks pointedly at another person near the door and says, "It sure is cold in here," the person near the door would have to be thickheaded not to realize that he has been asked to close the door.

However, the unequivocal form of a command in English is the imperative sentence:

Go away.
Stop that.
Bring me the file on Smith.

The obvious characteristic of the imperative sentence is that there is no overt subject. In traditional grammar, it was said that the subject of an imperative sentence was an understood *you.* Structural linguists tended to reject the "understood" subject on philosophical grounds. They did not approve of invoking imaginary elements to explain tangible data.

In this case, the transformational linguists side with the traditional grammarians. The chief piece of evidence that there is a *you* as the subject of the statement underlying the command is when we add a question tag to the commands:

Go away, *will you?* or *won't you?*
Stop that, *will you?* or *won't you?*
Bring me the file on Smith, *will you?* or *won't you?*

Since the form question tag is completely dependent upon the grammar of the underlying sentence, the underlying sentence must contain *you* as the subject noun phrase.

Answers to Exercise 20 / SENTENCE EMPHASIS

1. She *míght* be telling the truth!

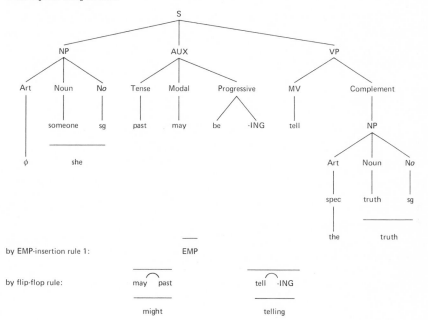

by EMP-insertion rule 1:

by flip-flop rule:

2. I *ám* coming!

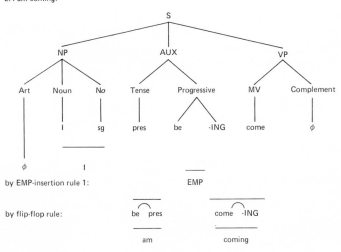

3. He *díd* have a car!

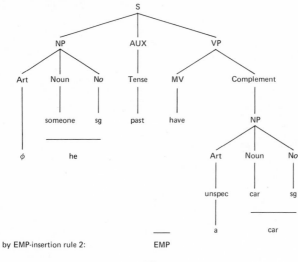

by EMP-insertion rule 2:   EMP

by *do*-insertion rule: do

by flip-flop rule: do͡ past

          did

4. He *hád* stolen a car!

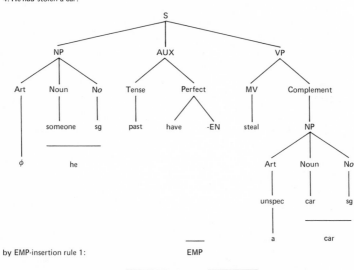

by EMP-insertion rule 1:   EMP

by flip-flop rule: have͡ past   steal͡ -EN

          had   stolen

5. The package *díd* turn up!

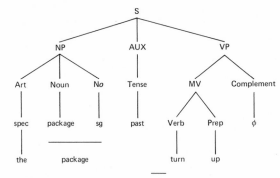

by EMP-insertion rule 2:   EMP

by *do*-insertion rule: do

by flip-flop rule: do   past

                                            did

part
three

SENTENCES
COMBINED BY
EMBEDDING RULES

Overview

The sentences we have dealt with up to now have been of a simplistic nature quite unlike the complex sentences that we encounter in real life. This is not a defect of the grammar. One of the basic tenets of transformational grammar is that complex sentences are made up of bundles of elementary simple sentences produced by the phrase structure rules. It may be useful for you to think of the phrase structure rules as producing the basic cells that more complex structures are composed of. The sentence combining rules govern the ways in which the simple sentences can be combined to produce new complex sentences.

There are two different types of sentence combining rules, embedding rules and joining rules. The difference between the two types of combining rules is in the relationship of the two underlying sentences that are combined. If the two underlying sentences retain a separate and equal identity even after they have been combined to produce a more complex new sentence, then the new combination is governed by the joining rules. However, if there is a clear distinction between a "main" sentence and a "subordinate" sentence, the combination is governed by embedding rules. In the terminology adopted here, we will refer to the "subordinate" sentence as being *embedded* in the "main" sentence.

In Part Three, we will deal with four types of embedding: sentences embedded in the verb phrase (Chapter 8), two ways of embedding sentences in the noun phrase (noun modification in Chapter 9; nominalization in Chapter 10), and sentences embedded in subordinating adverbs (Chapter 11).

CHAPTER 8

Sentences Embedded in the Verb Phrase Complement

Overview

In Chapter 3 we discussed various types of verb phrase complements. A complement, you recall, is the obligatory element that follows the main verb. The complements presented here all contain an embedded sentence. There are various restraints on what kinds of sentences are allowable as verb phrase complements. We will deal with three main sentence types: (1) noun clause sentences, (2) question-word sentences, and (3) tenseless sentences.

A noun clause sentence is an independent sentence which always may be preceded by *that*, for example:

I know (*that*) *we will win.*

When complements of this type contain the main verb *be*, the embedded sentence can be reduced to an infinitive phrase by replacing the tense with *to* by what is called the "infinitive phrase rule." For example, we can transform

I recognized *he was the house detective.*

into

I recognized *him to be the house detective.*

The question-word sentence is a closely related construction. Many of the main verbs that will take a noun clause sentence complement will also take a question-word sentence complement. In the case of the question-word sentence complement, the embedded sentence must have one of its grammatical elements replaced by an appropriate question word (for example, *who,* *what, where*), which is moved to the first position in the embedded sentence by the question-word switch rule. For example, the sentence

I know where John is.

is derived from an underlying sentence that contains *John is SOMEWHERE* as the complement. The SOMEWHERE is replaced by the appropriate question word, *where* in this case, and moved to the first position of its sentence.

The tenseless sentence complement must appear on the surface as either an infinitive or participial phrase, that is, with the tense of the embedded sentence replaced by either *to* or *-ing.* The main verb *begin,* for example, will accept both kinds of phrases:

Infinitive phrase: I began *to eat a peach.*
Participial phrase: I began *eating a peach.*

In this grammar the tenseless sentence complements are subclassified into three mutually exclusive types according to the relation of the subject noun phrase of the embedded sentence to the subject noun phrase of the main sentence.

Type 1: The subject noun phrase of the underlying embedded sentence *must* be identical with the subject noun phrase of the main sentence. Furthermore, the subject noun phrase of the embedded sentence always must be deleted from the surface. The examples of infinitive and participial phrase complements given above are type 1 complements. Notice that it is ungrammatical for the subject noun phrase of the embedded sentence to be different from the subject noun phrase of the main sentence:

° I began John to eat the peach.
° I began John eating the peach.

Likewise, it is ungrammatical to retain the subject noun phrase of the embedded sentence:

° I began I to eat the peach.
° I began I eating the peach.

Type 2: With tenseless sentence complements of this type it is possible for the subject noun phrase of the embedded sentence to be different from the subject noun phrase of the main sentence, for example:

I wanted John to see the humor in the situation.

However, like type 1 complements, if the subject noun phrase of the embedded sentence is the same as the subject noun phrase of the main sentence, the subject noun phrase of the embedded sentence must be deleted, for example, the surface sentence

I wanted to see the humor in the situation.

is derived from an underlying sentence

° I wanted I see the humor in the situation.

Type 3: Sentences of this complement type permit the subject noun phrase of the embedded sentence to be different from the subject noun phrase of the main sentence (like type 2). However, if the subject noun phrase of the embedded sentence is the same as the subject noun phrase of the main sentence, the subject noun phrase of the embedded sentence must be converted into the appropriate reflexive pronoun (unlike type 2). For example, we must change

° Alice told Alice to stop crying.

into

Alice told herself to stop crying.

SENTENCES EMBEDDED IN THE VERB PHRASE COMPLEMENT

A verb phrase complement is the obligatory element that follows the main verb. In the earlier discussion of the verb phrase, all the complements were what we might call "simple," that is, they did not contain any embedded sentences. To the list of structures that make up the verb phrase complement, we must now add these three "complex" complements that contain an embedded sentence:

> Noun Clause Sentence
> Question-Word Sentence
> Tenseless Sentence

NOUN CLAUSE SENTENCE

A noun clause sentence is an independent sentence, preceded by an optional *that*. Here are some sample sentences containing noun clause sentence complements:

I know (*that*) *we will win.*
We found out (*that*) *he was lying.*

He said *(that) he would be a little late.*
The lady realized *(that) she had the wrong party.*
I think *(that) you are mistaken.*

The noun clause sentence complement will be developed according to the following phrase structure rule: Noun Clause Sentence ⟶ (that) S. For example, here is a sample derivation of a sentence containing a noun clause sentence complement:

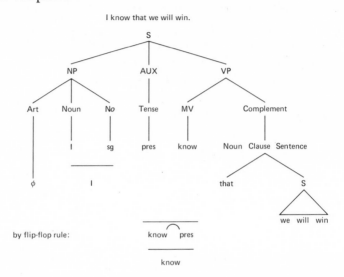

Notice that the embedded sentence *we will win* has not been derived in any detail. For the sake of simplicity, we will not as a general rule indicate the internal structure of embedded sentences except where we need to apply some rule to it.

When an embedded sentence (without the preceding *that*) contains the main verb *be,* many of the noun clause sentence complements can be reduced to an infinitive phrase by replacing the tense with *to:*

I recognized *he was the house detective* ⟹ I recognized *him to be the house detective.*
He demonstrated *the theory was incorrect* ⟹ He demonstrated *the theory to be incorrect.*
The patient found *his cough was much better* ⟹ The patient found *his cough to be much better.*
I understood *he was a doctor* ⟹ I understood *him to be a doctor.*
He knew *the answer was correct* ⟹ He knew *the answer to be correct.*

This rule, typical of the many transformational rules that convert clauses to phrases, is optional and does not appear to change the meaning of the sentence. A few verbs, however, that take a noun clause sentence complement do not permit the operation of this rule, for example:

I learned *he was the house detective* ⟹ ° I learned *him to be the house detective.*

He recalled *the theory was incorrect* ⟹ ° He recalled *the theory to be incorrect.*

The patient forgot *his cough was much better* ⟹ ° The patient forgot *his cough to be much better.*

I found out *he was a doctor* ⟹ ° I found out *him to be a doctor.*

He heard *the answer was correct* ⟹ ° He heard *the answer to be correct.*

The rule that converts a sentence into an infinitive phrase is a combination of two elementary rules: tense is deleted, and *to* inserted into the sentence. We will combine these under one roof and call it the "infinitive phrase rule." We may write this rule in the following form:

$$\text{NP}\frown \text{Tense}\frown \text{X} \implies \text{NP}\frown to\frown \text{X}$$

Here is a sample derivation of a sentence employing this rule:

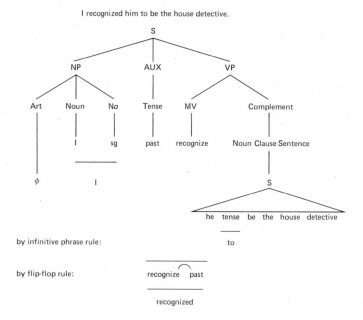

I recognized him to be the house detective.

The grammar would also have to specify those main verbs that will permit the noun clause sentence complement to undergo the infinitive phrase rule. Notice that the pronoun in the subject noun phrase of the embedded sentence must be converted from the subject form to the object form. Once the embedded sentence is transformed into a phrase, the case of pronouns is dependent on their function in the main sentence, not the original embedded sentence.

Exercise 21 / NOUN CLAUSE SENTENCE COMPLEMENTS

Draw phrase structure trees and apply the necessary transformational rules to generate the following sentences:

1. John decided that he would go after all.
2. He found out that it had started to rain.
3. I think he has moved back to Chicago.
4. The reports showed John to be in error.
5. I found him to be very alert.

Two Survivals of the Subjunctive with Noun Clause Complements

In Old English, verbs had a special set of endings that were used for talking about things that were not true or things that might or might not happen in the future, about wishes, about things that the speaker wanted to happen, and in talking about what people said or thought (as opposed to statement of facts about what they actually did). This set of endings is called the "subjunctive." When a verb is used with a subjunctive ending, it is said to be in the subjunctive mood. Even in Old English the modal auxiliaries (*can, may, should, might,* and so on) were taking over the various functions of the subjunctive mood. In Modern English the historical subjunctive survives only in some isolated bits and pieces. The clearest survival is the subjunctive form *were,* for example:

I wish that I *were* you.

In all other persons and numbers (besides the first person singular) the subjunctive form is identical with the past tense form *were,* and consequently, not recognizable as a separate form of the verb.

A second use of the subjunctive that has survived with noun clause complements is making statements about things we want to happen. These statements become a kind of polite command. The subjunctive is recognized by the fact that the embedded sentences have no apparent tense, for example:

Mr. Chairman, I move that the meeting *be* adjourned.
The court orders that the bill *be* paid.
They demanded that John *apologize.*

QUESTION-WORD SENTENCE COMPLEMENTS

Many of the same verbs that take a noun clause sentence complement also take a question-word sentence complement. In this case, the embedded sentence must have one of its elements replaced by an appropriate question word, for example, *who, what, which, where, why, when,* and *how often.* As in the development of question-word questions, the question word is moved to the first part of its sentence by the question-word switch rule. For example:

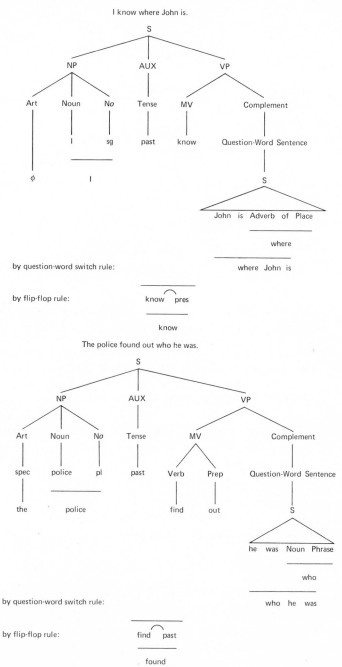

I know where John is.

by question-word switch rule:

by flip-flop rule:

know

The police found out who he was.

by question-word switch rule:

by flip-flop rule:

found

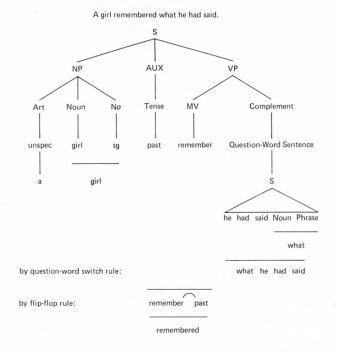

A girl remembered what he had said.

There are a few verbs that take the question-word sentence complement that do not also take the noun phrase sentence complement, for example, *wonder.*

I wondered when he might call.   (Question-Word Sentence Complement)
° I wondered that he might call.   (Noun Phrase Sentence Complement)

Exercise 22 / QUESTION-WORD SENTENCE COMPLEMENTS

Draw the phrase structure and apply the necessary transformational rules to generate the following sentences:

1. John realized where he was.
2. I know why he called.
3. The waitress remembered who ordered the iced tea.
4. The chairman couldn't recall who had been nominated.
5. We wondered how often we would have to go.

THE TENSELESS SENTENCE COMPLEMENT

Embedded sentences that belong to this complement type come to the surface in a bewildering variety of ways. However, all tenseless sentence complements share one important feature: the tense of the embedded sentence cannot come to the surface. The embedded sentence must come to the surface as either an infinitive phrase or a participial phrase. In this grammar we will attempt to group the embedded sentences into three distinct families or classes according to the relation of the subject noun phrase of the embedded sentence to the subject noun phrase of the main sentence.

Type 1: The subject noun phrase of the embedded sentence *must* be identical with the subject noun phrase of the main sentence. For example, the sentence

I failed to see the humor in the situation.

is derived from the underlying sentences

I *past* fail I *tense* see the humor in the situation.

If we change the subject of the embedded sentence to *John,* we generate an ungrammatical surface sentence:

° I failed John to see the humor in the situation.

Type 2: The subject noun phrase of the embedded sentence may be different from the subject noun phrase of the main sentence, for example:

I wanted John to see the humor in the situation.

However, if the subject noun phrase of the embedded sentence is the same as the subject noun phrase of the main sentence, it is deleted (as it is in type 1). For example,

I wanted to see the humor in the situation.

is derived from the underlying sentences

I *past* want I *tense* see the humor in the situation.

Type 3: The subject noun phrase of the embedded sentence may be different from the subject noun phrase of the main sentence (as in type 2). For example:

Alice told Humpty-Dumpty to stop crying.

However, the difference between type 3 and type 2 appears when the subject noun phrases of the embedded and main sentences are the same:

Alice told herself to stop crying.

In type 3, the subject noun phrase of the embedded sentence must be converted to the appropriate reflexive pronoun when it is the same as the subject noun phrase of the main sentence. If the embedded subject noun phrase were deleted from the surface as in type 2, the result would be ungrammatical:

° Alice told to stop crying.

Let us now consider each of the three types of complements in some detail.

Type 1

Complements of this type must always contain an underlying subject noun phrase identical to the subject noun phrase of the main sentence. The embedded sentence is turned into a surface phrase by deleting the subject noun phrase and replacing the tense with either *to* or *-ing*. If the tense is replaced by *to*, the phrase is called an "infinitive phrase." If the tense is replaced by *-ing* the phrase is called a "participial phrase." For example from the underlying sentence

I *tense* eat a peach.

we may generate either an infinitive phrase

to eat a peach

or a participial phrase

-*ING* eat a peach
   eating

This ability to convert tense to either *to* or *-ing* is apparently a peculiarity of type 1 complements. The other two types seem to allow only *to*. The participial phrase rule is obviously quite similar to the infinitive phrase rule. Both rules are really combinations of two elementary rules: a rule that deletes tense, and a rule that inserts the *to* or *-ing* in the same position that tense occupied. We may formalize the participial phrase rule in this manner:

$$\text{NP}\frown\text{Tense}\frown\text{X} \implies \text{NP}\frown\text{-ING}\frown\text{X}$$

The rule that deletes the subject noun phrase of the embedded sentence is even simpler. We may write this rule so that it will apply either before or after the rules that change tense to *-ing* or *to*. Since all embedded sentences of the tenseless sentence complement type must undergo either the infinitive phrase or the participial phrase rules, it seems natural to think of these rules applying first, though it should be stressed that this is a matter of convenience, not necessity. Let us call the rule that deletes the subject noun phrase of the embedded sentence the "subject NP deletion rule" and formalize it in this way:

$$\text{Main Verb}\frown\text{NP}\frown \begin{bmatrix} to \\ \text{-ING} \end{bmatrix} \implies \textit{Main Verb}\frown \begin{bmatrix} to \\ \text{-ING} \end{bmatrix}$$

Here are some sample sentences of type 1, first with the infinitive phrase rule, and second with the participial phrase rule:

Infinitive phrase

> Elliot hoped to eat a peach.
> I failed to see the humor in the situation.
> He hesitated to give his name.
> John pretended to be hurt.
> John refused to be annoyed by the reporters.

Participial phrase

> Elliot admitted eating a peach.
> I denied seeing the humor in the situation.
> He postponed giving his name.
> John avoided being hurt.
> He kept being annoyed by the reporters.

On the whole there does not seem to be any obvious semantic difference between the main verbs that take an infinitive phrase and those that take a participial phrase. A number of main verbs can take both an infinitive phrase and a participial phrase without any noticeable shift in meaning. For example,

> She began to laugh.
> She began laughing.
> He continued to shine his shoes.
> He continued shining his shoes.

A totally unrelated but superficially similar construction is often confused with the infinitive phrase type of embedded sentence. For example, consider the following three sentences:

> He started changing the flat tire.
> He started to change the flat tire.
> He stopped to change the flat tire.

The third sentence has a completely different structure from the second sentence. The phrase *to change the flat tire* comes from an adverbial prepositional phrase of reason or purpose. The *to* that begins this type of phrase is really a shortening of *in order to*. Thus we may paraphrase the third sentence as

> He stopped in order to change the flat tire.

If we make the same substitution for the second sentence, it becomes ungrammatical in its intended meaning:

> ° He started in order to change the tire.

In spite of their superficial differences, the second sentence is really much more like the first sentence than it is like the third sentence.

Here are some sample derivations of sentences of type 1:

John refused to be annoyed by the reporters.

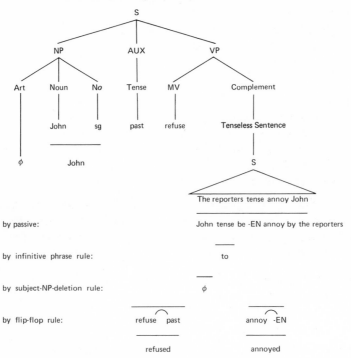

by passive: John tense be -EN annoy by the reporters

by infinitive phrase rule: to

by subject-NP-deletion rule: φ

by flip-flop rule: refuse past   annoy -EN

                          refused   annoyed

I enjoyed meeting your parents.

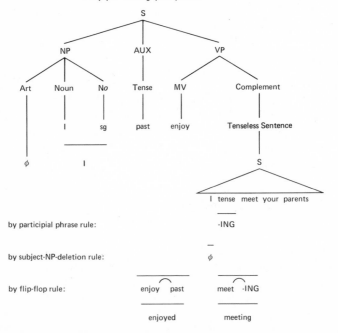

by participial phrase rule: -ING

by subject-NP-deletion rule: φ

by flip-flop rule: enjoy past   meet -ING

                          enjoyed   meeting

Exercise 23 / TYPE 1 COMPLEMENTS

Draw phrase structure trees and apply the necessary transformational rules to generate the following sentences:

1. He continued to receive threatening letters.
2. John hesitated to give his name.
3. I had finished reading the questions.
4. We started getting angry phone calls.
5. The firemen began to be bothered by the smoke.

Type 2 Complements

In complements of this type, the subject noun phrase of the embedded sentence may be different from the subject noun phrase of the main sentence. Here are several more examples of this type:

I wanted you to bring me the hammer.
He expected the baby to start crying at any minute.
We needed the experiment to be a success.
John played the long shot to win.

If the subject noun phrase of the embedded sentence is the same as the subject noun phrase of the main sentence, then the embedded subject noun phrase is deleted. For example,

I wanted to go home.
He expected to start crying at any minute.
We needed to be a success.
John played to win.

One of the characteristics of this complement type is that *for* may be inserted before the subject noun phrase of the embedded sentence if the subject noun phrase is not the same as the subject noun phrase of the main sentence. There appears to be considerable variation in the grammaticality of the resulting sentences. They are all grammatical for me, but I know that many speakers would reject some of them outright:

I wanted for you to bring me the hammer.
He expected for the baby to start crying at any minute.
We needed for the experiment to be a success.
John played for the long shot to win.

Here are some sample derivations of sentences of this complement type, first with the subject noun phrase of the embedded sentences different from the subject noun phrase of the main sentence, then with them the same:

I wanted you to bring me the hammer.

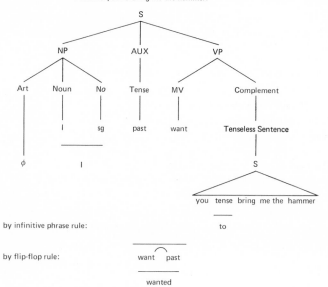

by infinitive phrase rule:

by flip-flop rule:

I wanted to go home.

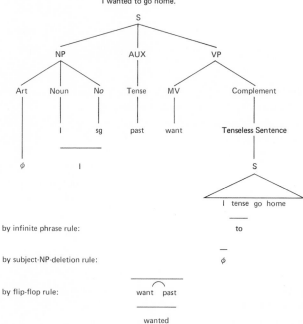

by infinite phrase rule:

by subject-NP-deletion rule:

by flip-flop rule:

A closely related construction employs an Adj͡ Tenseless Sentence Complement. Here are some examples where the subject noun phrase of the embedded sentence is the same as the subject noun phrase of the main sentence:

John was eager to please us.
The boy was happy to go.
The driver was reluctant to finish the race.
The workers were ready to begin.
I was glad to be of use to you.
Mary was ill-prepared to undertake the assignment.

When the subject noun phrase of the embedded sentence is not the same as the subject noun phrase of the main sentence, the *for* must be inserted before the embedded subject noun phrase:

John was eager for Bill to please us.
° John was eager Bill to please us.

The boy was happy for us to go.
° The boy was happy us to go.

The driver was reluctant for his assistant to finish the race.
° The driver was reluctant his assistant to finish the race.

The workers were ready for the signal to begin.
° The workers were ready the signal to begin.

I was glad for him to be of use to you.
° I was glad him to be of use to you.

Mary was ill-prepared for John to undertake the assignment.
° Mary was ill-prepared John to undertake the assignment.

Let us formalize the *for*-insertion rule. Assuming the rule to apply after the infinitive phrase rule, we may write it this way:

$$\text{Adj}\frown\text{NP}\frown to \implies \text{Adj}\frown for\frown\text{NP}\frown to$$

Notice that the rule is written in such a way that it cannot be used if the subject noun phrase deletion rule is used, that is, we cannot generate sentences of the form

° The boy was happy for to go.

Here are some sample derivations of Adj͡ Tenseless Sentence Complements, first with the subject of the embedded sentence different from the subject of the main sentence, then with them the same:

John was eager for Bill to please us.

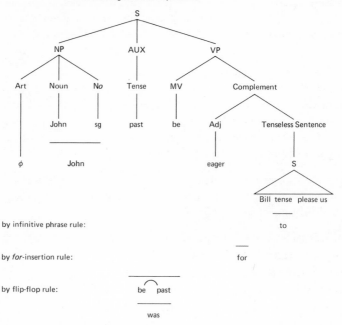

by infinitive phrase rule: to

by *for*-insertion rule: for

by flip-flop rule: be　past

                                                was

John was eager to please us.

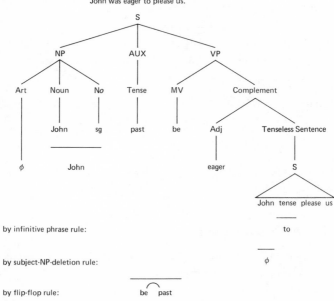

by infinitive phrase rule: to

by subject-NP-deletion rule: φ

by flip-flop rule: be　past

                                                was

Exercise 24 / TYPE 2 COMPLEMENTS

Draw phrase structure trees and apply the necessary transformational rules to produce the following sentences:

1. The girls wanted to become cheerleaders.
2. We were glad to see you do so well.
3. I expected you to be upset about it.
4. John was eager for Mary to take his place.
5. The boy was happy to be invited.

Type 3 Complements

Like type 2 complements, type 3 complements do not have the restriction that the subject noun phrase of the embedded sentence must be the same as the subject noun phrase of the main sentence. For example,

I persuaded John to go.
The coach advised him to quit.
The officer permitted the troops to return to the camp.
The lady told the little boy to stop making so much noise.
The company asked him to be examined by their doctor.

The difference between type 2 and type 3 complements appears when the subject noun phrase of the embedded sentence is the same as the subject noun phrase of the main sentence. When this happens, the subject noun phrase of the embedded sentence must be changed into a reflexive pronoun. For example:

I persuaded myself to quit.
The fat man allowed himself to take an extra dessert.
Alice told herself to stop crying.
They picked themselves to win.

If we apply the reflexive rule to sentences that take a type 2 complement, the result is ungrammatical:

° I wanted myself to go home.
° He expected himself to start crying at any minute.
° We needed ourselves to be a success.

Here are some sample derivations of type 3 complements, first with the subject noun phrase of the embedded sentence different from the subject noun phrase of the main sentence, then with them the same:

The coach persuaded him to quit.

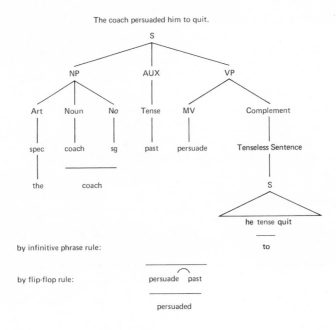

by infinitive phrase rule:

by flip-flop rule:

The coach persuaded himself to quit.

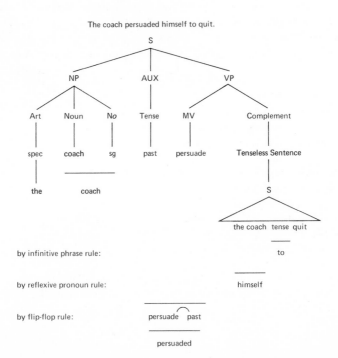

by infinitive phrase rule:

by reflexive pronoun rule:

by flip-flop rule:

For a limited number of verbs that take a type 3 complement, the embedded sentence can be reduced to a pair of noun phrases. For example,

We elected *Harry to be president of the club* ⟹
We elected Harry president of the club.
I chose *John to be the winner* ⟹ I chose John the winner.
They nominated *you to be the next chairman* ⟹
They nominated you the next chairman.
The president named *Mr. Quirk to be the vice-president* ⟹
The president named Mr. Quirk the vice-president.
We thought *John to be highly qualified* ⟹
We thought John highly qualified.

The optional deletion of the *to be* seems to have no effect on the meaning of the sentence. For many verbs that take a type 3 complement, the operation of this transformation produces an ungrammatical sentence in the intended meaning. For example,

The president asked Mr. Quirk to be the vice-president ⟹
° The president asked Mr. Quirk the vice president.
The president expected Mr. Quirk to be the vice-president ⟹
° The president expected Mr. Quirk the vice-president.

Let us formalize this rule as the "*to be*-deletion rule."

NP⌢ *to be*⌢ NP ⟹ NP⌢ NP

Here is a sample derivation of a sentence of this type:

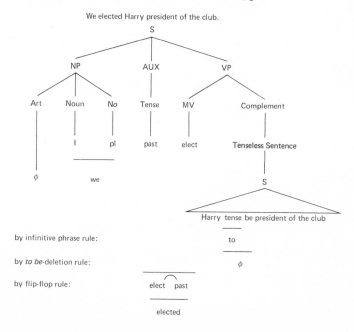

If the subject noun phrase of the embedded sentence is the same as the subject noun phrase of the main sentence, the embedded subject noun phrase must be changed into the proper reflective pronoun. For example,

I elected myself president of the club.
John nominated himself to be the next chairman.
Mary chose herself to be the secretary.
Mr. Quirk named himself the vice-president.
We thought ourselves ready for anything.

Exercise 25 / TYPE 3 COMPLEMENTS

Draw phrase structure trees and apply the necessary transformational rules to generate the following sentences:

1. The lawyer advised his client to plead guilty.
2. I chose myself to win.
3. We nominated John to be the candidate.
4. The judge considered him to be a menace to society.
5. Napoleon crowned himself emperor.

Answers to Exercise 21 / NOUN CLAUSE SENTENCE COMPLEMENTS

1. John decided that he would go after all.

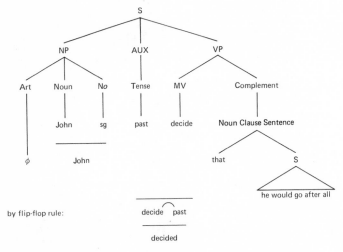

2. He found out that it had started to rain.

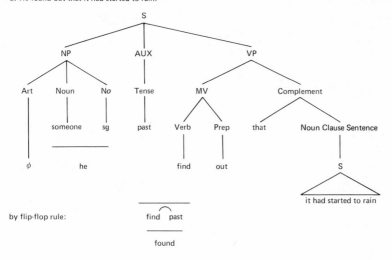

3. I think he has moved back to Chicago.

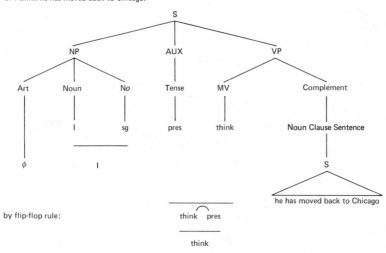

4. The reports showed John to be in error.

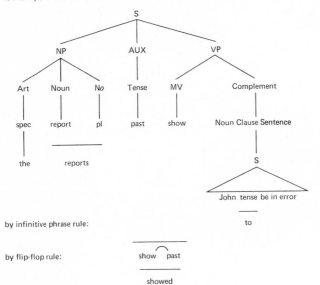

by infinitive phrase rule:

by flip-flop rule:

5. I found him to be very alert.

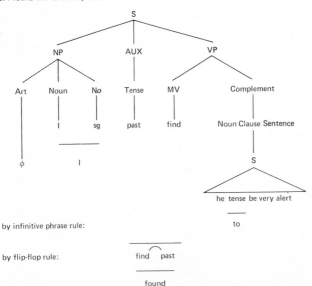

by infinitive phrase rule:

by flip-flop rule:

Answers to Exercise 22 / QUESTION-WORD SENTENCE COMPLEMENTS

1. John realized where he was.

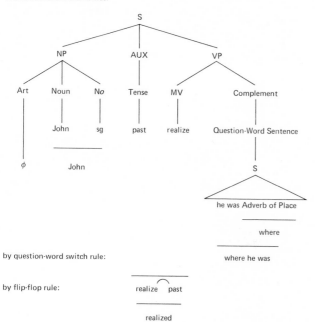

2. I know why he called.

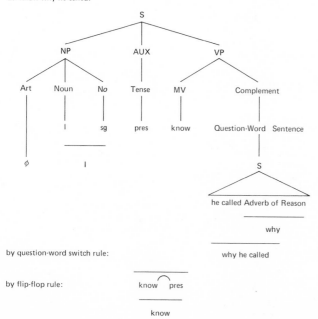

3. The waitress remembered who ordered the iced tea.

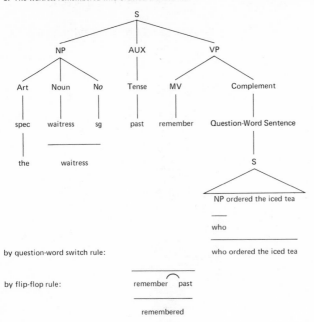

by question-word switch rule:

who ordered the iced tea

by flip-flop rule:

remember past

remembered

4. The chairman couldn't recall who had been nominated.

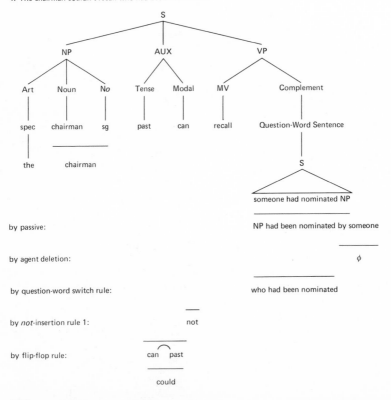

by passive:

NP had been nominated by someone

by agent deletion:

ϕ

by question-word switch rule:

who had been nominated

by *not*-insertion rule 1:

not

by flip-flop rule:

can past

could

5. We wondered how often we would have to go.

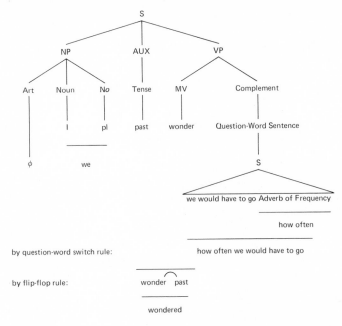

by question-word switch rule: how often we would have to go

by flip-flop rule: wonder past

                                            wondered

Answers to Exercise 23 / TYPE 1 COMPLEMENTS

1. He continued to receive threatening letters.

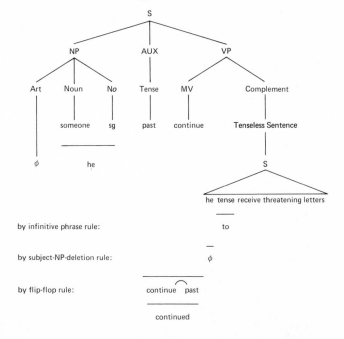

by infinitive phrase rule: to

by subject-NP-deletion rule: ϕ

by flip-flop rule: continue past

                                            continued

2. John hesitated to give his name.

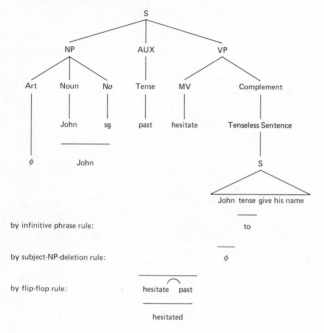

by infinitive phrase rule:	to
by subject-NP-deletion rule:	φ
by flip-flop rule:	hesitate past
	hesitated

3. I had finished reading the questions.

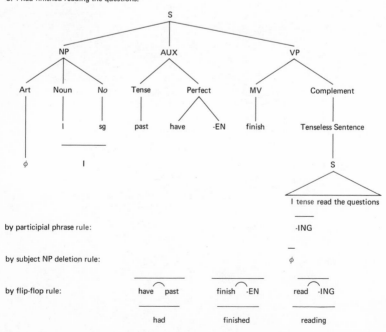

by participial phrase rule:	-ING
by subject NP deletion rule:	φ
by flip-flop rule:	have past finish -EN read -ING
	had finished reading

4. We started getting angry phone calls.

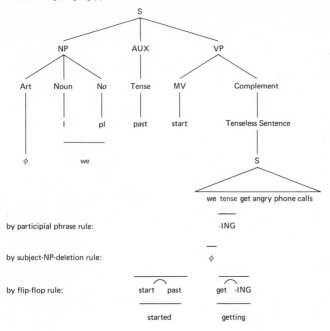

by participial phrase rule:	-ING
by subject-NP-deletion rule:	φ
by flip-flop rule:	start past	get -ING
	started	getting

5. The firemen began to be bothered by the smoke.

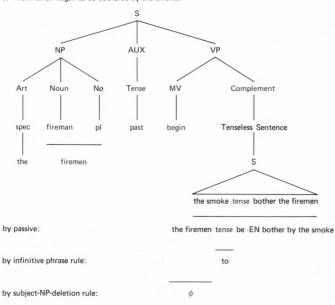

by passive:	the firemen tense be -EN bother by the smoke
by infinitive phrase rule:	to
by subject-NP-deletion rule:	φ
by flip-flop rule:	begin past	bother -EN
	began	bothered

Answers to Exercise 24 / TYPE 2 COMPLEMENTS

1. The girls wanted to become cheerleaders.

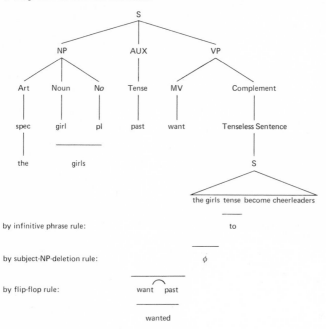

2. We were glad to see you do so well.

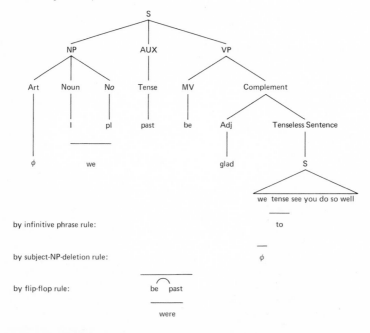

3. I expected you to be upset about it.

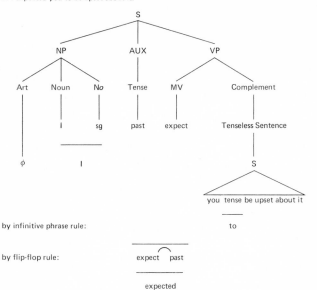

4. John was eager for Mary to take his place.

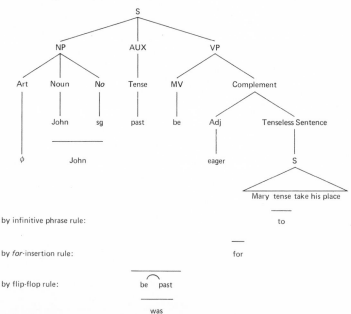

5. The boy was happy to be invited.

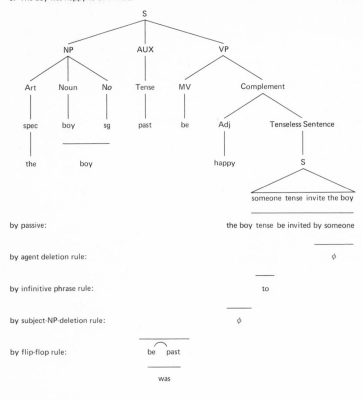

by passive: the boy tense be invited by someone

by agent deletion rule: φ

by infinitive phrase rule: to

by subject-NP-deletion rule: φ

by flip-flop rule: be   past

                            was

Answers to Exercise 25 / TYPE 3 COMPLEMENTS

1. The lawyer advised his client to plead guilty.

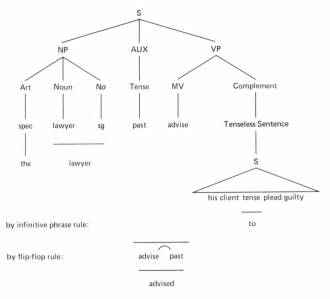

by infinitive phrase rule: to

by flip-flop rule: advise   past

                            advised

2. I chose myself to win.

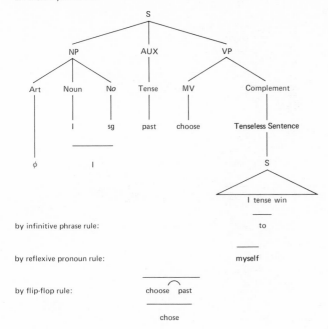

by infinitive phrase rule:

by reflexive pronoun rule:

by flip-flop rule:

3. We nominated John to be the candidate.

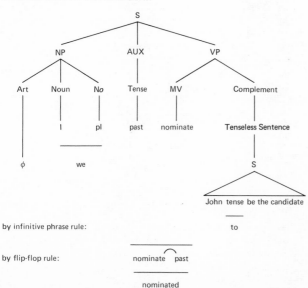

by infinitive phrase rule:

by flip-flop rule:

4. The judge considered him to be a menace to society.

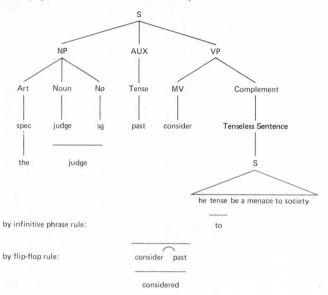

by infinitive phrase rule: to

by flip-flop rule: consider ⌢ past

                                                        considered

5. Napoleon crowned himself Emperor.

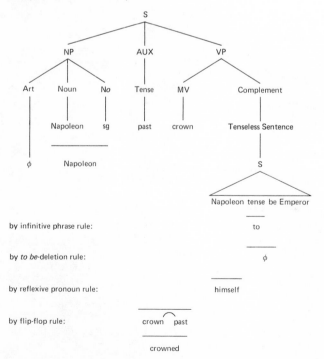

by infinitive phrase rule: to

by *to be*-deletion rule: φ

by reflexive pronoun rule: himself

by flip-flop rule: crown ⌢ past

                                                        crowned

CHAPTER 9

Noun Modification

Overview

In a transformational grammar, noun modifiers are derived from underlying full sentences that make an assertion about the noun. For example the sentence

> The *tall young man wearing a beret whom you introduced me to* borrowed my car last night.

contains four assertions about *man:*

> The *man* is tall.
> The *man* is young.
> The *man* was wearing a beret.
> You introduced me to the *man.*

Noun modification is built into the grammar by a recursive phrase structure rule which permits a noun to be modified by one or more embedded sentences. We can formalize this rule in the following way:

$$\text{NP} \longrightarrow \text{Art} \frown \text{Noun} \frown \text{No} \frown (\text{S})_1 \frown (\text{S})_2 \frown (\text{S})_3. \ldots$$

The only restraint on the embedded sentences is that they must contain within them the noun being modified (or else the embedded sentences would not be an assertion about the noun).

The embedded modifying sentence can come to the surface in one of two different ways: (1) as an adjectival clause or phrase, or (2) as an adjective, appositive, or prepositional phrase of place.

The first way appears to operate in two stages. The first stage converts the underlying full sentence into an adjectival clause. The second stage converts the adjectival clause into an adjectival phrase. The two operations may be applied to the following underlying embedded sentence

The man *the man wore a beret* borrowed my car last night.

The embedded modifying sentence can come to the surface as an adjectival clause by replacing its occurrence of the noun phrase being modified by the appropriate relative pronoun:

The man *who wore a beret* borrowed my car last night.

Though it is not apparent from this example, we must move the relative pronoun to the first position of the embedded sentence by a rule exactly parallel to the question-word switch rule. For example, if we were dealing with the embedded modifying sentence

You introduced me to the man.

we would have to move the relative pronoun that replaces *the man* (*whom* in this case) to the first position:

whom you introduced me to.

Under certain conditions we can move on to stage two and convert the adjectival clause into an adjectival phrase. We can do this by deleting the relative pronoun and replacing the tense with *-ing*. This operation would transform the adjectival clause

The man *who tense wear a beret* borrowed my car last night.

into the adjectival phrase

The man *wearing a beret* borrowed my car last night.

Embedded modifying sentences that have *be* as the main verb occupy a special status in the grammar. These embedded sentences can come to the surface in the second of the two ways: as adjectives, appositives, or prepositional phrases of place depending on the embedded sentence. If the embedded sentence contains the main verb *be* followed by an adjective, we can delete everything in the embedded sentence except the adjective. For example from the underlying sentence

The man *the man is tall* borrowed my car last night

we can delete the subject noun phrase, tense, and *be* (by what is called the *adjectival clause deletion rule*), producing:

The man *tall* borrowed my car last night.

We now need a second rule (called the *adjective switch rule*) to switch the order of the noun and adjective to produce the proper surface word order for English:

The *tall* man borrowed my car last night.

If the embedded modifying sentence contains the main verb *be* followed by a noun phrase, we can produce an appositive by deleting the subject noun phrase, tense, and *be* through the use of the adjectival clause deletion rule. For example if we take as an underlying sentence

The man *the man is an old friend of mine* borrowed my car last night.

we can reduce the modifying sentence to an appositive:

The man, *an old friend of mine*, borrowed my car last night.

If the embedded modifying sentence contains the main verb *be* followed by a prepositional phrase of place, we can produce a grammatical surface sentence by again applying the adjectival clause deletion rule. For example, from this underlying sentence

The man *the man is near the door* borrowed my car last night.

we can derive the following sentence

The man *near the door* borrowed my car last night.

The chapter closes with a brief discussion of *restrictive* and *nonrestrictive* modifiers. A restrictive modifier is one that, together with the noun it modifies, makes up a new semantic unit different in kind from the noun by itself. A nonrestrictive modifier is one that can be deleted from the sentence without radically changing the meaning of the whole sentence. A good example of a restrictive modifier is found in the adage

People *who live in glass houses* shouldn't throw stones.

If we were to take out the modifying clause, we would have a very different sentence:

People shouldn't throw stones.

Appositives are usually nonrestrictive modifiers. For example the appositive in the following sentence could be deleted without changing the basic sentence:

Mr. Mann, *my English teacher*, took a trip to Venice.

NOUN MODIFICATION

In the chapter on the noun phrase, the NP was seen to consist of three obligatory elements: Art Noun No. This is correct as far as it goes, but we now need to account for the expansion of the noun phrase through the process of modification. The basic idea of the transformational approach to noun modification is that all true modifiers make an assertion about the noun that they modify, and that this assertion can be expressed as a complete underlying sentence. For example, the italicized adjective in the following sentence

A *slender* boy stuck his head into the back room.

asserts that *the boy was slender.*

Similarly, the modifying adverb of place in this sentence

The picture *next to the window* needs to be straightened.

asserts that *the picture is next to the window.*

With adjectival participial phrases, the nature of the underlying assertion is easily seen, for example in this sentence

The tree, *being quite weather-beaten,* was uprooted.

It is clear that the phrase is understood as asserting that *the tree was quite weather-beaten.*

Finally, when an adjectival clause is used, the assertion appears on the surface of the sentence, for example,

The girl *whom you met last night* is a friend of my sister's.

We know that the *whom* could refer only to *the girl.* Thus the underlying assertion is *you met the girl last night.*

There is no upper limit on the number of times that a noun can be modified, for example the following sentence

The *tall young* man *wearing a beret whom you introduced me to* borrowed my car last night.

contains four underlying assertions about *the man:*

The man is tall.
The man is young.
The man wore a beret.
You introduced me to the man.

The one restriction on the underlying assertion is that it must contain the noun being modified (or else it would not be an assertion about that noun).

Modification is usually optional, that is, a sentence will not normally be un-grammatical solely because of the presence or absence of a modifier. We may incorporate all the above discussion into our rule for the development of the noun phrase by deriving the modifiers from an indefinite number of optional sentences. The new rule for the development of noun phrases would then look like this:

$$\text{NP} \longrightarrow \text{Art} \frown \text{Noun} \frown \text{No} \frown (S)_1, \frown (S)_2, \frown (S)_3. \dots$$

The embedded modifying sentence can come to the surface in either of two different ways: (1) as an adjectival clause or phrase, or (2) as an adjective, appositive, or prepositional phrase of place. The first way appears to operate in two stages. Stage I converts the underlying sentence into an adjectival clause. Stage II converts the adjectival clause to an adjectival phrase.

STAGE I: UNDERLYING SENTENCE INTO ADJECTIVAL CLAUSE

The first step in stage I is to replace the repetition of the noun being modified by the appropriate relative pronoun. Note that the class of relative pronouns is nearly identical with the class of question words. For example:

1. I met the man *the man knows your mother.*
   who

2. I met the man *your mother knows the man.*
   who(m)

3. I saw the trees *you told me about the trees.*
   which

4. I saw the tree *you told me about the tree.*
   that

5. We visited the island *they grow pepper on that island.*
   where

6. I remember the night *you pushed me into the pool that night.*
   when

The second step moves the relative pronoun to the first position in the modifying sentence. We will call this transformational rule the "relative pronoun switch rule." This rule is identical with the question-word switch rule. For example:

1.   I met the man *who knows your mother.*
     (no change; it was already in the first position)

2. I met the man *who(m) your mother knows.*
3.a. I saw the trees *which you told me about.*
  b. I saw the trees *about which you told me.*
4. I saw the tree *that you told me about.*
5. We visited the island *where they grow pepper.*
6. I remember the night *when you pushed me into the pool.*

At this point of development, the relative pronoun can be optionally deleted from many (but not all) of the sentences by the "relative pronoun deletion rule." For example:

1. ° I met the man *knows your mother.*
2. I met the man *your mother knows.*
3.a. I saw the trees *you told me about.*
  b. ° I saw the trees *about you told me.*
4. I saw the tree *you told me about.*
5. ° We visited the island *they grow pepper.*
6. I remember the night *you pushed me into the pool.*

As you are aware, sentences 1, 3.b, and 5 are ungrammatical; in other words, in these sentences we cannot apply the relative pronoun deletion rule.

Here are some sample derivations:

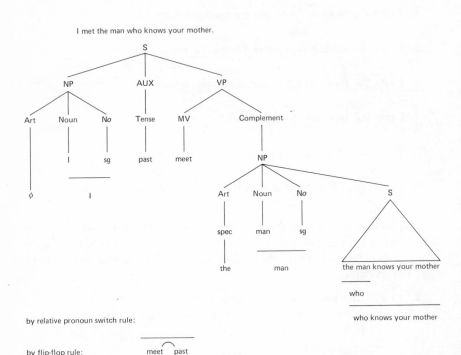

I met the man who knows your mother.

by relative pronoun switch rule:

by flip-flop rule:

I met the man whom your mother knows.

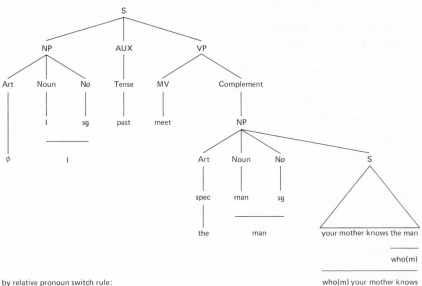

by relative pronoun switch rule:

by flip-flop rule:

I saw the trees you told me about.

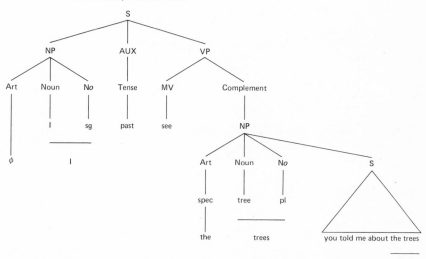

by relative pronoun switch rule:

by relative pronoun deletion rule:

by flip-flop rule:

STAGE II: ADJECTIVAL CLAUSE INTO ADJECTIVAL PHRASE

In the transformation from clause to phrase, the relative pronoun is deleted, and the verb is made into a present participle by replacing the tense with *-ing*. For example, the adjectival clauses in the sentences below are transformed to adjectival participial phrases:

the man, having drunk far too much, labored up the stairs.
The man, swearing at each step, labored up the stairs.
The man, looking very red in the face, labored up the stairs.

Let us call this operation the "adjectival phrase rule." It may be applied when the subject of the modifying sentence is the same as the noun being modified. We may formalize it this way

relative pronoun $\overset{\frown}{\text{Tense}}$ $\implies$ -ING

This formalization rests on a combination of elementary operations: the deletion of the relative pronoun and the replacement of tense with *-ing*. Here is a derivation involving this rule:

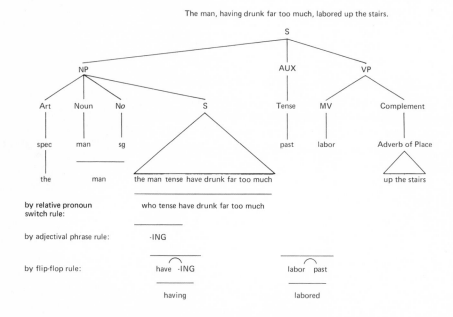

The man, having drunk far too much, labored up the stairs.

Exercise 26 / ADJECTIVAL CLAUSES AND PHRASES

Draw phrase structures and apply the necessary transformational rules to produce the following sentences:

1. I broke the watch that you gave me.
2. The children who live next door are watching television.
3. The children whom we invited over are watching television.
4. The tree you pruned will live.
5. I know a place where you can get tortillas.
6. The man, being short, stood on a box.
7. The boys, being warned of the danger, put on their shoes.

ADJECTIVES, APPOSITIVES, AND PREPOSITIONAL PHRASES OF PLACE

Modifying sentences that contain *be* as the main verb have a special status in the grammar. They undergo a transformational rule that deletes the subject noun phrase, the tense, and the *be*. For example, the following underlying sentences

A man *the man was tall* saw our distress signal.
A man *the man was a lifeguard* saw our distress signal.
A man *the man was on the shore* saw our distress signal.

are converted into

A man *tall* saw our distress signal.
A man, *a lifeguard,* saw our distress signal.
A man *on the shore* saw our distress signal.

The second and third sentences are grammatical as they stand. The modifying noun phrase *a lifeguard* in the second sentence is called an appositive.

The first sentence would be grammatical too if we were talking about French. In French, as you may know, most modifying adjectives occur after the noun they modify. A few survivals of the French order have survived in Modern English from the period after the Norman Conquest when French speakers ruled England. The clearest example is with a pair of adjectives. We can say

A girl, young and pretty, answered our knock.

as well as the more common

A pretty, young girl answered our knock.

For English, we need to reverse the order of the adjective and noun.

Let us call the rule that deletes the subject noun phrase, the tense, and the main verb *be* the "adjectival clause deletion rule." We may formalize the rule this way

Noun Phrase⌢Tense⌢*be* $\Longrightarrow$ Ø

We will call the rule that moves the modifying adjectives from a position following the noun to a position preceding it the "adjective switch rule." We may write the rule this way

$$\text{Art} \frown \text{Noun} \frown \text{N}o \frown \text{Adj} \implies \text{Art} \frown \text{Adj} \frown \text{Noun} \frown \text{N}o$$

Some sample derivations that employ this rule are shown below and on the opposite page.

We fixed the crack in the chimney.

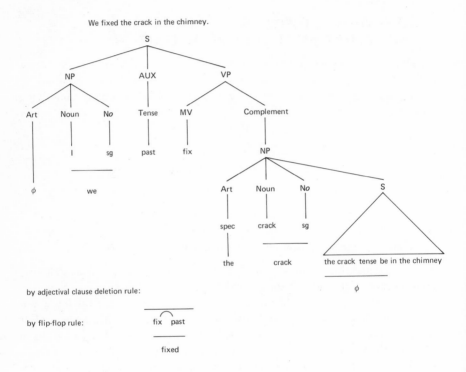

by adjectival clause deletion rule:

by flip-flop rule:

$$\overset{\frown}{\text{fix} \quad \text{past}}$$

fixed

A yellow owl stared at us.

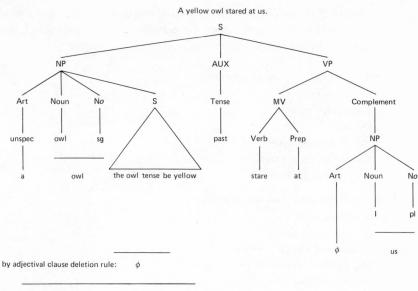

by adjectival clause deletion rule: φ

by adjective switch rule: a yellow owl

by flip-flop rule: stare past

                          stared

Mr. Brown, my teacher, reported the accident.

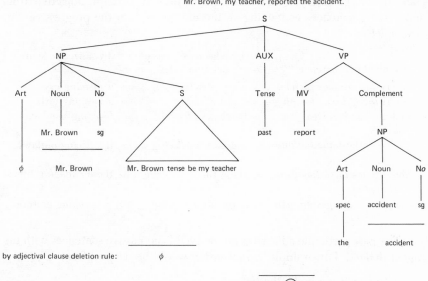

by adjectival clause deletion rule: φ

by flip-flop rule: report past

                              reported

The adjectival clause deletion and adjective switch rules also can be used in deriving adjectives from verbs. Both the present and past participle forms of verbs can be turned into modifying adjectives. For example:

Present participles used as adjectives:
    a *piercing* cry
    a *weeping* girl
    bleeding bandages
    the *fleeing* outlaws
    these *changing* times
    a *sweeping* gesture

Past participles used as adjectives:
    a *broken* toy
    an *unopened* letter
    a *canceled* check
    the *fallen* leaves
    a *hidden* treasure
    an *outraged* parent

It seems natural to assume that these derived adjectives come from modifying embedded sentences in much the same way as other adjectives do. That is, the noun being modified must appear as the subject of an underlying sentence and that the participle must occupy the position of a predicate adjective. Accordingly, we would derive the present participle adjectives from underlying sentences containing an intransitive verb in the progressive. For example:

Embedded sentence	by adjectival clause deletion rule:	by adjective switch rule:
a cry *the cry was piercing* $\Longrightarrow$	a cry *piercing*	$\Longrightarrow$ a *piercing* cry
a girl *the girl was weeping* $\Longrightarrow$	a girl *weeping*	$\Longrightarrow$ a *weeping* girl
bandages *the bandages were bleeding* $\Longrightarrow$	bandages *bleeding*	$\Longrightarrow$ *bleeding* bandages
The outlaws *the outlaws were fleeing* $\Longrightarrow$	the outlaws *fleeing*	$\Longrightarrow$ the *fleeing* outlaws
these times *these times are changing* $\Longrightarrow$	these times *changing* $\Longrightarrow$	these *changing* times
a gesture *the gesture was sweeping* $\Longrightarrow$	a gesture *sweeping*	$\Longrightarrow$ a *sweeping* gesture

The past participle adjectives are derived from passive sentences with the agent deleted. For example, *a broken toy* would be derived from

A toy *someone broke the toy.*

By the passive and agent deletion this would become

A toy *the toy was broken.*

The main verb of the embedded sentence now occupies the position of a predicate adjective, and the adjectival clause deletion and adjective switch rules may be applied. For example:

Embedded sentence (after passive and agent deletion)	by adjectival clause deletion rule:	by adjective switch rule:
a toy *the toy was broken* $\Longrightarrow$	the toy *broken* $\Longrightarrow$	the *broken* toy
a letter *the letter was unopened* $\Longrightarrow$	a letter *unopened* $\Longrightarrow$	an *unopened* letter
a check *the check was canceled* $\Longrightarrow$	a check *canceled* $\Longrightarrow$	a *canceled* check
the leaves *the leaves were fallen* $\Longrightarrow$	the leaves *fallen* $\Longrightarrow$	the *fallen* leaves
a parent *the parent was outraged* $\Longrightarrow$	a parent *outraged* $\Longrightarrow$	an *outraged* parent

A final point about modification that needs mentioning is the difference between restrictive and nonrestrictive modifiers. Dorothy Parker's famous couplet is a clear illustration of a restrictive modifier:

Boys seldom make passes
At girls who wear glasses.

Who do boys seldom make passes at? *Girls* or *girls who wear glasses?* Obviously, the second interpretation is the one intended. As its name suggests, a restrictive modifier restricts or limits the meaning of the noun in such a way that the noun plus the modifier means something quite different than the noun without the modifier. Here is an example of a nonrestrictive modifier:

Mr. Mann, my English teacher, took a trip to Venice.

The appositive *my English teacher* helps identify who Mr. Mann is. It is a useful piece of information, but it does not really alter the meaning of the sentence in any basic way.

Sometimes, a modifier can be either restrictive or nonrestrictive, according to the way we choose to interpret the sentence. For example:

The policeman *the policeman knew the area best* led the search.

How many policemen were there? If we interpret the modifying sentence as being restrictive, there were several policemen, and the one policeman who knew the area better than the other policemen led the search. If the modifying sentence is interpreted as nonrestrictive, there was only one policeman, and the modifying sentence is just giving some additional useful information about why the policeman led the search.

Not only does it make a difference in meaning, but the choice between making the underlying sentence restrictive or nonrestrictive also governs the pronunciation of the sentence. if the modifying sentence is restrictive, the whole sentence is pronounced like this:

The policeman who knew the area best led the search.

If the modifying sentence is nonrestrictive, the whole sentence is pronounced like this:

The policeman _____ led the search.
          who knew the area best

In the written sentence the nonrestrictive clause is set off by a pair of commas:

The policeman, who knew the area best, led the search.

Exercise 27 / ADJECTIVES, APPOSITIVES, AND PREPOSITIONAL PHRASES OF PLACE

Draw phrase structure trees and apply the necessary transformational rules to produce the following sentences:

1. The mailman delivered a brown envelope.
2. The train pulled onto a siding near the depot.
3. The tree, a huge oak, was uprooted by the storm.
4. The old house on the hill burned down.
5. You can't teach an old dog new tricks.

Answers to Exercise 26 / ADJECTIVAL CLAUSES

1. I broke the watch that you gave me.

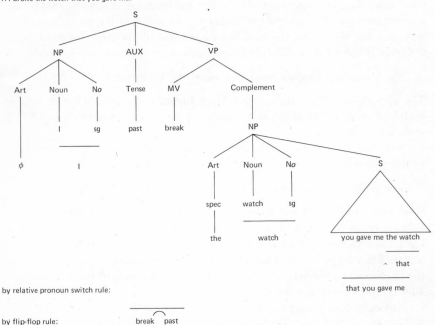

by relative pronoun switch rule:

by flip-flop rule:

2. The children who live next door are watching television.

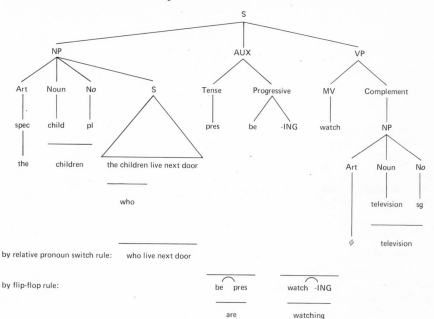

by relative pronoun switch rule: who live next door

by flip-flop rule:

3. The children whom we invited over are watching television.

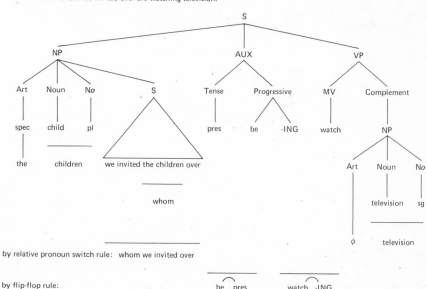

by relative pronoun switch rule: whom we invited over

by flip-flop rule:

4. The tree you pruned will live.

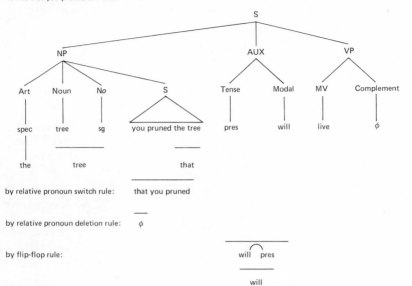

by relative pronoun switch rule: that you pruned

by relative pronoun deletion rule: φ

by flip-flop rule:

5. I know a place where you can get tortillas.

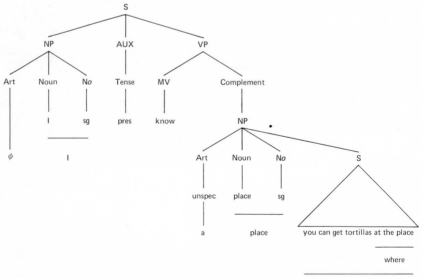

by relative pronoun switch rule:

by flip-flop rule:

6. The man, being short, stood on a box.

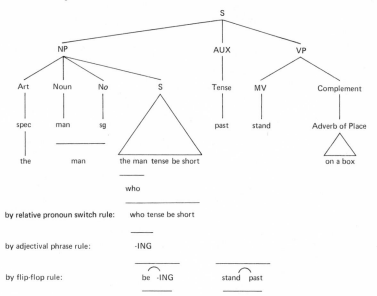

by relative pronoun switch rule: who tense be short

by adjectival phrase rule: -ING

by flip-flop rule: be -ING   stand past

                 being   stood

7. The boys, being warned of the danger, put on their shoes.

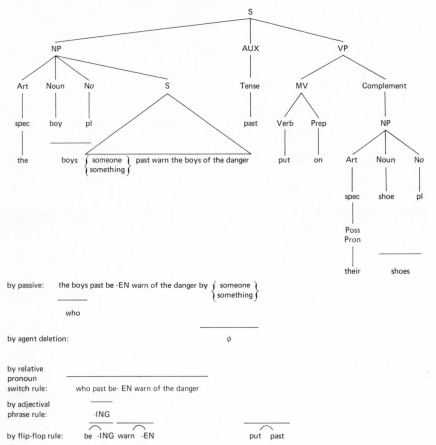

by passive: the boys past be -EN warn of the danger by ⎰ someone ⎱
                _____   ⎱ something ⎰
                      who

by agent deletion: _____
                                                    φ

by relative
pronoun   _____
switch rule: who past be- EN warn of the danger

by adjectival   _____
phrase rule: -ING

by flip-flop rule: ⌒   ⌒   ⌒
                    be -ING warn -EN   put past
                    ____   _____   _____

                    being   warned   put

Answers to Exercise 27 / ADJECTIVAL PHRASES

1. The mailman delivered a brown envelope.

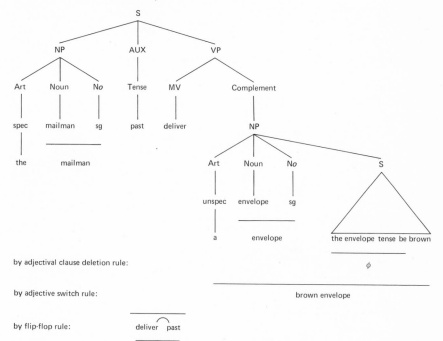

by adjectival clause deletion rule:

by adjective switch rule: brown envelope

by flip-flop rule: deliver past

                                      delivered

2. The train pulled onto a siding near the depot.

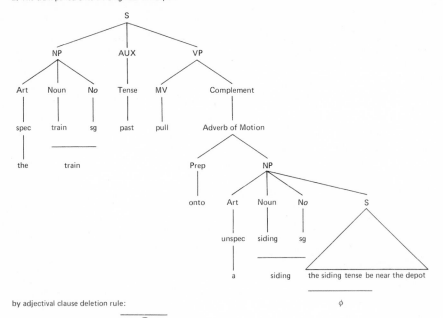

by adjectival clause deletion rule: φ

by flip-flop rule: pull past

                       pulled

3. The tree, a huge oak, was uprooted by the storm.

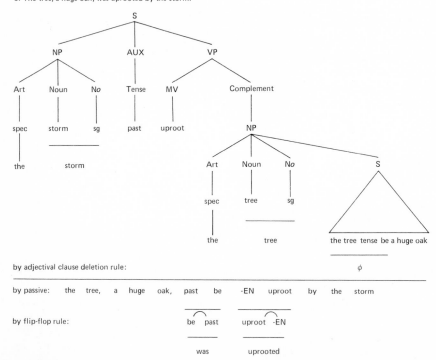

by adjectival clause deletion rule: φ

by passive: the   tree,   a   huge   oak,   past   be   -EN   uproot   by   the   storm

by flip-flop rule: be past   uproot -EN

                                   was   uprooted

238

4. The old house on the hill burned down.

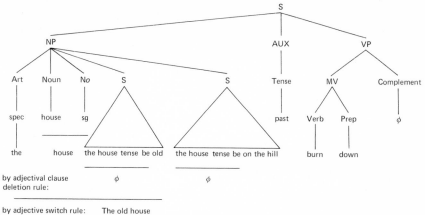

by adjectival clause
deletion rule: φ   φ

by adjective switch rule: The old house

by flip-flop rule: burn past

                            burned

5. You can't teach an old dog new tricks.

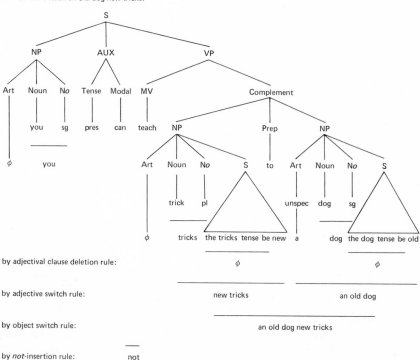

by adjectival clause deletion rule: φ   φ

by adjective switch rule: new tricks   an old dog

by object switch rule: an old dog new tricks

by *not*-insertion rule: not

by flip-flop rule: can pres

                            can

CHAPTER 10

Nominalized Sentences

Overview

When the grammar of a sentence will permit the use of a singular, abstract noun, the entire noun phrase of which that noun is a part can be replaced by an embedded sentence, which can come to the surface in a variety of superficially different forms. Let us take as an example the main sentence

The audience applauded NP.

We may replace the object NP in this sentence with an embedded sentence, for example,

John rebutted the speaker.

The embedded sentence can come to the surface in the following ways (among many others):

The audience applauded
$$\begin{cases} \text{the fact that John rebutted the speaker.} \\ \text{John's rebutting the speaker.} \\ \text{John's rebutal of the speaker.} \end{cases}$$

There are several different types of nominalized sentences. The most common type can be paraphrased as beginning with "the fact that . . . ."

The fact that-nominalization can be broken down into four subtypes according to what happens to the tense of the embedded sentence:

Subtype 1: Tense is retained, for example:
The fact that John rebutt*ed* the speaker $\Longrightarrow$
　　that John rebutt*ed* the speaker (pleased us).
Subtype 2: Tense is replaced by *-ing*, for example:
The fact that John rebutt*ed* the speaker $\Longrightarrow$
　　John's rebutt*ing* the speaker (pleased us).
Subtype 3: Tense is replaced by *to*, for example:
The fact that John rebutt*ed* the speaker $\Longrightarrow$
　　for John *to* rebut the speaker (pleased us).
Subtype 4: Tense is lost, for example:
The fact that John rebutt*ed* the speaker $\Longrightarrow$
　　John's rebutal of the speaker (pleased us).

Only certain embedded sentences can come to the surface as subtype 4 nominalizations, that is, with tense lost. In subtype 4 nominalizations the main verb of the embedded sentence is converted into a noun. Consequently, only those main verbs that have corresponding noun forms can undergo the subtype 4 nominalization. For example, we can transform the embedded sentence

The company published the book.

into the nominalized surface form

The company's publication of the book,

but we cannot transform a similar appearing embedded sentence

The company printed the book.

into a grammatical nominalization of subtype 4

＊ The company's print of the book

because the main verb *print* does not have a corresponding noun form.

Of the many different forms that *the fact that*-nominalized sentence can take, two particular forms stand apart: a subtype 1 nominalization with *that* followed by the entire embedded sentence, and the subtype 3 nominalization with tense changed to *to*. Taking as an example the underlying sentence

The fact that John refused the offer surprised me.

we can produce the two forms in question:

That John refused the offer ⎫
For John to refused the offer ⎬ surprised me.

These two forms can undergo a special transformational operation called the "*it*-inversion rule":

It surprised me $\begin{cases} \textit{that John refused the offer.} \\ \textit{for John to refuse the offer.} \end{cases}$

When the subject of the embedded sentence is the same as the object of the main sentence, we must replace the repetition of *John* in the first nominalized sentence by the appropriate pronoun:

It surprised John that *he* received the offer.

In the second nominalized sentence, however, we must delete both the repeated noun phrase and the *for* that precedes it, producing

It surprised John to receive the offer.

NOMINALIZED SENTENCES

A nominalized sentence is a sentence used as a noun phrase. For example in the sentence

The audience applauded John's rebutting the speaker.

the noun phrase object of the transitive verb *applaud* is *John's rebutting the speaker*. This noun phrase comes from an underlying sentence

John rebutted the speaker.

There are many restrictions as to which noun phrases can be developed as nominalized sentences. Perhaps the most important restraint is that the noun in the noun phrase be abstract. For example, all of the following uses of the same nominalized sentence are ungrammatical because they are used in a position where an animate noun must be used:

* John's rebutting the speaker applauded the audience.
* John's rebutting the speaker was hungry.
* The event surprised John's rebutting the speaker.

When a nominalized sentence is used in place of a concrete noun, the results are even more outlandish:

* John's rebutting the speaker tipped over.
* The fisherman hooked his line on John's rebutting the speaker.

A key restriction of nominalized sentences, then, is that they can be used only in positions where abstract nouns are grammatical. A useful test word is *outcome*. *Outcome* is an abstract noun that is semantically compatible with almost any verb that will take abstract nouns. It can be used, for example, in the first sentence in this section:

The audience applauded the outcome.

A second restraint on the use of nominalized sentences is that they can be used only in the singular. For example, the verbs in the following sentences will accept abstract nouns, but the sentences are ungrammatical because the nominalized sentences cannot be made plural to agree with the verb:

*John's rebutting the speaker are surprising.
*John's rebutting the speaker were announced over the radio.

Another advantage in using the word *outcome* as a test case is that it is a mass (or noncount) noun, and consequently is inherently singular. In summary, any sentence that will accept a singular abstract noun will also accept a nominalized sentence in that same position. We may derive the embedded sentence by adding on the noun phrase rule:

$$\text{NP} \longrightarrow \begin{Bmatrix} \text{Art} \frown \text{Noun} \frown \text{No} \frown (S)_1 \frown (S)_2 \cdots \\ \text{the fact that} \frown S \end{Bmatrix}$$

Notice that the noun phrase rule now has two different types of embedded sentences. The "$(S)_1 \frown (S)_2 \ldots$" in the first line of the rule is the source of all noun modification, as was discussed in the preceding chapter. The S in the second line is the source of nominalized sentences.

One of the most striking facts about the nominalizing process is the bewildering variety of ways the underlying sentence can come to the surface. For example, let us take the sentence

The boy is tall.

and substitute it in place of the *outcome* in the sentence

The outcome surprised me.

This sentence can come to the surface in at least ten different ways:

The fact that the boy is tall surprised me.
That the boy is tall surprised me.
The fact of the boy's being tall surprised me.
The boy's being tall surprised me.
The boy's tallness surprised me.
The boy being tall surprised me.
The fact of the tallness of the boy surprised me.
The tallness of the boy surprised me.
The fact of the boy's tallness surprised me.
For the boy to be tall surprised me.

It is possible to break down the nominalized surface sentences into four subtypes on the basis of what happens to the tense of the underlying nominal sentence. In subtype 1, the tense is preserved intact. Examples of this would be:

The fact that the boy *is* tall
That the boy *is* tall

In subtype 2 the tense is replaced by *-ing*, changing the underlying sentence into a participial phrase, for example:

> The fact of the boy's *being* tall
> The boy's *being* tall
> The boy *being* tall

In subtype 3 the tense is replaced by *to*, changing the underlying sentence into an infinitive phrase, for example:

> For the boy *to be* tall.

In subtype 4 the tense disappears altogether, for example:

> The fact of the boy's tallness
> The boy's tallness
> The fact of the tallness of the boy
> The tallness of the boy

Here are the same nominalization processes applied to the underlying intransitive sentence *John died:*

> Subtype 1; Tense retained:
> > *The fact that John died* surprised me.
> > *That John died* surprised me.
>
> Subtype 2; Tense changed to *-ing:*
> > *The fact of John's dying* surprised me.
> > *John's dying* surprised me.
> > *The dying of John* surprised me.
>
> Subtype 3; Tense changed to *to:*
> > *For John to be dead* surprised me.
>
> Subtype 4; Tense lost:
> > *The fact of John's death* surprised me.
> > *John's death* surprised me.
> > *The fact of the death of John* surprised me.
> > *The death of John* surprised me.

Finally, here are the nominalization processes applied to the underlying transitive sentence *John refused the offer:*

> Subtype 1 Tense retained:
> > *The fact that John refused the offer* surprised me.
> > *That John refused the offer* surprised me.
>
> Subtype 2; Tense changed to *-ing:*
> > *The fact of John's refusing the offer* surprised me.
> > *John's refusing (of) the offer* surprised me.
> > *The refusing of the offer (by John)* surprised me.

Subtype 3; Tense changed to *to:*
> *For John to refuse the offer* surprised me.

Subtype 4; Tense lost:
> *The fact of John's refusal of the offer* surprised me.
> *John's refusal of the offer* surprised me.
> *The fact of the refusal of the offer (by John)* surprised me.
> *The refusal of the offer (by John)* surprised me.

As the above examples indicate, the nominalization process produces a variety of surface forms with the same underlying meaning. From a stylistic standpoint, many of the above sentences are clumsy and would be avoided in actual practice. Nevertheless, as far as I know, nominalizations of subtypes 1, 2, and 3 are always open to the user. Subtype 4 is somewhat idiomatic. It can only be applied when the main verb (or when the main verb is *be*, the predicate adjective) can be changed into an abstract noun. In the first example, the adjective *tall* was changed into the noun *tallness;* in the second example, the verb *die* was changed into the noun *death;* and in the third example, the verb *refuse* was changed into the noun *refusal.* If the verb has no related noun form, then the subtype 4 nominalization process will be ungrammatical. For example the verb *print* and *publish* mean roughly the same things in the sentence

The company printed the book.
The company published the book.

The verb *publish* can be turned into the noun *publication,* and consequently subtype 4 nominalization can be applied to it, for example:

> *The fact of the company's publication of the book* surprised me.
> *The company's publication of the book* surprised me.
> *The fact of the publication of the book by the company* surprised me.
> *The publication of the book by the company* surprised me.

However, there is no noun derived from the verb *print,* and consequently the underlying sentence *the company printed the book* cannot grammatically undergo subtype 4 nominalization, for example:

> ° *The fact of the company's print of the book* surprised me.
> ° *The company's print of the book* surprised me.
> ° *The fact of the print of the book by the company* surprised me.
> ° *The print of the book by the company* surprised me.

Yet, all the other nominalization processes apply normally, for example:

Subtype 1; Tense retained:
> *The fact that the company printed the book* surprised me.
> *That the company printed the book* surprised me.

Subtype 2; Tense changed to *-ing:*
>*The fact of the company's printing the book* surprised me.
>*The company's printing the book* surprised me.
>*The printing of the book (by the company)* surprised me.

Subtype 3; Tense changed to *to:*
>*For the company to print the book* surprised me.

All of the examples of nominalization that we have discussed so far have been in position of the subject noun phrase. Most, but not all, nominalized sentences can also appear in the object noun phrase position. Some examples follow.

With the underlying sentence *John past be rich:*

Subtype 1; Tense retained:
>She based her hopes on *the fact that John was rich.*
>° She based her hopes on *that John was rich.*

Subtype 2; Tense changed to *-ing:*
>She based her hopes on *the fact of John's being rich.*
>She based her hopes on *John's being rich.*

Subtype 3; Tense changed to *to:*
>° She based her hopes on *for John to be rich.*

Subtype 4; Tense lost:
>She based her hopes on *the fact of John's richness.*
>She based her hopes on *John's richness.*
>She based her hopes on the fact of *the richness of John('s).*
>She based her hopes on *the richness of John('s).*

With the underlying sentence *John past die.*

With subtype 1; Tense retained:
>She based her hopes on *the fact that John died.*
>° She based her hopes on *that John died.*

With subtype 2; Tense changed to *-ing:*
>She based her hopes on *the fact of John's dying.*
>She based her hopes on *John's dying.*
>She based her hopes on *the dying of John.*

With subtype 3; Tense changed to *to:*
>° She based her hopes on *for John to be dead.*

With subtype 4; Tense lost:
>She based her hopes on *the fact of John's death.*
>She based her hopes on *John's death.*
>She based her hopes on *the fact of the death of John.*
>She based her hopes on *the death of John.*

With the underlying sentence *John refused the offer.*

With subtype 1; Tense retained:
> She based her hopes on *the fact that John refused the offer.*
> * She based her hopes on *that John refused the offer.*

With subtype 2; Tense changed to *-ing:*
> She based her hopes on *the fact of John's refusing the offer.*
> She based her hopes on *John's refusing (of) the offer.*
> She based her hopes on *the refusing of the offer (by John).*

With subtype 3; Tense changed to *to:*
> * She based her hopes on *for John to refuse the offer.*

With subtype 4; Tense lost:
> She based her hopes on *the fact of John's refusal of the offer.*
> She based her hopes on *John's refusal of the offer.*
> She based her hopes on *the fact of the refusal of the offer (by John).*
> She based her hopes on *the refusal of the offer (by John).*

As you can see, two of the ten different surface forms of the nominalized sentence cannot be used in the object position: the *that* S nominalization of subtype 1 and the *for. . .to* nominalization of subtype 3. This pair of nominalizations needs to be treated as a special subclass. More about them later.

Since the underlying sentence can come to the surface in such a variety of superficially different ways, we will make no attempt to write a separate transformational rule for each of them. Instead, we will merely state which of the four subtypes of nominalizations governs the derivation. Here are sample derivations of each subtype:

Subtype 1: That John knew the answer pleased Mary.

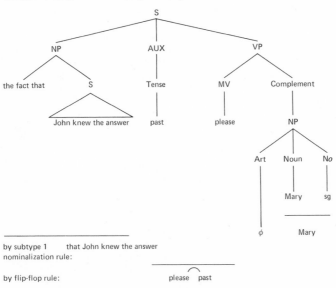

by subtype 1 that John knew the answer
nominalization rule:

by flip-flop rule: please past

pleased

Subtype 2:   We heard about John's dying.

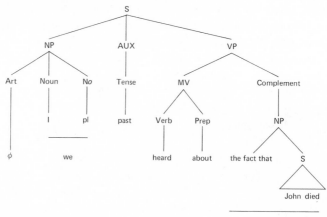

by subtype 2 nominalization rule: John's dying

by flip-flop rule:

heard

Subtype 3:   For John to be broke amused me.

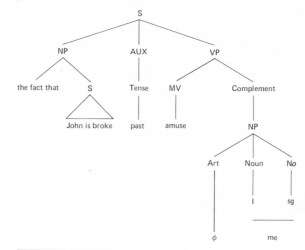

by subtype 3 nominalization
rule: For John to be broke

by flip-flop rule:

amused

Subtype 4: I was saddened by John's death.

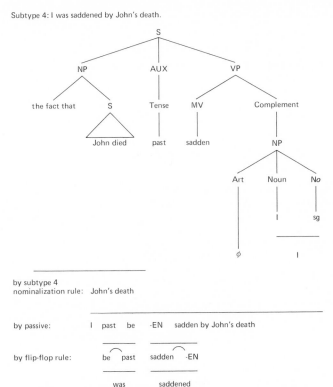

by subtype 4
nominalization rule: John's death

by passive: I   past   be   -EN   sadden by John's death

by flip-flop rule: be⌢past   sadden⌢-EN

              was   saddened

Exercise 28 / THE FACT THAT⌢S

Draw phrase structure trees and apply the necessary transformational rules to produce the following sentences:

1. The crowd anticipated the jury's announcement of the decision.
2. For John to nominate himself was absurd.
3. We worried about the fact of his being absent.
4. John's repetition of the questions annoyed the examiners.
5. The landlady reported John's taking the car to the police.
   (That is, she reported to the police that John took the car.)

It-Inversion

Of the ten different surface forms of the nominalized sentence, two can undergo an optional transformational process that inverts the sentence and supplies an *it* as the superficial subject noun phrase. For example, taking the underlying sentence *John refused the offer,* we can transform

> *That John refused the offer* surprised me.
> *For John to refuse the offer* surprised me.

into

> It surprised me *that John refused the offer.*
> It surprised me *for John to refuse the offer.*

If the *it*-inversion is applied to the other forms of the nominalized sentence, the result is ungrammatical unless said in a special way:

> Subtype 1; Tense retained:
>> ° It surprised me the fact that John refused the offer.

> Subtype 2; Tense changed to *-ing:*
>> ° It surprised me the fact of John's refusing the offer.
>> ° It surprised me John's refusing the offer.
>> ° It surprised me the refusing of the offer (by John).

> Subtype 4; Tense lost:
>> ° It surprised me the fact of John's refusal of the offer.
>> ° It surprised me John's refusal of the offer.
>> ° It surprised me the fact of the refusal of the offer (by John).
>> ° It surprised me the refusal of the offer (by John).

Notice that the two nominalized sentences that can undergo the *it*-inversion are the same two sentences that cannot occur in the object noun phrase position. As was pointed out above, these two forms of the nominalized sentence seem to belong to a very special class.

The *it*-inversion rule is a combination of an insertion rule (for the *it*) and a switch rule for the rest of the sentence. We may formalize the *it*-inversion rule in the following way:

$$\text{NP} \frown \text{Aux} \frown \text{VP} \implies it \frown \text{Aux} \frown \text{VP} \frown \text{NP}$$

A more formal rule would make explicit that the NP must be a nominalized sentence that has been turned into a surface structure by subtype 1 or subtype 3 nominalization rules. A sample derivation of each type of rule is shown on the opposite page.

It surprised me that John refused the offer.

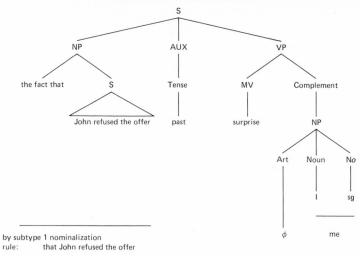

by subtype 1 nominalization
rule: that John refused the offer

by *it*-inversion rule: it past surprise me that John refused the offer

by flip-flop rule: surprise past
            surprised

It surprised me for John to refuse the offer.

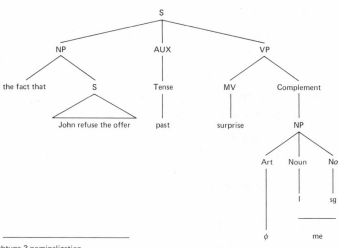

by subtype 3 nominalization
rule: for John to refuse the offer

by *it*-inversion rule: it past surprise me for John to refuse the offer

by flip-flop rule: surprise past
            surprised

The two subtypes of nominalized sentences that can undergo the *it*-inversion behave differently when the subject noun phrase of the nominalized sentence is the same as the object noun phrase of the underlying main sentence. For example, given the underlying sentence

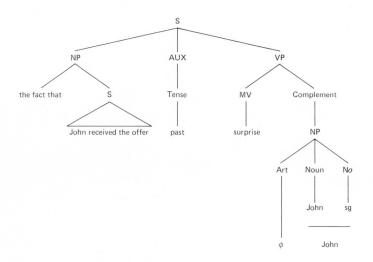

we can produce, by the nominalization rules,

> That John received the offer surprised John.
> For John to receive the offer surprised John.

By the *it*-inversion, we rearrange the above sentences to produce

> It surprised John that John received the offer.
> It surprised John for John to receive the offer.

Assuming that we are talking about just one John and not two different people both named John, then we must make certain changes in both sentences. In the first sentence we must apply the normal rule that changes the second occurrence of the same noun to the appropriate pronoun:

> It surprised John that John received the offer $\Longrightarrow$
> It surprised John that he received the offer.

If we apply this same rule to the second sentence, the result is grammatical, but the meaning is completely different:

> It surprised John for John to receive the offer $\Longrightarrow$
> It surprised John for him to receive the offer.

In this case, the *him* does not refer to John, but to somebody else. In order for the sentence to mean what we want, we must delete both the *for* and the subject noun phrase of the nominalized sentence:

> It surprised John for John to receive the offer ⟹
>   It surprised John to receive the offer.

Let us call the rule that makes this deletion the "*for-NP*-deletion rule":

> *for* ⌒NP ⟹ Ø

Here is a sample derivation employing the *for-NP*-deletion rule:

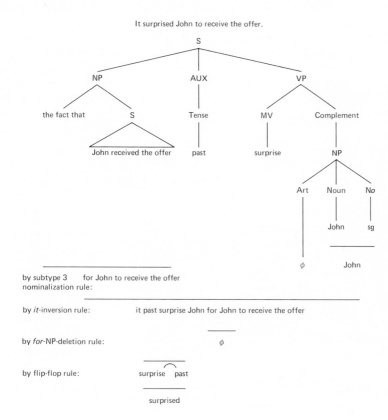

by subtype 3   for John to receive the offer
nominalization rule:

by *it*-inversion rule: it past surprise John for John to receive the offer

by *for*-NP-deletion rule: Ø

by flip-flop rule: surprise ⌒past

surprised

Exercise 29 / *IT-INVERSION*

Draw phrase structure trees and apply the necessary transformational rules to produce the following sentences:

1. It tickled me that John wouldn't come.
2. It overwhelmed Cinderella to get an invitation to the ball.

3. It amused me for John to be invited.
4. It makes us happy that tomorrow is a holiday.
5. It made me mad to be insulted by John.

Not only can nominalizations be stylistically clumsy; they are often ambiguous as well. For example, notice in one of the examples of subtype 4 nominalizations we had this sentence:

The refusal of the offer (by John) surprised me.

If we retain the *by John*, the embedded sentence has two possible meanings:

1. John refused the offer.
2. John gave someone an offer which that person refused.

The classic case of ambiguity in nominalized sentences occurs when the embedded sentence contains a transitive verb that can take subject and objects of the same type. Chomsky's well-known example from *Syntactic Structures* is

The shooting of the hunters

This nominalized sentence can be derived from either: (1) *the hunters shot something* or (2) *someone shot the hunters*. A similar looking nominalization

The growling of the lions

is not ambiguous because in the underlying sentence, *lions* can only be the subject noun phrase because the verb *growl* is intransitive: *lions growl*. In order for the nominalized sentence to be ambiguous it would have to have this possible underlying sentence:

° Something growls lions.

The contrast between the two nominalized sentences

The shooting of the hunters
The growling of the lions

is a clear illustration of the need to interpret surface forms in terms of their underlying source sentences. A grammar that did not incorporate such abstract information would be totally incapable of telling *why* the first nominalized sentence was ambiguous and the second one was not, since on their surface, the two nominalized sentences appear to have exactly the same structure.

Answers to Exercise 28 / THE FACT THAT S

1. The crowd anticipated the jury's announcement of the decision.

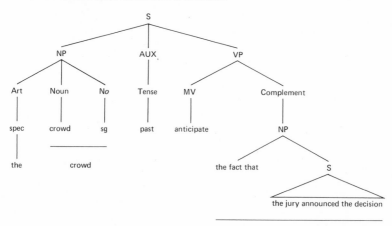

by subtype 4 nominalization rule: the jury's announcement of the decision

by flip-flop rule: anticipate ⌒ past

                    anticipated

2. For John to nominate himself was absurd.

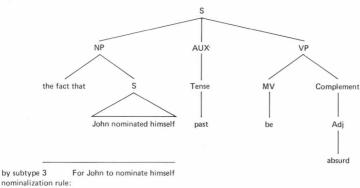

by subtype 3   For John to nominate himself
nominalization rule:

by flip-flop rule: be ⌒ past

                    was

3. We worried about the fact of his being absent.

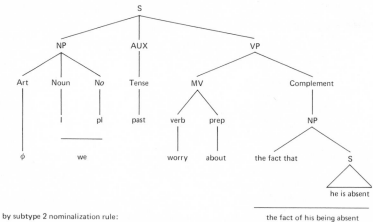

by subtype 2 nominalization rule: the fact of his being absent

by flip-flop rule:

4. John's repetition of the questions annoyed the examiners.

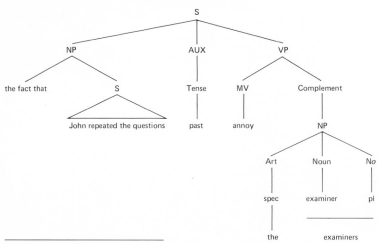

by subtype 4   John's repetition of the questions
nominalization rule:

by flip-flop rule:

5. The landlady reported John's taking the car to the police.

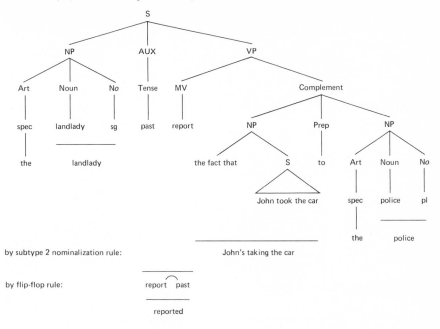

by subtype 2 nominalization rule: John's taking the car

by flip-flop rule: report‿past

                       reported

Answers to Exercise 29 / *IT*-INVERSION

1. It tickled me that John wouldn't come.

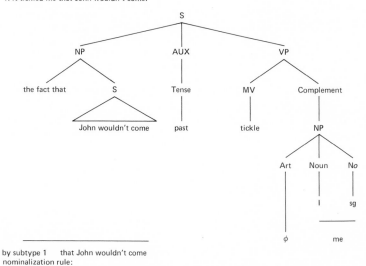

by subtype 1   that John wouldn't come
nominalization rule:

by *it*-inversion rule: it past tickle me that John wouldn't come

by flip-flop rule: tickle‿past

             tickled

2. It overwhelmed Cinderella to get an invitation to the ball.

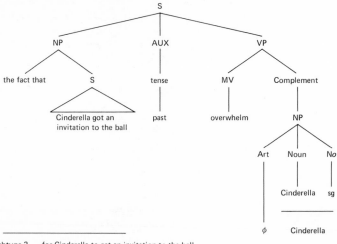

by subtype 3   for Cinderella to get an invitation to the ball
nominalization rule:

by *it*-inversion rule: it past overwhelm Cinderella for Cinderella to get an invitation to the ball

by *for*-NP-deletion rule: φ

by flip-flop rule: overwhelm ⌒ past

               overwhelmed

3. It amused me for John to be invited.

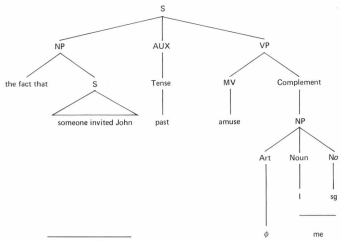

by passive: John was invited by someone

by agent deletion: ∅

by subtype 3   for John to be invited
nominalization rule:

by *it*-inversion rule: it past amuse me for John to be invited

by flip-flop rule: amuse past

                            amused

4. It makes us happy that tomorrow is a holiday

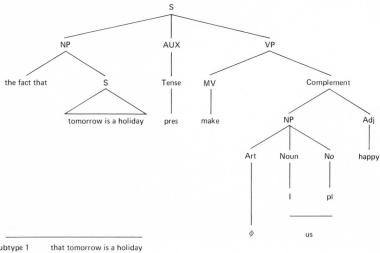

by subtype 1   that tomorrow is a holiday
nominalization rule:

by *it*-inversion rule: it pres make us happy that tomorrow is a holiday

by flip-flop rule: make   pres

          makes

5. It made me mad to be insulted by John.

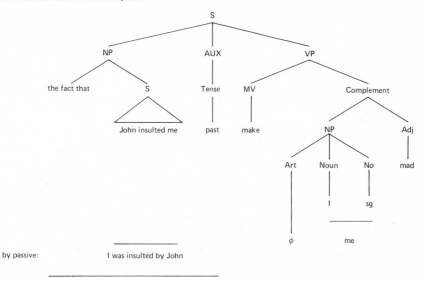

by passive: I was insulted by John

by subtype 3 nominalization rule: for I to be insulted by John

by *it*-inversion rule: it past make I mad for I to be insulted by John

by *for*-NP-deletion rule: φ

by flip-flop rule: make   past

                                                      made

CHAPTER 11

Sentences Embedded in Subordinating Adverbs

Overview

Certain types of adverbs can contain embedded sentences. The types discussed in this section are adverbs of reason, condition, time, and place. Sentences embedded in adverbs of reason and of condition are introduced by subordinating conjunctions, words like *because, as, since, unless, although, if.* For example:

Adverb of reason: We had to abandon the search, *as it was getting dark.*
Adverb of condition: You had better quit *unless you can do better than that.*

Sentences embedded in adverbs of time and of place, however, themselves begin with an adverb of time or place. For example:

Adverb of time: It was midnight *when he got back.*
Adverb of place: He saw ruined houses *everywhere he looked.*

It is reasonable to assume that sentences embedded in adverbs of time and of place contain, as part of their own structure, an adverb which is moved to the first position of the embedded sentence by a rule very similar to the question-word switch rule. For example, the embedded sentences given above would be derived from

He got back <u>SOMETIME</u> $\implies$ when he got back.
      when

He looked everywhere $\implies$ everywhere he looked.

This rule is called the "adverb switch rule."

This rule moves adverbs to the first position in the embedded sentence. This same rule also has another important use. It can also be optionally applied to the main sentence, that is, it can move the adverbs to the first position of main sentences. For example:

We had to abandon the search, *as it was getting dark* $\implies$
  As it was getting dark, we had to abandon the search.

SENTENCES EMBEDDED IN SUBORDINATING ADVERBS

Subordination is a process in which sentences embedded in certain types of adverbs are transformed into subordinating adverb clauses. There appear to be at least four such types of adverbs: *reason, condition, time,* and *place*. Here are some examples of each type:

Adverb of reason
  I stopped off for a hamburger *since I had missed my dinner.*
  He picked tuna *because it was cheaper.*
  We had to abandon the search, *as it was getting dark.*

Adverb of condition
  We will leave without him *if he does not get here soon.*
  You had better quit *unless you can do better than that.*
  I took my umbrella *even though it was not raining.*
  I decided to help him out *although it was against my better judgment.*
  She will come *even if you can't.*

Adverb of time
  Drop over *whenever you are free.*
  It was midnight *when he got back.*
  The phone started ringing *as soon as I stepped into the shower.*
  I noticed it was missing *after he left.*
  He called *before he came.*

Adverb of place
They bought fresh supplies *wherever they could.*
He collected samples *where the vegetation was especially thick.*

There seems to be a difference between sentences embedded as adverbs of reason and condition on the one hand and sentences embedded as adverbs of time and place on the other. The embedded sentences that function as adverbs of reason and condition are introduced by words like *because, since, unless,* and *although.* These introductory words are sometimes called subordinating conjunctions. These conjunctions do not appear to be an internal constituent of the embedded sentence. Let us agree, then, to represent adverbs of reason and condition as consisting of two subcomponents: a subordinating conjunction and an embedded sentence. For example,

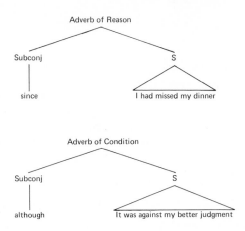

The adverbs of time and place do not contain conjunctive adverbs. Instead, the embedded sentence begins with question word, *when(ever)* or *where(ever)* or with a time expression, such as *before, as, as soon as, after.* Probably the most natural way to treat adverbs of time and place would be to assume that the embedded sentence must itself contain an adverb of time or place which is replaced by the appropriate question word or time expression. The question word or time expression is moved to the first position within its sentence by a rule parallel to the question-word switch rule. Let us call this new rule the "adverb switch rule." We may formalize the rule in the following way:

NP⌢Aux⌢MV⌢Comp⌢Adverb ⟹ Adverb⌢NP⌢Aux⌢MV⌢Comp

Some sample derivations employing this rule are shown on the opposite page.

It was midnight when he got back.

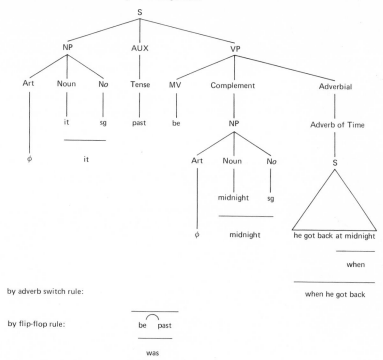

He collected samples where the vegetation was especially thick.

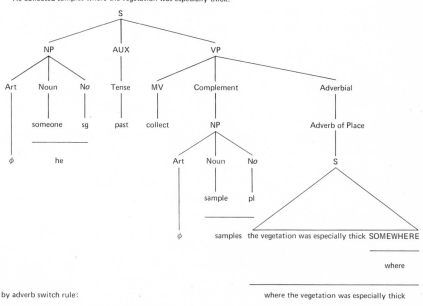

One of the basic characteristics of subordinating adverb clauses is that they can always be inverted, that is, they can be moved, as a unit, in front of the main sentence. For example,

Adverb of reason
> *Since I had missed my dinner,* I stopped off for a hamburger.
> *Because it was cheaper,* he picked tuna.
> *As it was getting dark,* we had to abandon the search.

Adverb of condition
> *If he does not get here soon,* we will leave without him.
> *Unless you can do better than that,* you had better quit.
> *Even though it was not raining,* I took my umbrella.
> *Although it was against my better judgment,* I decided to help him out.
> *Even if you can't,* she will come.

Adverb of time
> *Whenever you are free,* drop over.
> *When he got back,* it was midnight.
> *As soon as I stepped into the shower,* the phone started ringing.
> *After he left,* I noticed it was missing.
> *Before he came,* he called.

Adverb of place
> *Wherever they could,* they bought fresh supplies.
> *Where the vegetation was especially thick,* he collected samples.

The formalization of this rule should look quite familiar:

$$\overset{\frown}{NP} \overset{\frown}{AUX} \overset{\frown}{MV} \overset{\frown}{Comp} Adverb \implies Adverb \overset{\frown}{NP} \overset{\frown}{AUX} \overset{\frown}{MV} \overset{\frown}{Comp}$$

This rule is simply another application of the adverb switch rule that we applied to embedded sentences containing either an adverb of place or an adverb of time. In the first case, it is an obligatory rule for the embedded sentence. In the second case, it is an optional rule for the main sentence. The dual use of the same basic rule is a vivid example of the enormous generalizing power of transformational rules. Some sample derivations of inverted sentences are shown on pages 267–268.

Notice that in the derivation of the first sentence we have an option about which of the two identical noun phrases to replace by a pronoun; we can have either

Because tuna was cheaper, he picked it.

or

Because it was cheaper, he picked tuna.

Because it was cheaper, he picked tuna.

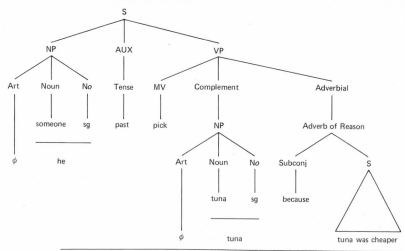

by adverb switch rule: because tuna was cheaper he past pick tuna

by flip-flop rule: pick   past

                                                          picked

Wherever there was a good hotel, we spent the night.

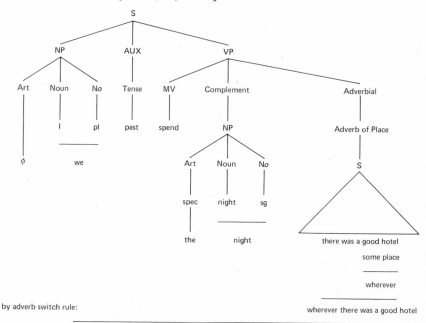

by adverb switch rule: wherever there was a good hotel

by adverb switch rule: wherever there was a good hotel, we past spend the night

by flip-flop rule: spend   past

                                                       spent

Even though it was not raining, I took my umbrella.

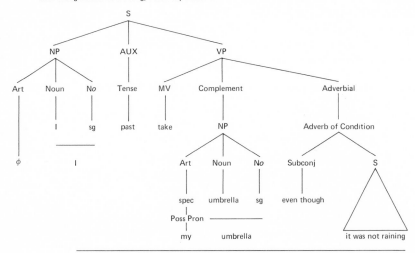

by adverb switch rule: even though it was not raining, I past take my umbrella

by flip-flop rule: take ⌢ past

                                                      took

Before he came, he called.

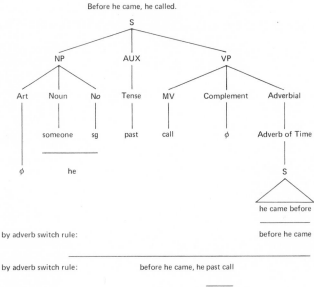

by adverb switch rule: before he came

by adverb switch rule: before he came, he past call

by flip-flop rule: call ⌢ past

                                              called

**Exercise 30 / SENTENCES EMBEDDED IN
SUBORDINATING ADVERBS**

Draw phrase structures and apply the necessary transformational rules to
produce the following sentences.

1. The soldiers pitched their tents wherever they could get the stakes in
   the ground.
2. He failed the exam because he didn't study hard enough.
3. If you can't come, John will give me a call.
4. Whenever I wash my car, it starts raining.
5. Every time I drive into Baltimore, I lose my way.

**Answers to Exercise 30 / SENTENCES EMBEDDED IN
SUBORDINATING ADVERBS**

1. The soldiers pitched their tents wherever they could get the stakes in the ground.

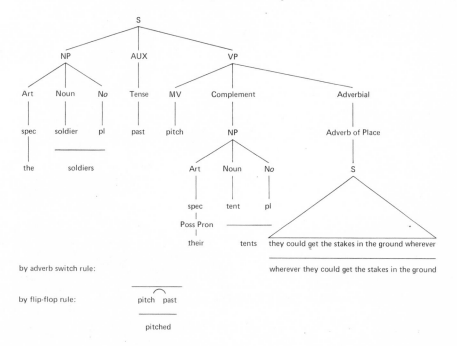

2. He failed the exam because he didn't study hard enough.

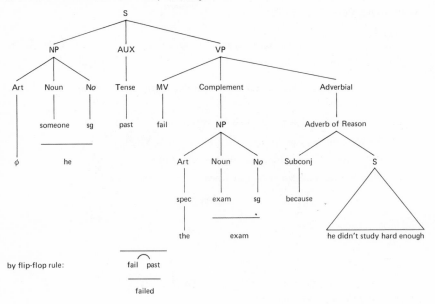

by flip-flop rule:

fail ⌢ past

failed

3. If you can't come, John will give me a call.

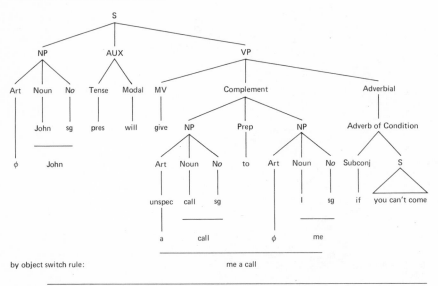

by object switch rule: me a call

by adverb switch rule: if you can't come, John pres will give me a call

by flip-flop rule: will ⌢ pres

will

4. Whenever I wash my car, it starts raining.

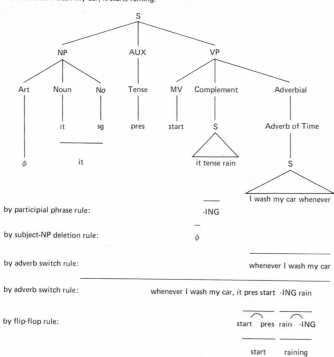

by participial phrase rule:		-ING
by subject-NP deletion rule:		φ
by adverb switch rule:		whenever I wash my car
by adverb switch rule:	whenever I wash my car, it pres start -ING rain	
by flip-flop rule:	start pres rain -ING	
	start raining	

5. Every time I drive into Baltimore, I lose my way.

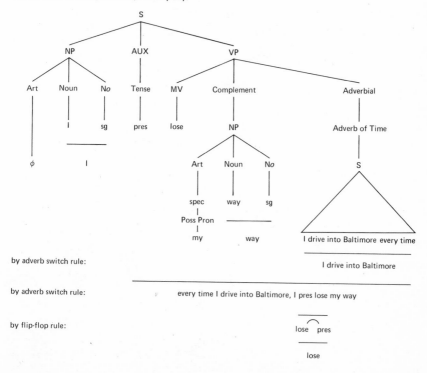

by adverb switch rule:	I drive into Baltimore
by adverb switch rule:	every time I drive into Baltimore, I pres lose my way
by flip-flop rule:	lose pres
	lose

271

part

four

SENTENCES
COMBINED BY
JOINING RULES

Overview

The joining rules combine together two independently generated sentences in such a way that one sentence is not subordinated to the other. Three different ways of joining sentences are discussed: (1) coordination, (2) conjunction, and (3) comparison.

Coordination is undoubtedly the most commonly used way of joining two independent sentences together; the two sentences are merely placed side by side with a coordinating conjunction (*and, but, or*) between them. That part of the operation is certainly simple enough. However, the process of coordination becomes much more complex when the second sentence contains one or more elements that are identical with the corresponding elements of the first sentence. In this case, we produce what traditional grammar calls a "compound sentence." A compound sentence contains two elements of the same grammatical type joined by *and*. For example, we can have compound noun phrases *John and Mary* or compound verb phrases, as in the sentence

She *married the prince* and *lived happily ever after.*

The process of conjunction joins two sentences together with what are called conjunctive adverbs (*however* and *therefore*, for example). The discussion in this section deals with the difference between conjunction and sentences embedded in adverbs or, put another way, the difference between conjunctive adverbs and subordinating conjunctions (words like *because* and *although*).

The last chapter in the book deals with comparison. There are two quite distinct kinds of comparison: the comparative (*John is older than his sister*); and the superlative (*John is the oldest in his family*). Strangely enough, the ways the two different kinds of comparison are formed have virtually nothing to do with each other.

CHAPTER 12

Coordination

Overview

In this chapter, the process of joining two independent sentences together by means of the coordinating conjunction *and* is discussed. Coordination involves three operations: (1) joining the two sentences together with *and* (the "coordination joining rule"), (2) deleting all parts of the second sentence that are identical with the corresponding parts of the first sentence (the "duplicate deletion rule"), and (3), if necessary, moving what is left of the second sentence into the proper place in the first sentence (the "residue switch rule"). For example, the sentence

The crowd laughed and jeered at the fighters

is derived from two underlying sentences:

S_1: The crowd laughed at the fighters.
S_2: The crowd jeered at the fighters.

By the coordination joining rule the two sentences are joined by *and:*

The crowd laughed at the fighters *and* the crowd jeered at the fighters.

By the duplicate deletion rule all parts of the second sentence that are duplicates of the corresponding parts of the first sentence are deleted, producing

The crowd laughed at the fighters and jeered.

Finally, the *and* along with the surviving part of the original second sentence (*jeered* in this case) are moved to the proper place in the first sentence by the residue switch rule.

A type of ambiguity results from an adjective that may or may not modify the second of two coordinated noun phrases. The classic example is *old men and women*. It is unclear whether *old* modifies just *men* or both *men* and *women*. The final topic in the chapter also involves coordinated noun phrases. Certain noun phrases joined with *and* have the meaning 'together with'. A clear-cut example is found in the sentence

If you combine hydrogen and oxygen, you will get water.

This *and* is assumed not to be originated by the process of coordination at all, but rather from a phrase structure rule of this sort

NP $\longrightarrow$ NP and NP.

COORDINATION

Coordination means joining two sentences with the coordinating conjunctions *and, or, but.* Each of the three coordinating conjunctions has its own special range of meanings and privileges of occurrence. In this discussion we will be concerned only with *and.*

The basic process of coordination is simple: the two sentences being coordinated are matched with each other. All elements of the second sentence that are the same as the corresponding elements of the first sentence are deleted while all elements of the second sentence that are different from the corresponding element in the first sentence are retained. Let us take as our first example a pair of sentences that have no elements in common.

S_1: John sang.
S_2: Mary danced.
S_1 and S_2: John sang and Mary danced.

Here is an example where the subject noun phrases of the two sentences are identical while the verb phrases are not:

S_1: John sang.
S_2: John danced.
S_1 and S_2: John sang and John danced $\Longrightarrow$ John sang and danced.

Here is an example with identical verb phrases:

S_1: John sang.
S_2: Mary sang.
S_1 and S_2: John sang and Mary sang $\Longrightarrow$ John and Mary sang.

Here is an example with identical subjects and identical verb phrases, but with different modal auxiliaries:

S_1: John can sing.
S_2: John will sing.
S_1 and S_2: John can sing and John will sing $\Longrightarrow$ John can and will sing.

The process of coordination depends on our ability to recognize when an element in one sentence "corresponds" to an element in the second sentence. Chomsky gives an example in *Syntactic Structures* of a pair of sentences that cannot be grammatically coordinated because the corresponding elements play different grammatical roles in their underlying sentences:

S_1: The scene of the movie was in Chicago.
S_2: The scene that I wrote was in Chicago.
S_1 and S_2: The scene of the movie was in Chicago and the scene that
    I wrote was in Chicago $\Longrightarrow$ °The scene of the movie and that I
                                    wrote was in Chicago.

One of the side effects of coordination is that the resulting sentence is often ambiguous. One type of ambiguity results from two different underlying second sentences producing the same surface. A classic example is the phrase *old men and women,* which is ambiguous because *old* may modify both *men* and *women* or just *men* alone. The surface sentence

Save the old men and women first!

has two different interpretations depending on the nature of the second underlying sentence. One interpretation would derive from this pair of underlying sentences containing *old* in the second sentence:

S_1: Save the old men first!
S_2: Save the old women first!
S_1 and S_2: Save the old men first and save the old women first $\Longrightarrow$
    Save the old men and women first!

The other interpretation would derive from an underlying second sentence that did not contain *old* at all:

S_1: Save the old men first!
S_2: Save the women first!
S_1 and S_2: Save the old men first and save the women first $\Longrightarrow$
    Save the old men and women first!

Certain noun phrases joined with *and* have a special meaning of 'together with'. For example:

If you combine hydrogen *and* oxygen, you will get water.
John *and* Mary sang a duet together.
Mix one part of vinegar *and* two parts of olive oil.

Probably the simplest way to account for this use of *and* would be to derive it from a single underlying sentence, that is, the subject noun phrase *John and Mary* in the sentence

John and Mary sang a duet together

would *not* be derived from the coordination of these two underlying sentences:

S₁: ° John sang a duet together.
S₂: ° Mary sang a duet together.
S₁ and S₂: ° John sang a duet together and ° Mary sang a duet to-
gether $\Longrightarrow$ John and Mary sang a duet together.

Rather it would be derived from an optional phrase structure rule of this sort:

NP $\Longrightarrow$ NP *and* NP.

In a phrase structure tree, we would represent the operation of the rule like this:

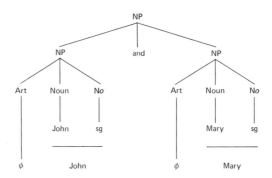

Since the two different rules produce exactly the same surface strings, sentences containing the sequence *Noun Phrase and Noun Phrase* are often ambiguous. For example, the sentence

I called up John and Mary

can mean either (a) that I made one call to John and another call to Mary: a total of two calls, or (b) that I made a single call to John and Mary's house. Here is how the grammar would reflect the two different interpretations:

Meaning (a) (two calls)
  S_1: I called up John.
  S_2: I called up Mary
  S_1 and S_2: I called up John and I called up Mary $\Longrightarrow$ I called up
                                                    John and Mary.

Meaning (b) (one call)

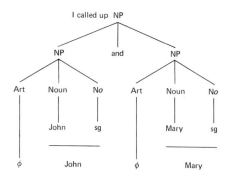

Up to this point we have not attempted to formalize the rules for coordinating sentences. Let us begin by drawing a possible phrase structure tree for the sentence we have just discussed—*I called up John and Mary*—in its first meaning of two separate calls:

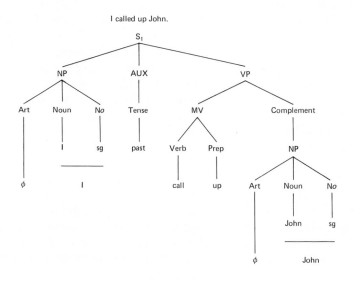

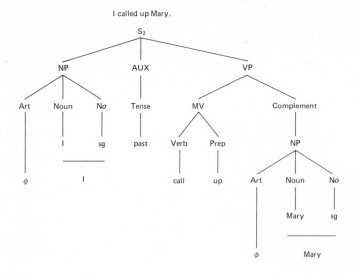

I called up Mary.

Let us call the rule that joins two sentences together with a coordinating conjunction "the coordination joining rule." This rule merely inserts one of the coordinating conjunctions between the two sentences. For example, when applied to the two underlying sentences above, it would produce

I past call up John *and* I past call up Mary.

We now need a deletion rule which will remove from the second sentence all those elements that are an exact duplicate of the corresponding element in the first sentence. Notice that "exact duplicate" implies not only identity of actual words, but also identity of function, that is, the duplicate words must come from exactly the same abstract elements (for example, Noun Phrase, Aux, Verb Phrase, and so on). This rule needs to be so general that it is difficult to formalize. Accordingly, we will simply invoke this rule as needed without further formalization. Let us call it the "duplicate deletion rule." Applying this rule to our sentence, we produce

I past call up John and I past call up Mary $\implies$ I past call up John and Mary.

It is now necessary to add another rule. We need to attach whatever remains of the second sentence to the corresponding element of the first sentence. Let us call this rule the "residue switch rule." Applying this rule to the sentence on the opposite page, we produce the derived phrase structure tree shown on page 282.

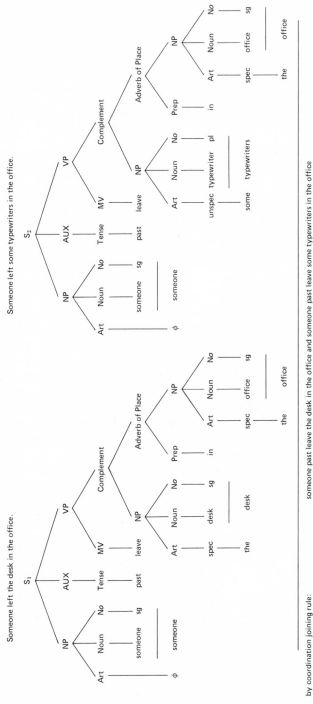

281

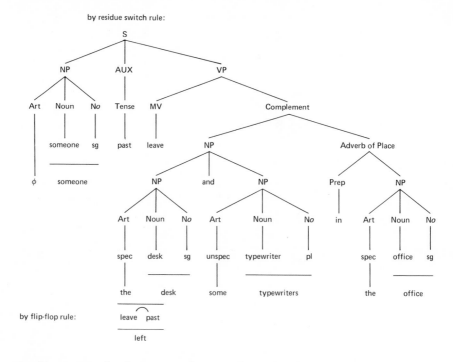

by residue switch rule:

by flip-flop rule:

At this point in the derivation, the second sentence has been obliterated. The parts of it that were identical with the first sentence have been deleted, and the parts that are not identical have been inserted in the phrase structure tree of the first sentence. Here are some more sample derivations:

The author and the producer collaborated on the script.

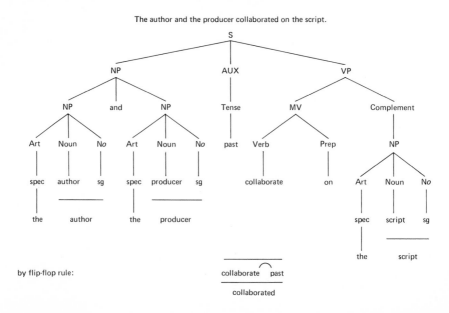

by flip-flop rule:

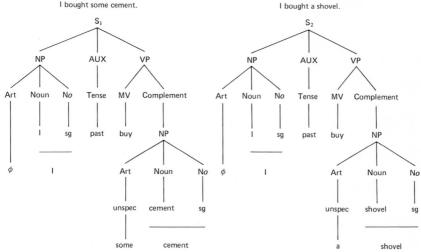

by coordination joining rule: I past buy some cement and I past buy a shovel

by duplicate deletion rule: ϕ

by flip-flop rule: buy ⌒ past
                                 _____
                                   bought

John and Mary are cousins.

by flip-flop rule: be ⌒ pres
                                 _____
                                   are

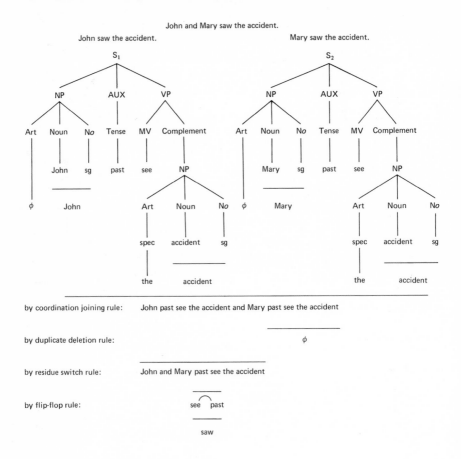

by coordination joining rule: John past see the accident and Mary past see the accident

by duplicate deletion rule: φ

by residue switch rule: John and Mary past see the accident

by flip-flop rule: see past

                          saw

Exercise 31 / COORDINATION

Draw the phrase structures and apply the necessary transformational rules to produce the following sentences:

1. John smiled and shrugged his shoulders.
2. I went up this side and down that side.
3. John and Mary are similar.
4. A fire truck and a police car followed the ambulance.
5. He mailed the package and the bills to the store. (separately)

Answers to Exercise 31 / **COORDINATION**

1. John smiled and shrugged his shoulders.

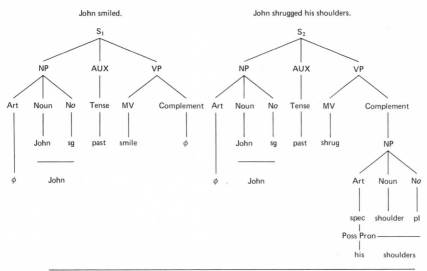

John smiled.　　　　　　　　John shrugged his shoulders.

---

by coordination joining rule:　　　John past smile and John past shrug his shoulders

by duplicate deletion rule:　　　　　　　　　φ

by flip-flop rule:　　　　smile⌢past　　shrug⌢past

　　　　　　　　　　　　　smiled　　　　shrugged

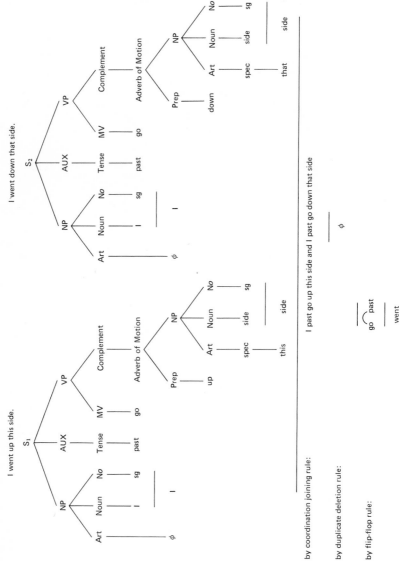

2. I went up this side and down that side.

I went up this side.

I went down that side.

by coordination joining rule:

I past go up this side and I past go down that side

by duplicate deletion rule:

ϕ

by flip-flop rule:

3. John and Mary are similar.

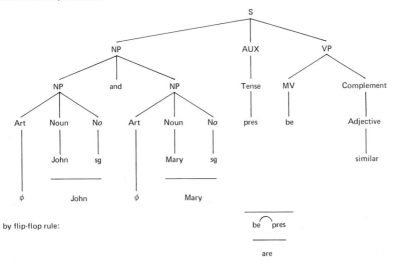

by flip-flop rule:

$$be \frown pres$$

$$are$$

4. A fire truck and a police car followed the ambulance.

A fire truck followed the ambulance. A police car followed the ambulance.

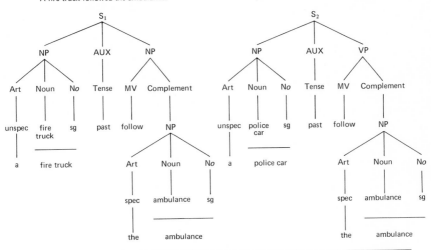

by coordination joining rule: a fire truck past follow the ambulance and a police car past follow the ambulance

by duplicate deletion rule: ϕ

by residue switch rule: a fire truck and a police car past follow the ambulance

by flip-flop rule: $follow \frown past$

$followed$

5. He mailed the package and the bills to the store.
   He mailed the package to the store.
   He mailed the bills to the store.

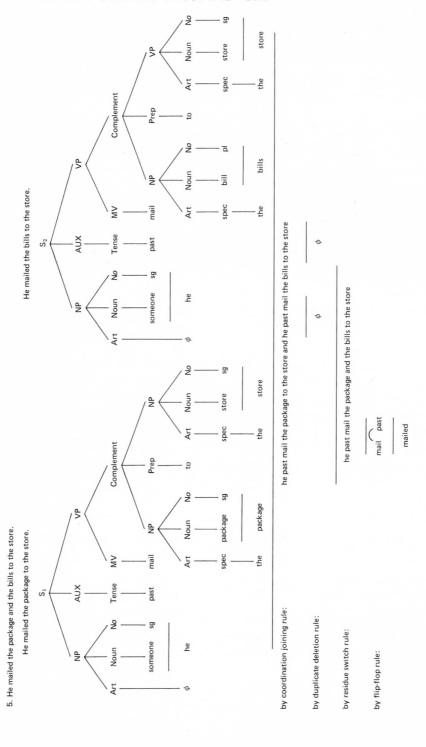

by coordination joining rule: he past mail the package to the store and he past mail the bills to the store

by duplicate deletion rule: φ   φ

by residue switch rule: he past mail the package and the bills to the store

by flip-flop rule: mail ⌢ past → mailed

CHAPTER 13

Conjunction

Overview

Conjunction joins two independent sentences together with a conjunctive adverb, (*however, therefore,* and *consequently,* for example). Conjunctive adverbs superficially resemble subordinating conjunctions (*because, since,* and *although,* for example). Recall that sentences containing subordinating conjunctions can undergo the adverb switch rule which places the embedded adverb clause at the beginning of the sentence. For example:

John was at the scene, although he did not see the accident.

is transformed into

Although John did not see the accident, he was at the scene.

When this same rule is applied to sentences joined together by a conjunctive adverb, the result is ungrammatical:

John was at the scene; however, he did not see the accident $\Longrightarrow$
° However John did not see the accident, he was at the scene.

Sentences joined together by conjunctive adverbs differ in another respect from embedded sentences functioning as adverbs. The conjunctive adverb can be moved to any of several positions within the second sentence. For example we can change

John was at the scene; however, he did not see the accident.

into

John was at the scene; he did not, however, see the accident.
John was at the scene; he did not see the accident, however.

When we attempt to change the position of the subordinating conjunction within its sentence, the result is ungrammatical:

° John was at the scene, he did not, although, see the accident.
° John was at the scene, he did not see the accident, although.

CONJUNCTION

By the process known as conjunction, two independent sentences are joined together by a "conjunctive adverb." Conjunctive adverbs are words like *consequently, however, moreover, nevertheless,* and *therefore.* Here are some examples of sentences linked by conjunction:

S_1: John was at the scene.
S_2: He did not see the accident.
S_1 conjunction S_2: John was at the scene; *however,* he did not see the accident.

S_1: John was at the scene.
S_2: He must have seen the accident.
S_1 conjunction S_2: John was at the scene; *consequently,* he must have seen the accident.

S_1: John was at the scene.
S_2: He must have seen the accident.
S_1 conjunction S_2: John was at the scene; *therefore,* he must have seen the accident.

S_1: John was at the scene.
S_2: He did not see the accident.
S_1 conjunction S_2: John was at the scene; *nevertheless,* he did not see the accident.

S_1: John was at the scene.
S_2: He saw the accident.
S_1 conjunction S_2: John was at the scene; *moreover,* he saw the accident.

Notice that the second sentence does not undergo any deletion of elements that are identical with elements in the first sentence. In this respect, conjunction differs from both coordination and comparison. The only difficult thing about conjunction is telling conjunctive adverbs apart from subordinating conjunctions (words like *because, since, unless,* and *although*).

In the discussion of sentences embedded in subordinating adverbs, it was pointed out that one of the characteristics of embedded subordinating adverbs was the ability of the entire subordinating adverb to undergo the adverb switch rule. This rule converts a sentence from this form

John was at the scene, although he did not see the accident.

into this form

Although he did not see the accident, John was at the scene.

When we apply the adverb switch rule to the conjoined sentences above, the results are ungrammatical:

   ° However, John did not see the accident, he was at the scene.
   ° Consequently, John must have seen the accident, he was at the scene.
   ° Therefore, John must have seen the accident, he was at the scene.
   ° Nevertheless, John did not see the accident, he was at the scene.
   ° Moreover, John saw the accident, he was at the scene.

The second (or conjoined) sentence cannot be moved, but the conjunctive adverb can. By what we will call the "conjunctive adverb switch rule," the conjunctive adverb usually can be moved to any of several positions in the middle of the second sentence or clear to the end. For example:

Middle of the embedded sentence:
   John was at the scene; he did not, *however,* see the accident.
   John was at the scene; he must, *consequently,* have seen the accident.
   John was at the scene; he, *therefore,* must have seen the accident.
   John was at the scene; he did not, *nevertheless,* see the accident.
   John was at the scene; he, *moreover,* saw the accident.

End of the embedded sentence:
   John was at the scene; he did not see the accident, *however.*
   John was at the scene; he must have seen the accident, *consequently.*
   John was at the scene; he must have seen the accident, *therefore.*
   John was at the scene; he did not see the accident, *nevertheless.*
   John was at the scene; he saw the accident, *moreover.*

If we apply this switching rule to the subordinating conjunctions that introduce subordinated embedded sentences, the results are always clearly ungrammatical:

Middle of the embedded sentence:
   ° He picked tuna, it, *because,* was cheaper.
   ° He picked tuna, it was, *because,* cheaper.
   ° You had better quit, you, *unless,* can do better than that.
   ° You had better quit, you can, *unless,* do better than that.

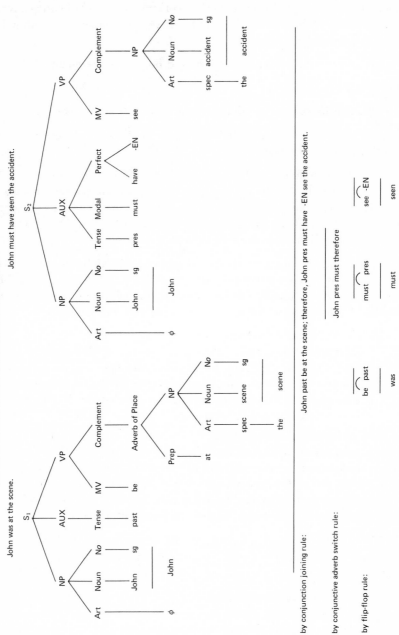

John was at the scene; he must, therefore, have seen the accident.

John was at the scene.

John must have seen the accident.

by conjunction joining rule: John past be at the scene; therefore, John pres must have -EN see the accident.

by conjunctive adverb switch rule: John pres must therefore

by flip-flop rule:

End of the embedded sentence:

   ° He picked tuna, it was cheaper, *because.*
   ° You had better quit, you can do better than that, *unless.*

A sample derivation of conjoined sentences is shown on page 292.

Exercise 32 / CONJUNCTION

Relying on the adverb switch rule and the conjunctive adverb switch rule, establish for each of the following sentences whether the italicized word or phrase is a subordinating conjunction or a conjunctive adverb:

1. John answered the phone *therefore* he knew it wasn't for him.
               although
               however
               nevertheless
               even though
               despite the fact that
2. I was discouraged *consequently* I was coming down with a cold.
               because
               also
               since
               moreover
               as

Answers to Exercise 32 / CONJUNCTION

1. *therefore*—conjunctive adverb
although—subordinating conjunction
however—conjunctive adverb
nevertheless—conjunctive adverb
even though—subordinating conjunction
despite the fact that—subordinating conjunction

2. *consequently*—conjunctive adverb
because—subordinating conjunction
also—conjunctive adverb
since—subordinating conjunction
moreover—conjunctive adverb
as—subordinating conjunction

CHAPTER 14

Comparison

Overview

All adjectives and a few adverbs can enter into the process of comparison. There are two basically different types of comparison: the comparative and the superlative. Here is an example of each type:

Comparative: John is taller than Mary.
Superlative: John is the tallest boy in his class.

The rules governing the two types are quite different. We will deal here only with the comparative.

The basic assumption in the analysis presented here is that the comparative is derived from two underlying sentences joined together by *-er than, more than, as . . . as,* and a few other similar expressions. For example, the comparative sentence

John is taller than Mary.

is presumed to be derived from these two underlying sentences:

S_1: John is tall.
S_2: Mary is tall.

The first step in the process of comparison is to combine the two underlying sentences by the "comparative joining rule":

S_1 comparative S_2: John is tall *-er than* Mary is tall.

The next step is to apply the duplicate deletion rule to delete elements in the second sentence that are duplicates of the corresponding elements in the first sentence, producing the correct surface structure

John is taller than Mary.

However, it turns out that in a number of cases the duplicate deletion rule must be prohibited from applying. Considerable attention is given to stating the conditions under which the duplicate deletion rule applies to the second sentence. It is proposed that there is a right-to-left ordering of the application of the deletion rule. In other words, only the rightmost element in the second sentence may be deleted if it is a duplicate of the corresponding element in the first sentence. After the old rightmost element has been deleted, there is a new rightmost element, which may be deleted if it is a duplicate of the corresponding element in the first sentence, and so on until the duplicate deletion rule cannot apply, at which point the whole process must halt.

One consequence of this right-to-left ordering is that no deletion of elements from the middle of the second sentence can take place unless the rightmost element is identical and has been deleted. For example, the following comparative sentence is ungrammatical because the rightmost element of the second sentence has not been deleted but a duplicate element from the middle of the sentence has been deleted:

 * John is taller than his father wide.

Notice that similar sentences joined by coordination allow the deletion of duplicate elements from the middle of the second sentence:

John is tall and his father wide.

THE COMPARATIVE

Here are some sentences formed by the comparative process:

With adjectives:
    John is taller than his father is wide.
    John looks as mean as his father did.
    John looks older than he is.
    John is as tall as his father.
    John seems to be taller than his father.
    John is less tall than his father.

With adverbs:
    John goes fishing more often than his father does.
    John behaved as badly as his father.
    John plays golf better than his father.

The comparative process involves two underlying sentences, which we will call S_1 and S_2. Both sentences must contain a predicate adjective or both must have one of the adverbs that can be compared. For example, the comparative sentence

John is taller than his father is wide.

is composed of these two underlying sentences:

S_1: John is tall.
S_2: His father is wide.

In this case we will join S_1 and S_2 together with the sequence *-er than* by a rule we will call the "comparative joining rule." Other ways we might have joined them together are *as . . . as; more . . . than; less . . . than.* Both *-er than* and *more than* mean the same thing. All one-syllable adjectives and adverbs form their comparative by using *-er than.* All three syllable adjectives and adverbs form their comparative by using *more . . . than.* With two-syllable adjectives, the rule of thumb is that if the adjective ends in *-y*, the comparative will be *-er than,* for example, *busy–busier; happy–happier.* If the two-syllable adjective ends in anything besides *-y*, it normally takes the *more . . . than* form, for example, *serious–more serious than; rapid–more rapid than.* From this point on we will assume the correct selection and placement of the words that join the two underlying sentences.

As with coordination, elements of the second sentence that are identical with the corresponding elements of the first sentence are deleted. However, in the case of the comparative, this deletion takes place only under certain conditions.

In order to show the difference between comparative and coordination, let us take the same two underlying sentences given above and join them with *and:*

S_1: John is tall.
S_2: His father is wide.
S_1 and S_2: John is tall and his father is wide.

Under the duplicate deletion rule, repetitions of identical elements in the second sentence, (*pres be* in this case) are deleted, producing:

John is tall and his father wide.

If we apply the same deletion operation to the second sentence when the two sentences are joined by the comparative, the result is ungrammatical. For example,

S_1: John is tall.
S_2: His father is wide.
S_1 comparative S_2: John is taller than his father is wide.

Deleting the repetition of *pres be,* we get

     * John is taller than his father wide.

On the basis of this example, it would appear that the duplicate deletion rule is not used in the comparative. However, let us now take the case where the two predicate adjectives are identical:

S_1: John is tall.
S_2: His father is tall.
S_1 comparative S_2: John is taller than his father is tall.

Here we must apply the duplicate deletion rule to the repeated adjective, producing

     John is taller than his father is.

Notice that now we may also delete the repeated *pres be,* producing

     John is taller than his father.

In this example it was possible to delete the tense and main verb from the second underlying sentence while in the previous example it was not, even though in both cases the tense and main verb in the second underlying sentence were identical with the tense and main verb in the first underlying sentence. We may conclude that the duplicate deletion rule operates under more complex conditions in the comparative than it did when sentences were joined with coordination.

At this point we might be led to the conclusion that the deletion of the tense and main verb is permitted only on the condition that the predicate adjective is also deleted. This is correct as far as it goes. However, consider the following comparative sentence:

S_1: John *pres* look mean.
S_2: His father *pres* look mean.
S_1 comparative S_2: John *pres* look as mean as his father *pres* look mean.

The surface sentence must delete the duplicate predicate adjective *mean,* producing

     John looks as mean as his father looks.

While this sentence is grammatical, as it stands, we can also delete the duplicate main verb *look,* producing either

     John looks as mean as his father.

if the duplicate tense is deleted also, or

     John looks as mean as his father does.

if the tense is retained. (The *do*-insertion rule applies automatically.)

We may account for the use of the duplicate deletion rule with comparative sentences by means of a single general condition: in comparative sentences, only the rightmost identical element can be deleted. In other words if the two predicate adjectives are not identical, no deletion can take place from the second sentence. This is why the repeated $\underset{\text{is}}{\underline{pres\ be}}$ cannot be deleted from *John is taller than his father is wide*. However, when the repeated adjective is deleted, the verb is now the rightmost element, and can be deleted if it is identical to the verb in the first sentence. For example:

S_1: John *pres* look mean.
S_2: His father *pres* look mean.
S_1 comparative S_2: John *pres* look as mean as his father *pres* look mean.

Since the rightmost element is identical with the corresponding element in the first sentence, we may delete the second *mean*, producing

John *pres* look as mean as his father *pres* look.

Now the rightmost element in the second sentence is the main verb *look*, which is a repetition of the main verb in the first sentence. By applying the duplicate deletion rule again we generate

John *pres* look as mean as his father *pres*.

By the *do*-insertion (and flip-flop) rule, the above sentence would be transformed into

John $\underset{\text{looks}}{\underline{pres\ look}}$ as mean as his father $\underset{\text{does}}{\underline{pres\ do}}$.

The above sentence can come to the surface in still another way. Before the *do*-insertion rule is applied, the tense is the rightmost element in the second sentence. If the tense in the second sentence is identical with the tense in the first sentence, the repeated tense may be deleted producing

John $\underset{\text{looks}}{\underline{pres\ look}}$ as mean as his father.

Here are some sample derivations:

John is older than he looks.

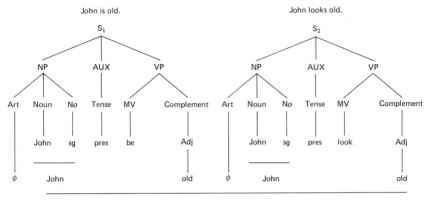

John is old.

John looks old.

by comparative joining rule: John pres be old -ER than John pres look old
                                                                                        he

by duplicate deletion rule: φ

by flip-flop rule: be pres   look pres

                               is   look

John is older than Mary.

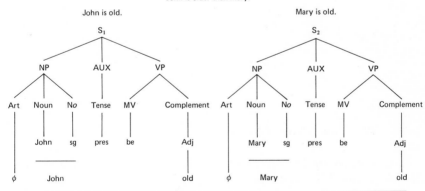

John is old.

Mary is old.

by comparative joining rule: John pres be old -ER than Mary pres be old.

by duplicate deletion rule: φ   φ   φ

by flip-flop rule: be pres

                               is

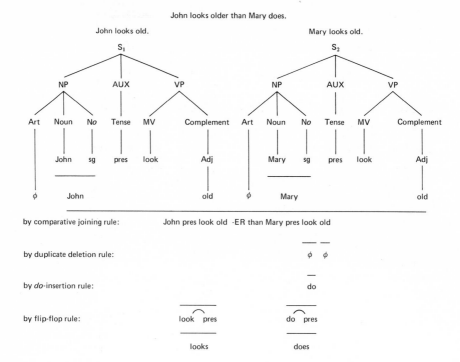

John looks older than Mary does.

John looks old.

Mary looks old.

by comparative joining rule: John pres look old -ER than Mary pres look old

by duplicate deletion rule: φ φ

by *do*-insertion rule: do

by flip-flop rule: look pres   do pres

                            looks   does

Exercise 33 / THE COMPARATIVE

Draw the phrase structures and apply the necessary transformational rules to produce the following sentences:

1. John is dumber than Bill is smart.
2. John is faster than Bill was.
3. John is quicker than Bill.
4. John seemed younger than Bill.
5. John acted braver than Bill did.

Answers to Exercise 33 / THE COMPARATIVE

1. John is dumber than Bill is smart.

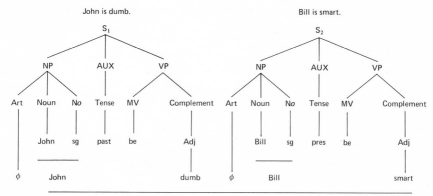

by comparative joining rule: John pres be dumb -ER than Bill pres be smart

2. John is faster than Bill was.

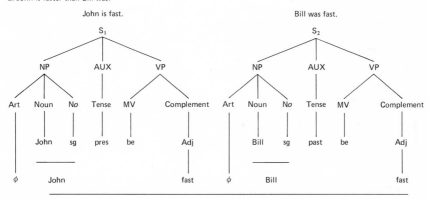

3. John is quicker than Bill.

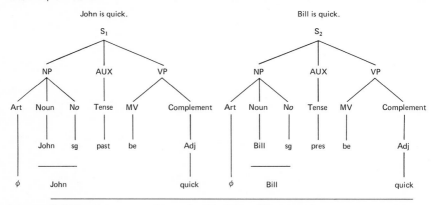

John is quick.   Bill is quick.

by comparative joining rule: John pres be quick -ER than Bill pres be quick

by duplicate deletion rule: φ   φ   φ

by flip-flop rule: be   pres

                                        is

4. John seemed younger than Bill.

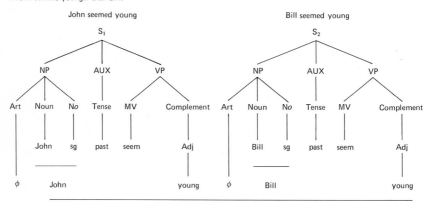

John seemed young   Bill seemed young

by comparative joining rule: John past seem young -ER than Bill past seem young

by duplicate deletion rule: φ   φ   φ

by flip-flop rule: seem   past

                                        seemed

5. John acted braver than Bill did.

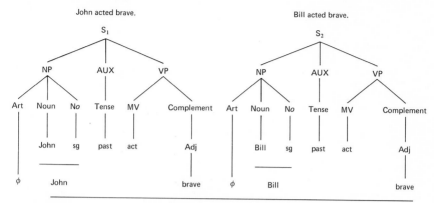

John acted brave.   Bill acted brave.

by comparative joining rule: John past act brave -ER than Bill past act brave

by duplicate deletion rule: φ   φ

by *do*-insertion rule: do

by flip-flop rule: act⌢past   do⌢past

                                acted   did

APPENDIXES

Summary of Rules

PART ONE / SIMPLE PHRASE STRUCTURE RULES

S $\longrightarrow$ NP͡ Aux͡ VP (p. 33)

Chapter 1 / The Noun Phrase

NP $\longrightarrow$ Art͡ Noun͡ No (p. 36)

Art $\longrightarrow$ $\left\{\begin{array}{l} \text{Specified} \\ \text{Unspecified} \\ \emptyset \end{array}\right\}$

Specified $\longrightarrow$ $\left\{\begin{array}{l} \textit{the, this, that,} \\ \textit{these, those;} \\ \text{possessive nouns} \\ \text{and possessive} \\ \text{pronouns} \end{array}\right\}$

Unspecified $\longrightarrow$ $\left\{\begin{array}{l} \textit{a/an, some, a few,} \\ \textit{a couple, several,} \\ \textit{much, many} \ldots . \end{array}\right\}$

Noun $\longrightarrow$ {*boy, tree, idea, Mr. Brown, America* . . . . }

No $\longrightarrow$ $\left\{\begin{array}{l} \text{Sg} \\ \text{Pl} \end{array}\right\}$

Chapter 2 / The Auxiliary

Aux $\longrightarrow$ Tense⌒(Modal)⌒(Perfect)⌒(Progressive) (p. 54)

Tense $\longrightarrow$ $\begin{Bmatrix} \text{pres} \\ \text{past} \end{Bmatrix}$

Modal $\longrightarrow$ {*can, may, must, shall, will*}

Perfect $\longrightarrow$ *have*⌒-EN

Progressive $\longrightarrow$ *be*⌒-ING

Flip-flop rule (p. 71)

    Let Af = Tense, -EN, or -ING

    Af⌒Verb $\Longrightarrow$ Verb⌒Af

    Example: pres⌒*do* $\Longrightarrow$ $\underline{do⌒\text{pres}}$

                          does

Chapter 3 / Verb Phrase

VP $\longrightarrow$ Main Verb⌒Complement⌒(Adverbial) (p. 83)

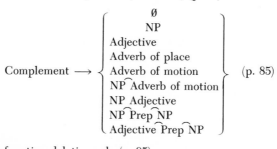

Complement $\longrightarrow$ $\left\{\begin{array}{l} \varnothing \\ \text{NP} \\ \text{Adjective} \\ \text{Adverb of place} \\ \text{Adverb of motion} \\ \text{NP⌒Adverb of motion} \\ \text{NP Adjective} \\ \text{NP⌒Prep⌒NP} \\ \text{Adjective⌒Prep⌒NP} \end{array}\right\}$ (p. 85)

Adverb-of-motion deletion rule (p. 95)

    MV⌒(NP)⌒prep$_1$⌒(prep$_2$)⌒NP $\Longrightarrow$ MV⌒(NP)⌒prep$_1$

    Example: The train pulled into the station $\Longrightarrow$ The train pulled in.

               I drove my car into the garage $\Longrightarrow$ I drove my car in.

Object switch rule (p. 99)

       (DO)   (IO)   (IO) (DO)

    MV⌒NP⌒Prep⌒NP $\Longrightarrow$ MV⌒NP⌒NP

    Example: He sent some flowers to her $\Longrightarrow$ He sent her some flowers.

Separable preposition switch rule (p. 106)

    MV⌒Prep⌒NP $\Longrightarrow$ MV⌒NP⌒Prep

    Example: John looked up the word $\Longrightarrow$ John looked the word up.

PART TWO / SIMPLE TRANSFORMATIONAL RULES

Chapter 4 / The Passive

Passive (p. 132)
    (1) NP switch rule: the subject NP and object NP change places.
    (2) *by*-insertion rule: *by* is inserted between MV and following NP.
    (3) *be* -EN insertion rule: *be* -EN is inserted between the last element of the Aux and the MV.

    Example: John *past* break the glass.
    by (1): The glass *past* break John.
    by (2): The glass *past* break by John.
    by (3): The glass *past be -EN break* by John
                        was   broken

Agent deletion rule (p. 133)
    be $\frown$ -EN $\frown$ MV $\frown$ by $\frown$ NP $\Longrightarrow$ be $\frown$ -EN $\frown$ MV
    Example: The glass was broken by John $\Longrightarrow$ The glass was broken.

Chapter 5 / Questions

Yes-no question switch rule 1 (p. 146)
    Let V_{aux} = the first optional element in the Aux *or*, if no optional element has been selected, the Main Verb *be*.
    NP $\frown$ Tense $\frown$ V_{aux} $\Longrightarrow$ Tense $\frown$ V_{aux} $\frown$ NP
    Example: John past may come $\Longrightarrow$ past may John come?
                                  might
             John pres be crazy $\Longrightarrow$ pres be John crazy?
                                    is

Yes-no question switch rule 2 (p. 146)
    NP $\frown$ Tense $\Longrightarrow$ Tense $\frown$ NP
    Example: John past laugh $\Longrightarrow$ past John laugh?

Do-insertion rule (p. 147)
    Let X = any element *except* a verb
    Tense $\frown$ X $\Longrightarrow$ Tense $\frown$ *do* $\frown$ X
    Example: past John laugh $\Longrightarrow$ past do John laugh?
                                  did

Question-word switch rule (p. 151)
    Question word is moved to the first position of the sentence.
    Example: pres have you -EN be where $\Longrightarrow$ where pres have you -EN be?
                                           have   been

Chapter 6 / Negative Statements

Not-insertion rule (p. 162)

Let V_{aux} be defined as in the *yes-no* question switch rule 1.

1: Tense V_{aux} $\Longrightarrow$ Tense $\frown$ V_{aux} $\frown$ *not*

2: Tense $\frown$ MV $\Longrightarrow$ Tense $\frown$ *not* $\frown$ MV

Example 1: Mary pres have -EN finish $\Longrightarrow$ Mary pres have not -EN finish.
               has   finished

2: I past listen $\Longrightarrow$ I past not listen.

Question tag rule (p. 164)

(a) The main sentence contains *not*:

$$\text{NP} \frown \text{Tense} \frown \begin{bmatrix} do \\ V_{aux} \end{bmatrix} \frown not \frown \text{X} \Longrightarrow \text{NP} \frown \text{Tense} \frown \begin{bmatrix} do \\ V_{aux} \end{bmatrix} \frown not \frown \text{X} \frown \text{Tense} \frown \underbrace{\begin{bmatrix} do \\ V_{aux} \end{bmatrix} \frown \text{NP}}_{\text{tag}}$$

Example: It isn't hot $\Longrightarrow$ It isn't hot, is it?
              It didn't rain $\Longrightarrow$ It didn't rain, did it?

(b) The main sentence does not contain *not*:

1: $\text{NP} \frown \text{Tense} \frown V_{aux} \frown \text{X} \Longrightarrow \text{NP} \frown \text{Tense} \frown V_{aux} \frown \text{X} \frown \underbrace{\text{Tense} \frown V_{aux} \frown not \frown \text{NP}}_{\text{tag}}$

Example: It is hot $\Longrightarrow$ It is hot, isn't it?

2: $\text{NP} \frown \text{Tense} \frown \text{X} \Longrightarrow \text{NP} \frown \text{Tense} \frown \text{X} \frown \underbrace{\text{Tense} \frown not \frown \text{NP}}_{\text{tag}}$

Example: It rained $\Longrightarrow$ It rained, past not it?

Chapter 7 / Emphasis and Commands

EMP insertion rule (p. 176)

Let V_{aux} be defined as in the *yes-no* question switch rule 1.

1: Tense $\frown$ V_{aux} $\Longrightarrow$ Tense $\frown$ V_{aux} $\frown$ EMP

Example: You must be quiet $\Longrightarrow$ You *múst* be quiet!

2: Tense $\frown$ MV $\Longrightarrow$ Tense $\frown$ EMP $\frown$ MV

Example: I past know the answer $\Longrightarrow$ I past EMP know the answer!

Cleft (p. 178)

The cleft is a way of emphasising whole grammatical elements. Here are several clefts applied to the sentence *the plane circled the field:*

Subject NP: What circled the field was *the plane.*
Object NP: What the plane circled was *the field.*
Whole VP: What the plane did was (to) *circle the field.*

Predicate (p. 179)

The predicate is a way of emphasising whole grammatical elements. Here are several predicate transformations applied to the sentence *John saw Mary at the park yesterday:*

Subject NP: It was *John* who saw Mary at the park yesterday.
Object NP: It was *Mary* that John saw at the park yesterday.
Adverb of Place: It was *at the park* that John saw Mary yesterday.
Adverb of Time: It was *yesterday* that John saw Mary at the park.

PART THREE / SENTENCES COMBINED BY EMBEDDING RULES

Chapter 8 / Sentences Embedded in the VP Complement

$$\text{Complement} \longrightarrow \left\{ \begin{array}{l} \text{Noun Clause Sentence} \\ \text{Question Word Sentence} \\ \text{Tenseless Sentence} \end{array} \right\} \text{(p. 189)}$$

Noun Clause Sentence $\longrightarrow$ (that)$\frown$S (p. 189)

Example: I know *that we will win.*
Question-Word Sentence (p. 192)

Example: I know *where John is.*

Tenseless Sentence (p. 195)

Type (1) Subject NP of embedded S must be identical with subject NP of main S.

Example: Alice failed to stop crying.

Type (2) Subject NP of embedded S may be different from subject NP of main S. If they are identical, the subject NP of the embedded S must be deleted.

Example: Alice wanted Humpty Dumpty to stop crying.
Alice wanted to stop crying. (Alice was crying.)

Type (3) Like (2) except if subject NP of embedded S is identical with subject NP of main S, subject NP of embedded S must be changed into a reflexive pronoun.

Example: Alice told herself to stop crying.

Infinitive phrase rule (p. 191)

NP$\frown$Tense$\frown$X $\Longrightarrow$ NP$\frown$*to*$\frown$X

Example: I recognized *he* Tense *be the house detective* $\Longrightarrow$
I recognized *him to be the house detective.*

Participial phrase rule (p. 196)

NP$\frown$Tense$\frown$X $\Longrightarrow$ NP$\frown$-ING$\frown$X

Example: Elliot admitted Elliot past eat a peach $\Longrightarrow$
Elliot admitted Elliot -ING eat a peach.

Subject NP deletion rule (p. 196)

$$\text{MV} \frown \text{NP} \frown \begin{bmatrix} to \\ \text{-ING} \end{bmatrix} \implies \text{MV} \frown \begin{bmatrix} to \\ \text{-ING} \end{bmatrix}$$

Example: Elliot admitted Elliot -ING eat a peach $\implies$
Elliot admitted <u>-*ING*</u> eat a peach.
eating

Adjective $\frown$ Tenseless Sentence Complement (p. 201)

Example: John was *eager to please us*.

For-insertion rule (p. 201)

$$\text{Adj} \frown \text{NP} \frown to \implies \text{Adj} \frown for \frown \text{NP} \frown to$$

Example: John was eager Bill to please us $\implies$
John was eager for Bill to please us.

To be-deletion rule (p. 205)

$$\text{NP} \frown to \; be \frown \text{NP} \implies \text{NP} \frown \text{NP}$$

Example: We elected Harry to be President $\implies$
We elected Harry President.

Chapter 9 / Noun Modification

NP modification (p. 223)

$$\text{NP} \longrightarrow \text{Art} \frown \text{Noun} \frown \text{No} \frown (\text{S})_1, \frown (\text{S})_2, \frown (\text{S})_3 \dots$$

Example: NP $\longrightarrow$ the boy sg *the boy is tall*.

Relative pronoun switch rule (p. 223)

Identical with the question-word switch rule.

Example: I saw the tree you told me about *that* $\implies$
I saw the tree *that* you told me about.

Relative pronoun deletion rule (p. 224)

Certain relative pronouns, after the application of the relative pronoun switch rule, may be deleted.

Example: I met a man *whom* your mother knows $\implies$
I met a man your mother knows.

Adjectival phrase rule (p. 226)

relative pronoun $\frown$ Tense $\implies$ -ING

Example: The man *who* Tense have drunk far too much $\implies$
The man <u>-*ING*</u> have drunk far too much.
having

Adjectival clause deletion rule (p. 227)

$$\text{NP} \frown \text{Tense} \frown be \implies \emptyset$$

Example: We fixed the crack *the crack is* in the chimney.
We fixed the crack in the chimney.

Adjective switch rule (p. 228)

Art⌢Noun⌢No⌢Adj ⟹ Art⌢Adj⌢Noun⌢No

Example: the owl sg yellow ⟹ the yellow <u>owl</u> sg.

owl

Chapter 10 / Nominalized Sentences

Nominalization rule (p. 243)

NP ⟶ the fact that⌢S

The fact that⌢S nominalizations (p. 243)

Type (1)   Tense retained:
: the fact that the boy is tall
: that the boy is tall

Type (2)   Tense replaced by -ING:
: the fact of the boy's being tall
: the boy's being tall
: the boy being tall

Type (3)   Tense replaced by *to:*
: for the boy to be tall

Type (4)   Tense lost:
: the fact of the boy's tallness
: the boy's tallness
: the fact of the tallness of the boy
: the tallness of the boy

It-inversion rule (p. 250)

NP⌢Aux⌢VP ⟹ *it*⌢Aux⌢VP⌢NP

Example: That John refused the offer surprised me ⟹
: It surprised me that John refused the offer.

: For John to refuse the offer surprised me ⟹
: It surprised me for John to refuse the offer.

For⌢NP deletion rule (p. 253)

for⌢NP ⟹ Ø

Example: It surprised John *for John* to receive the offer ⟹
: It surprised John to receive the offer.

Chapter 11 / Sentences Embedded in Subordinating Adverbs

Adverb switch rule: (p. 264)

NP⌢Aux⌢MV⌢Comp⌢Adverb ⟹ Adverb⌢NP⌢Aux⌢MV⌢Comp

Example: It was midnight he got back *when* ⟹
: It was midnight *when* he got back.

: It was midnight *when he got back* ⟹
: *When he got back*, it was midnight.

PART FOUR / SENTENCES COMBINED BY JOINING RULES

Chapter 12 / Coordination

Coordination joining rule (p. 280)
> This rule merely inserts one of the coordinating conjunctions between two independent sentences.
>
> Example: S_1: John saw the movie.
> S_2: I saw the movie.
> S_1 and S_2: John saw the movie *and* I saw the movie.

Duplicate deletion rule (p. 280)
> Deletes the elements in S_2 that are identical with the corresponding elements of S_1.
>
> Example: John saw the movie and I *saw the movie* $\Longrightarrow$
> John saw the movie and I.

Residue switch rule (p. 280)
> This rules attaches whatever remains of S_2 to the corresponding element in S_1 (along with the *and*).
>
> Example: John saw the movie *and I* $\Longrightarrow$ John *and I* saw the movie.

Compound NP's that mean 'together with' (p. 278)
> NP $\longrightarrow$ NP *and* NP
>
> Example: John and Mary sang a duet together.

Chapter 13 / Conjunction

Conjunction joining rule (p. 290)
> Two independent sentences are joined together by a conjunctive adverb.
>
> Example: S_1: John was at the scene.
> S_2: He did not see the accident.
> S_1 conjunction S_2: John was at the scene; *however*, he did not see the accident.

Conjunctive adverb switch rule (p. 291)
> The conjunctive adverb can be moved to the middle or end of the second sentence.
>
> Example: John was at the scene; *however*, he did not see the accident $\Longrightarrow$
> John was at the scene; he did not, *however*, see the accident.
>
> *or* he did not see the accident, *however*.

Chapter 14 / Comparison

Comparative joining rule (p. 296)

Two sentences are joined together by *-er than, as* . . . *as,* or some other comparative expression.

Example: S_1: John is tall.

S_2: His father is wide.

S_1 comparative S_2: John is tall*er than* his father is wide.

Sample Analysis of a Paragraph

The following paragraph is from Sinclair Lewis' novel *Babbitt*. It has been very slightly adapted.

He finished shaving in a growing testiness increased by his spinning headache and by the emptiness in his stomach. When he was done, his round face smooth and streamy and his eyes stinging from soapy water, he reached for a towel. The family towels were wet, wet and clammy and vile, all of them wet, he found, as he blindly snatched them—his own face-towel, his wife's, Verona's, Ted's, Tinka's and the lone bath-towel with the huge welt of initial. Then George F. Babbitt did a dismaying thing. He wiped his face on the guest-towel! It was a pansy-embroidered trifle which always hung there to indicate that the Babbitts were in the best Floral Heights society. No one had ever used it. No guest had ever dared to. Guests secretively took a corner of the nearest regular towel.

The paragraph may be broken down into nine sentences:

1. He finished shaving in a growing testiness increased by his spinning headache and by the emptiness in his stomach.
2. When he was done, his round face smooth and streamy and his eyes stinging from soapy water, he reached for a towel.

3. The family towels were wet, wet and clammy and vile, all of them wet, he
   found, as he blindly snatched them—his own face-towel, his wife's, Verona's,
   Ted's, Tinka's and the lone bath-towel with the huge welt of initial.
4. Then George F. Babbitt did a dismaying thing.
5. He wiped his face on the guest-towel!
6. It was a pansy-embroidered trifle which always hung there to indicate that
   the Babbitts were in the best Floral Heights society.
7. No one had ever used it.
8. No guest had ever dared to.
9. Guests secretively took a corner of the nearest regular towel.

1. He finished shaving in a growing testiness increased by his spinning headache and by the emptiness in his stomach.

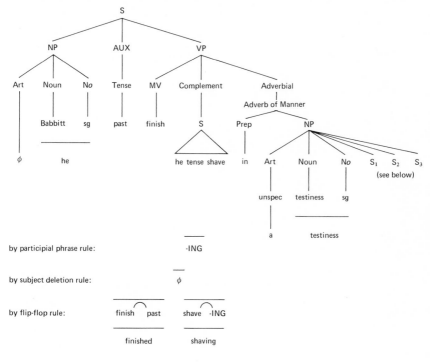

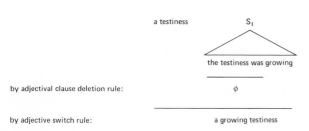

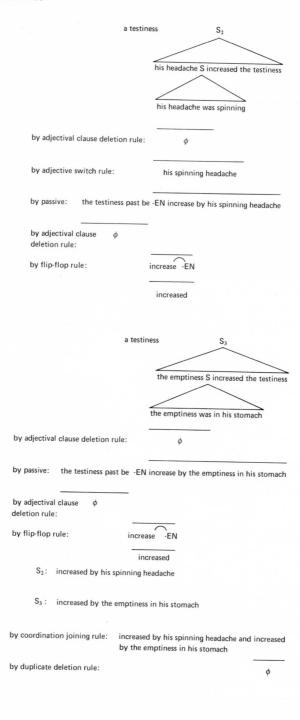

a testiness　　　　　　　　S_2

his headache S increased the testiness

his headache was spinning

by adjectival clause deletion rule:　　　　ϕ

by adjective switch rule:　　　　his spinning headache

by passive:　　the testiness past be -EN increase by his spinning headache

by adjectival clause　　　ϕ
deletion rule:

by flip-flop rule:　　　　increase ⌒ -EN

increased

a testiness　　　　　　　　S_3

the emptiness S increased the testiness

the emptiness was in his stomach

by adjectival clause deletion rule:　　　　ϕ

by passive:　　the testiness past be -EN increase by the emptiness in his stomach

by adjectival clause　　　ϕ
deletion rule:

by flip-flop rule:　　　　increase ⌒ -EN

increased

S_2:　increased by his spinning headache

S_3:　increased by the emptiness in his stomach

by coordination joining rule:　　increased by his spinning headache and increased
by the emptiness in his stomach

by duplicate deletion rule:　　　　　　　　　ϕ

2. When he was done, his round face smooth and streamy and his eyes stinging from soapy water, he reached for a towel.

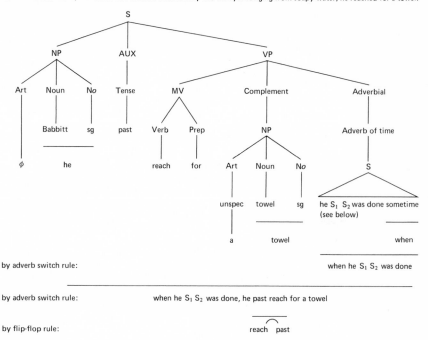

by adverb switch rule: when he S_1 S_2 was done

by adverb switch rule: when he S_1 S_2 was done, he past reach for a towel

by flip-flop rule: reach   past

                                                              reached

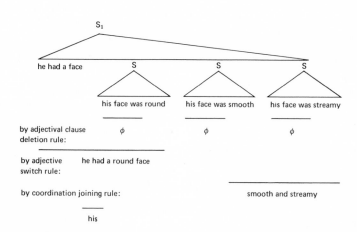

by adjectival clause ϕ ϕ ϕ
deletion rule:

by adjective   he had a round face
switch rule:

by coordination joining rule: smooth and streamy

                            his

[*Comment:* We have not discussed the rules that would convert NP $\widehat{have}$ into a pos-sive appositive, that is, *he had* into *his*.]

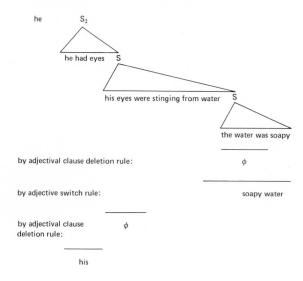

[*Comment: he had eyes* would be changed into *his eyes* by the same rule needed for S_1.]

S_2:   his round face smooth and streamy

S_3:   his eyes stinging from soapy water

by coordination joining rule: his round face smooth and streamy and his eyes stinging from soapy water

3. The family towels were wet, wet and clammy and vile, all of
   them wet, he found, as he blindly snatched them—his own face-
   towel, his wife's, Verona's, Ted's, Tinka's and the lone bath-
   towel with the huge welt of initial.

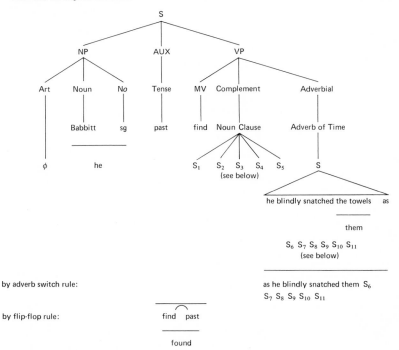

by adverb switch rule: as he blindly snatched them S₆
                                              S₇ S₈ S₉ S₁₀ S₁₁

by flip-flop rule: find past

                                      found

S₁: The family towels were wet.

S₂: The family towels were wet.

S₃: The family towels were clammy.

S₄: The family towels were vile.

S₅: All of the family towels were wet.

by coordination joining rule: The family towels were wet and the family
                                 towels were wet and the family towels were
                                 clammy and the family towels were vile and
                                 all of the family towels were wet.

by duplicate deletion rule: The family towels were wet, wet and clammy and
                                 vile, all of the family towels wet.

                                 them

[*Comment:* If we applied the duplicate deletion mechanically all the repetitions of *wet* would be deleted. We also need a rule that would optionally switch the complement to the first position in the sentence.]

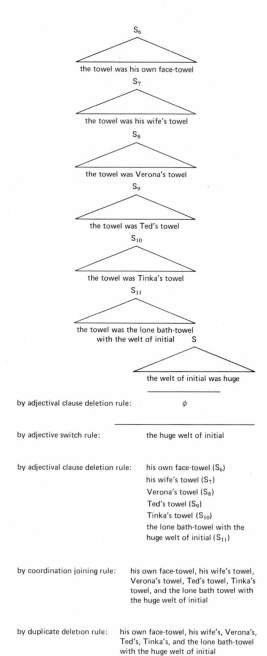

S_6

the towel was his own face-towel

S_7

the towel was his wife's towel

S_8

the towel was Verona's towel

S_9

the towel was Ted's towel

S_{10}

the towel was Tinka's towel

S_{11}

the towel was the lone bath-towel
with the welt of initial   S

the welt of initial was huge

by adjectival clause deletion rule: ϕ

by adjective switch rule: the huge welt of initial

by adjectival clause deletion rule: his own face-towel (S_6)
his wife's towel (S_7)
Verona's towel (S_8)
Ted's towel (S_9)
Tinka's towel (S_{10})
the lone bath-towel with the
huge welt of initial (S_{11})

by coordination joining rule: his own face-towel, his wife's towel,
Verona's towel, Ted's towel, Tinka's
towel, and the lone bath towel with
the huge welt of initial

by duplicate deletion rule: his own face-towel, his wife's, Verona's,
Ted's, Tinka's, and the lone bath-towel
with the huge welt of initial

4. Then George F. Babbitt did a dismaying thing.

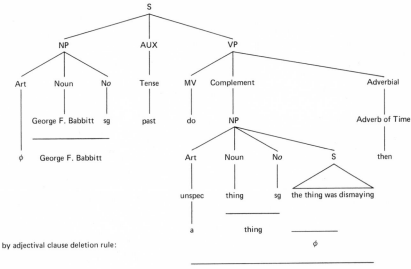

by adjectival clause deletion rule: φ

by adjective switch rule: a dismaying thing

by adverb switch rule: Then George F. Babbitt past do a dismaying thing

by flip-flop rule: do past

did

5. He wiped his face on the guest-towel!

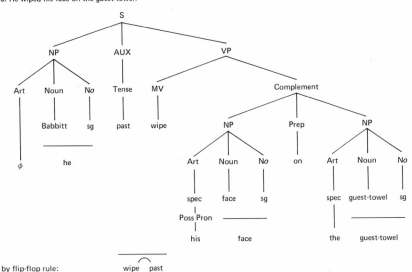

by flip-flop rule: wipe past

wiped

6. It was a pansy-embroidered trifle which always hung there to
   indicate that the Babbits were in the best Floral Heights
   society.

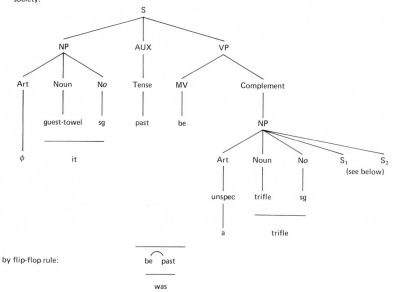

by flip-flop rule:

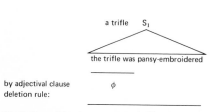

by adjectival clause   φ
deletion rule:

by adjective switch rule: a pansy-embroidered trifle

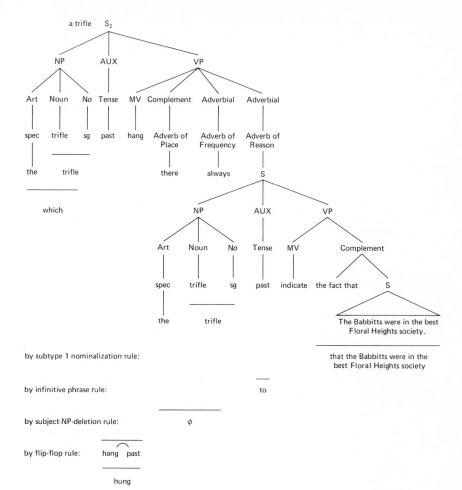

a trifle S₂

NP AUX VP

Art Noun No Tense MV Complement Adverbial Adverbial

spec trifle sg past hang Adverb of Place Adverb of Frequency Adverb of Reason

the trifle there always S

which

NP AUX VP

Art Noun No Tense MV Complement

spec trifle sg past indicate the fact that S

the trifle The Babbitts were in the best Floral Heights society.

by subtype 1 nominalization rule: that the Babbitts were in the best Floral Heights society

by infinitive phrase rule: to

by subject-NP-deletion rule: φ

by flip-flop rule: hang past

hung

7. No one had ever used it.

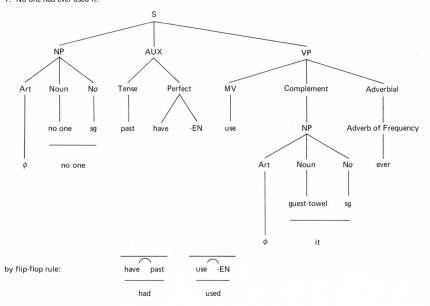

by flip-flop rule:

have͡past   use͡-EN

had   used

8. No guest had ever dared to.

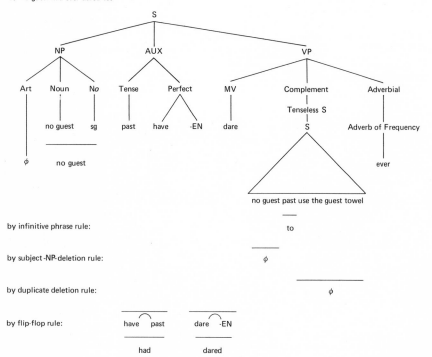

by infinitive phrase rule:

by subject -NP-deletion rule:

by duplicate deletion rule:

by flip-flop rule:

have͡past   dare͡-EN

had   dared

[*Comment:* Notice that the duplicate deletion rule applies across sentence boundaries.]

9. Guests secretively took a corner of the nearest regular towel.

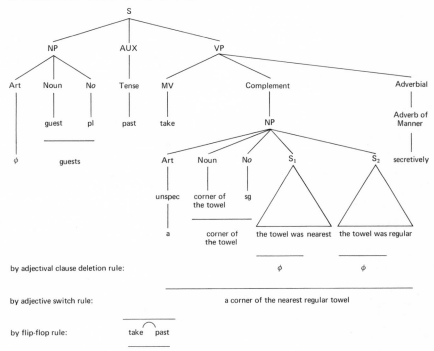

by adjectival clause deletion rule:

by adjective switch rule:

by flip-flop rule:

INDEX